D0170614

Novelist of Three Worlds
FORD MADOX FORD

Novelist of Three *Worlds*
FORD MADOX FORD

PAUL L. WILEY

SYRACUSE UNIVERSITY PRESS · 1962

PR
6011
.O53
Z97

COPYRIGHT © 1962 BY SYRACUSE UNIVERSITY PRESS
SYRACUSE, NEW YORK

ALL RIGHTS RESERVED

*This work has been published with the
assistance of a Ford Foundation grant.*

Library of Congress Catalog Card: 62-18928

MANUFACTURED IN THE UNITED STATES OF AMERICA
BY THE VAIL-BALLOU PRESS, INC., BINGHAMTON, NEW YORK

For Jean

5595

Preface

BACK SOMEWHERE in the 1930's, as an undergraduate with time in plenty for browsing, I happened to stumble in a San Francisco bookstore upon a crate of used novels by a Ford Madox Ford of whom I had heard nothing except his oddly circular name. The box was spilling over—evidently the backwash of a local best selling wave—and mostly with books notable for sameness: *No More Parades, The Last Post,* titles suggesting the war theme which in those years had not yet grown stale. Feeling a little sorry for the books, which no one seemed to think worth the bother of carting to whatever place discarded novels eventually go, I reached for *No More Parades* and read the opening paragraph. I read it again. It was not description; you were somehow brought inside a hot but soaking Great War army hut "shaped like the house a child draws" and ominously "transfused with a brown-orange dust that was light." Today, when those books no longer require sympathy, that paragraph must be common knowledge to an audience that is re-discovering the Tietjens novels. Yet read it as often as one will and the style refuses to fade. Whatever its secret, the vitality persists.

Perhaps, subconsciously, the first notion of writing a study of Ford occurred to me at that moment of random encounter with a single page not yet tied to context. At least I would like to think so; for although I did not until years later, and after completing a manuscript on Conrad, begin reading him assiduously and from end to end in the congenial atmosphere of a small English town, I believe that before everything else one comes to Ford by way of the style which he thought the element most original in his art and which is, indeed, the solvent for so much that we isolate regretfully as technique, subject, or theme. As his critical writings show, Ford was an expert and sensitive judge of fictional prose; and had he chosen to be more pontifical as well as less generous, perhaps, to

vii

other members of a hard craft, he might now rank among major interpreters of novelists like James, Crane, Conrad, and Lawrence. His own style, exhibiting distinction almost from the outset, is clearly modern—spare, allusive, delicate in response to the shades and tensions of the contemporary psyche. Yet although this is surely a primary reason for wanting to know Ford better, it remains true, I think, that emphasis upon the language of his text and all that it has to yield could be pressed further so as to remove a good deal of individual and even critical misunderstanding or doubt of this gifted and singular novelist. Consequently I have, in what follows, quoted liberally from Ford's work; and whereas this study is, I hope, more than a "reading," it does pursue the subsidiary aim of demonstrating style in all phases of the writer's career. Other aims, possibly, can better take care of themselves.

Since, moreover, the scope and general bearing of Ford's effort are neither widely known nor fully appraised, I have tried to do some justice to the bulk of his novels without giving special weight or assigning a pivotal function to *The Good Soldier* or to the *Parade's End* tetralogy. Both publicly available and highly respected, the latter books have received and should rightly go on attracting skilled analysis; yet until we have fuller knowledge and agreement concerning Ford's many other works and of his literary position generally, it would seem premature and perhaps hazardous to associate permanence too strictly with two novels of assured merit, certainly, but of comparatively recent popularity. To Ford a new novel was always a try at something new, so that despite the lapses incidental to prolific writing, he is interesting as a rule because he continues to surprise. A few of his unfamiliar books are, no doubt, still to be found in local libraries; and the reader willing to experiment may acquire a personal taste for some of the less recognized manifestations of Ford's talent—for example, as Edwardian satirist, as historical novelist, or as elaborator of a symbolic geography. In the end, too, I think, extensive reading enables one to discern better the shape and development of Ford's convictions which, although inevitably the convictions of an artist, proceed from a mind informed, trained in close observation, and increasingly reflective with regard to the deeper anxieties of this century. What certain of his views may have been I have attempted to suggest while considering at the same time the unified effect of any particular work; for, in his method, meaning seldom emerges complete as theme or argument but rather in a final and cumulative impression which, for ultimate success, every line should justify.

That the preparation of this book was so little wearisome may be attributed not only to a subject engrossing in itself but also to the help and stimulation given me by so many friends. My colleagues in English at the University of Wisconsin were invariably ready with encouragement and needed advice; and in the Department of French and Italian Professor William T. Bandy, with his store of recollections of the 1920's Paris days and of the *bouts rimés* in which Ford excelled, enabled me frequently to view the past as living. Likewise the graduate students with whom I once read Ford in seminar gave greater moral support than they may have realized by their alert response to a novelist in some respects new to them. While indispensable for her attention to details too numerous to mention, my wife deserves thanks of a special kind for indefatigable patience and a sense of humor. For large material assistance I acknowledge an important debt to the University Graduate School for granting me an invaluable research leave in England and to those members of the staff of the Memorial Library who so promptly and efficiently answered requests for books and microfilm not available in the general Ford collection.

PAUL L. WILEY

Madison, Wisconsin
May, 1962

Acknowledgments

To Miss Janice Biala, Ford Madox Ford's literary executrix, the author wishes to express particular thanks for her generous permission to quote illustrative material from the following among Ford's works:

The Shifting of the Fire, Rossetti, The Soul of London, The Benefactor, Hans Holbein the Younger, An English Girl, The Spirit of the People, Mr. Apollo, The 'Half Moon,' The Portrait, The Simple Life Limited, The Critical Attitude, Mr. Fleight, When Blood Is Their Argument, Thus to Revisit, The Marsden Case, Women and Men, Some Do Not, Joseph Conrad: A Personal Remembrance, No More Parades, A Man Could Stand Up—, The Last Post, A Little Less than Gods, No Enemy, Return to Yesterday, When the Wicked Man, The Rash Act, Vive Le Roy, Mightier than the Sword, and *Great Trade Route.*

For other passages from books by Ford quoted in the text, the author gratefully owes permissions to: William Blackwood Sons Ltd for *The Cinque Ports;* The Bodley Head Ltd for *The Fifth Queen, Privy Seal,* and *The Fifth Queen Crowned;* Chatto and Windus Ltd for *A Call;* Constable and Co. Ltd for *Ladies Whose Bright Eyes* and *The Panel;* Dodd, Mead and Co. for *Henry James: A Critical Study;* Alfred A. Knopf, Inc. for *The Good Soldier* and *Parade's End;* J. B. Lippincott Co. for *The English Novel, It Was the Nightingale, Henry for Hugh,* and *Provence.*

J. M. Dent and Sons Ltd courteously permitted quotations from the following works by Ford in collaboration with Joseph Conrad: *The Inheritors, Romance,* and *The Nature of a Crime.*

For a passage from *The Journals of Arnold Bennett,* permission by the copyright owner, Mrs. Cheston Bennett, is gratefully acknowledged. Thanks, likewise, are due to Charles Scribner's Sons for the use of a quotation from *The Wings of the Dove* by Henry James.

Contents

You go to books to be taken
out of yourself, I to be shown
where I stand.

Ford Madox Ford
A Call

Chapter I

Introduction

THOUGH his art was meticulous, Ford Madox Ford's talk was deliberately casual, yet often more cogent than it appeared—a fact of some bearing on his literary reputation. His habit, for example, of saying that one book was enough for any man to write seems at odds with his actual output of seventy-five volumes of fiction and miscellanea of one sort or another; yet what he affirmed in this instance, as frequently in others, makes important sense when weighed carefully. When he talked of one book, Ford evidently meant creative work in the strictest sense or, more specifically, a superior accomplishment in the novel form which he believed the literary art of brightest promise in the twentieth century. Ardent modernist that he always was, his aim was to produce such a book himself, a novel representative of the temper of modern life, while at the same time pressing others to engage in the same venture, an objective that accounts for the existence of a great part of his purely discursive writing in the cultural or critical line. In this respect his attitude contrasts essentially, perhaps necessarily, with that of the novelists of a slightly older generation, James and Conrad, despite the fact that he constantly asserted his attachment to them in a common school and freely acknowledged what he owed them on the score of fictional theory and technique. Where James and Conrad, like Yeats as a poet, seem bent primarily on the shaping of their careers to establish an enduring literary monument, Ford appears deficient in this sense of métier, his efforts sporadic though intense and his energies diverted into byways of pamphleteering and controversy. Temperamental in great measure as this disposition undoubtedly was, it may be attributed likewise to his not unjustifiable belief that in the present century the

1

novel, if it were to hold the public status that he thought it deserved, must not only seek new aesthetic dimensions but also constantly affirm and demonstrate its indispensability to a culture that Ford regarded as radically altered from the past in both its habits and tastes. On this account he deserves particular recognition not so much as a major theorist in the art of fiction, like James, nor even as the technician that he has so often been called, but as a main advocate of the novel as a cultural force, in which role he may well stand alone among English writers of his time. Excellent critic of the craftsman type as he could be on occasion, he was essentially the partisan of a special cause, a fact that does much to explain his numerous erratic or biased, and frequently stimulating, pronouncements on the novel from a historical point of view.

In a sense, therefore, he was always more or less a novelist whether he happened to be writing fiction in order to reflect the cultural atmosphere around him or issuing polemical or observational works designed to arouse a keener critical sense or to promote a readier acceptance of the arts in general. The same tone of cultural enquiry and speculation carries over from his expository prose to his novels, sometimes providing them with content and, despite his interest in formal problems, endowing them with the qualities of satire and intellectual debate that set them apart from so much of the blander English fiction of the earlier years of the century. Yet if Ford was, in his own way, bringing up to date Arnold's aesthetic-cultural preoccupation and so facing a dilemma to be explored in varied fashion by Yeats, Eliot, and Lawrence, his position is exceptional in that instinct directed him to absorb himself in the quest for a certain kind of literary absolute, for a positive formula which might become standard for the contemporary novel. In seeking this he disparaged unduly the intelligence and expert craftsmanship that he brought to novels which he considered inferior to his perfect measure, a result being that out of his thirty or more works of fiction perhaps three or four at most have been generally known in the period since his death in 1939. As an incidental cause for this obscurity one might well count the simple fact of unfortunately chosen titles; for whether or not through carelessness or sheer bad luck, with which Ford was conspicuously endowed, it remains that the bulk of his titles have either little seeming relevance to the substance of the novels behind them or, what is worse, the unfortunate tendency to mislead the reader curious enough to inspect the contents themselves. Granting that his books vary in merit, it may be regretted that Ford, who even when least inspired was seldom a dull and never a naïve writer, should have permitted a satire on pulp fiction to be insipidly titled in America *Ring for Nancy;* a caustic portrayal of 1920's confusion to be named *When the Wicked Man;* or a subtle late novel of double identity to be called vapidly *Henry for Hugh.* Happier as he might have been with no titles at all, his comparative casualness or indifference regarding the naming of so many of his books seems in tune with his attitude of exact discrimination. The two novels that he thought worth notice were, in his order of preference, *The Good Soldier* and the tetralogy eventually called *Parade's End.* The public at large has acquiesced in the verdict. They are among his few novels which continue to circulate widely.

On this point Ford's judgment, as an indicator of highest success, appears correct. Yet to know his work by these two novels alone is to have no more idea of the character of his development—or, in fact, of the full nature of his mind and temperament—than if one were, say, to restrict acquaintance with James to *The Ambassadors* and *The Golden Bowl.* As Kenneth Young has indicated in his British Council monograph on Ford, several novels other than *The Good Soldier* and *Parade's End* are well worth study in and for themselves; and one might venture the further opinion that a selective edition of ten or so books from throughout Ford's career would, in present conditions of critical enlightenment, prove welcome. Meantime, however, it remains to determine, especially in view of his own inconclusive or casual statements, what Ford accomplished as a writer and along what lines his literary course proceeded, an undertaking reasonably initiated, as the following study maintains, by an analysis and commentary in general chronological sequence of the fiction composed throughout his working life, which extended virtually to the time of his death. This method recommends itself for two reasons at least. For one thing it clears the novels from the tangle of much occasional writing, such as art criticism and cultural speculation or propaganda, that surrounds them. Whereas Ford's output of the latter sort often has independent interest and illuminates aspects of his thought in a manner that might well justify separate consideration of him as a belletrist of almost Victorian amplitude, it would seem injudicious to deny primary consideration to his effort in the novel, the one literary form which, in the end, he admired unreservedly. Occasional poet though he was, his shrewd appraisal in the preface to his *Collected Poems* of 1914 of the failure of verse to equal fiction in contemporary tone during the opening years of the century amply explains his permanent allegiance to the fortunes of the novel.

More importantly, a separate examination of Ford's novels in temporal order makes plain almost at once several fundamental matters concerning his course as a writer which would not emerge from a reading of selected books or from a view of his work as an irregular alternation of fiction and general prose. It becomes clear, first of all, that his progress is not haphazard, as might have been true had he considered the novel a sideline, but shows, like the work of most serious writers, a discernible pattern of development leading from experiment to maturity and exhibiting evidence of consistency both in personal outlook and aesthetic intent. Since Ford sought to advertise only those novels which satisfied his exacting taste, he says almost nothing of a public kind to suggest that ordinary development applied to him but inclines, instead, to create the impression that the books he wished remembered sprang into being on a sudden tide of creative energy and confidence.

Of crucial concern in this respect is *The Good Soldier* which Ford represented as an almost magical feat performed by him in his fortieth year, thereby enhancing the prestige always rightly accorded the novel but also largely ignoring the sixteen works preceding it, in one of which, *A Call* in 1910, he had most certainly attempted and very nearly mastered the form ultimately perfected in *The Good Soldier*. Although he had every reason to place high value upon this remarkable novel, which demonstrated his arrival at full maturity, Ford so isolated *The Good Soldier* that it became easy to overlook the struggle to achieve form as well as exact statement of attitude which he had been conducting for twenty or so years. By acquaintance with this earlier evolution a reader not only better understands Ford's purpose and achievement in this unique work of contra-Victorian irony but also sees *The Good Soldier* not as a solitary tour de force but as a keystone in a continuing literary development which entered a new phase in the final decade of Ford's career.

The special place which Ford assigned to *The Good Soldier* reflects his conviction that in this novel he had devised at last the positive formula that he wanted for the recording of contemporary experience and that, in so doing, he had contributed in an original way to modern fiction. The term that he applied to this form was "Affair," a usable piece of critical nomenclature that appears with notable regularity throughout his critical writing. What Ford meant by an Affair this study will endeavor to demonstrate, since it is here contended that this concept supplied the control principle for his most characteristic work and brought forth the collection of supplementary techniques that have fostered the mistaken opinion that he was merely a technician, in itself a dubious title, rather than a practicing artist employing the means necessary to render a centralized vision. In brief, however, he conceived the Affair, perhaps with a slight overtone of the "Affaire Dreyfus" which had startled him like so many others of his generation, as an epitome of the habits of contemporary existence with its hid-

den complexities and intrigues and hence as a form opposed
to the broad surface panorama of naturalism. For making the
Affair his own, Ford need not be credited with the complete
originality which he never claimed, since he directed attention
to the presence of the form in the later work of James and in
the Conrad of *The Secret Agent* period. Yet he was original
in classifying the Affair as a distinct fictional mode and thus
making it available to the modern novelist as well as in adapt-
ing it to the requirements of his own temperament which
sought expression in the labyrinthine and in meticulous workmanship. Even though he considerably modified his treatment
of the Affair in his postwar novels, it remained his basic structural design, in historical fiction as elsewhere; and since its
comprehension is essential to appreciating his aims and effects,
chapters III and IV of this study discuss the factors in its
genesis and make-up.

It may, therefore, be assumed, as this study likewise maintains, that Ford, despite his adherence to the Impressionist
wing in fiction, was in his own right an independent artist
and not, as oftentimes asserted by his antagonists, one who
battened on the reputations of his literary superiors. In the
latter regard his collaboration with Conrad, however advantageous at the time, was not altogether favorable to his posthumous reputation which invariably fastens upon the point
that Ford was collaborator to Conrad while rarely suggesting
that the terms of the equation might in certain respects be
reversed. The present study inclines to view the partnership as
mutual but also to some extent as one of mutual discomfort
caused by the friction between two personalities as divided in
temperament as they may have been allied in theory. The
truth of Ford's own opinion that the temperamental difference
between himself and Conrad was too sharp to allow for any
really fruitful creative interchange seems corroborated by the
few works resulting from the association, since these novels,
mentioned in the chapters to follow, display evidence of
strained composition and perhaps, one may suspect, of the

dominating voice of the senior partner. Much, in any case, as Ford owed to Conrad, and it cannot be said that the debt was grudgingly acknowledged, it is apparent that Ford's particular manner had begun to take form prior to the collaboration and that it was afterwards to grow into a style not only less robust than Conrad's but also, possibly, in its deliberately muted effects better attuned to the range of a modern ear. As a novelist working alone, Ford moved naturally towards a contemporary historical outlook focused upon the social, cultural, and aesthetic situation which had little in common with Conrad's special vision; and in his final years he turned to the elaboration of a personal myth both singular and revelatory of long-standing private beliefs.

Limited as it is to Ford's accomplishment in the novel, this study makes no attempt to depart markedly from the texts themselves, although many of his general prose works have been cited for information bearing importantly on matters of literary analysis. Although one discovers, in the end, that nearly everything written by Ford illuminates in one way or another his character as a novelist, it is impossible to proceed without reference to his autobiographical and critical writings and, when dealing with his last novels, without consulting late books of a semi-prophetic kind such as *Provence* and *Great Trade Route*. Moreover, the interpreter must, of course, avail himself of the help provided by other students of Ford. Among those responsible for maintaining interest in his personality and work during times when Ford needed remembrance have been writers such as Graham Greene, Frank MacShane, R. P. Blackmur, Mark Schorer, Hugh Kenner, and Robie Macauley. More recently critics and scholars like Richard Cassell, R. W. Lid, John Meixner, and Richard M. Ludwig have advanced measurably the closer inspection that Ford's novels warrant or have cast additional light on the important problem of his literary reputation. Difficult questions of a biographical nature, some of which have been noted by Douglas Goldring in his pioneering accounts of Ford's life, have been excluded not only as beyond the aims of a study of this kind but also for lack at present of more conclusive evidence, even though the temptation to speculate on certain apparently direct connections between elements in the novels and the personal history of Ford himself is admittedly strong, particularly in the case of recurrent or obsessive themes. With respect to Ford's private embarrassments, which were evidently numerous, no judgment is offered, unless it be to say that he must in the course of a life that endured war and other hardships have atoned for a great deal. Whatever his faults may have been, it is difficult to round out a literary evaluation without concluding that he possessed a certain magnanimity, a talent for absorbing himself in issues of impersonal scope. Lacking this trait, he could not have attained the mature vision which enabled him to comprehend at once the errors of the late Victorian world and the desolation of its collapse in the Great War.

Chapter II

Ford—*en route*

THE READER should be struck at once by two qualities of Ford's novels that often account particularly for their hold upon the attention: the speed and compression of the narrative and a prevailing sense of restless movement, of shifting scene and characters in transit. Main incidents occur on ships or trains, between one country and another, or involve people hurrying through streets or corridors or even running frantically. While this is, to be sure, a familiar trait of the modern novel by contrast with the fixed or stable locality of much past fiction, the transitional note is also in key with Ford's own unsettled life and in some measure with his literary principles, as he suggests in a reflection set down towards the end of his career:

> I am neither sociologist nor politician. I am an onlooker stating the result of conclusions that have taken me half a century to arrive at. . . . During these years I have rarely been still for more than three or four months on end. I have rolled my hump along, on mule back, in dog-carts, on liners, in carriers' carts, on trains, autobuses, army waggons, on my feet, looking at things and listening to men talking. And all the while growing something in soup dishes or aware that something was growing itself for me on the slopes above the Mediterranean—or the Channel. . . . And now putting down what I think about it all.[1]

This, like so many of Ford's statements, can be read not as bare fact but rather as a heightened image of personal experience conveying at the same time his Impressionist conviction that the writer draws primarily upon firsthand insights from life in progress with its variety and unexpectedness. To some

9

extent Ford's often seemingly unpredictable manner of existence can be attributed to factors of temperament and circumstance; yet conscious will determined many of the choices,
especially when maturity enabled him to make creative use
of changing environment and to write virtually anywhere.
Through restlessness he became an "international" novelist of a
different sort than James, and the interest that his books evoke
derives in considerable part from their accumulation of precise detail recreating vividly the contrasting and often curious
areas of contemporary society which he came to know between
his birth in England in 1873 and his death in France in 1939.
Irregularity in movement represented gain to a novelist resolved on making himself a mirror to his age, however uneasy
the road proved to be over troublesome stretches.

Characteristically, Ford began by repudiating the milieu
into which he had been born while recording it later with a
customary fluency in anecdote. As Ford Hermann Hueffer,
the elder son of a naturalized German who had married the
daughter of the eminent painter, Ford Madox Brown, and
become respected in London as a music critic and author of
learned works on Wagner and the troubadours, he entered by
chance of birth a circle of individuals distinguished or influ-
ential in the arts and hence strong as patrons to fortunate
young talent. Close to Ford on the one hand were Morris and
the Rossettis and their numerous connections, and on the other
Richard Garnett of the British Museum and his family including, in particular, Edward Garnett, rising in esteem as a publisher's reader. After an education conducive to sound taste
though not directed towards a university, Ford satisfied the
expectations of his elders by writing two children's stories,
one of which had a remarkable popular success, and a first
novel, *The Shifting of the Fire*, all in print by 1892. While
talent he obviously had, it does not seem to have been accompanied by any pronounced ambition for a professional
literary career under pre-Raphaelite auspices, perhaps because
as a boy he had seen enough of the vanities of the great and

of artists in general to leave him unexcited at the prospect. Throughout his life he retained his affection and respect for his grandfather, Madox Brown, who besides being a man of generous temper and an engaging conversationalist probably helped stimulate Ford's appreciation of new currents in literature and of such foreign novelists as Stendhal, Flaubert, and Turgenev, later to receive his mature critical approval. But that Ford cared little for what others of the pre-Raphaelite generation represented may be gathered from his often ironical retrospective observations in such books as *Ancient Lights* and in the first volume of the Tietjens tetralogy. In any case, he broke immediate ties with London in 1894 by marrying his young school friend, Elsie Martindale, without the formal blessing of her parents, and taking her to settle in a Kentish village near the Romney Marsh, a section of England that he especially favored.

Although he was to state that from 1894 to 1903 he was hardly at all in London, Ford was by no means in rural hiding; and these years were formative in his development as a novelist. While maintaining domestic habits—two daughters being born in 1897 and 1900—he and his wife, who also possessed literary ability, were intellectually active; and besides changing residence to suit their mood, Ford made occasional trips to the Continent and probably accustomed himself to that attentive study of the drift of contemporary events which was to make him an opponent of the Boer War and the jingoistic deterioration in English politics and culture for which he blamed it. Temporarily, however, and apparently at ease financially, he seemed content to delay any limiting choice of profession and to spend his creative impulses on poetry and musical composition and the writing of casual articles. Yet the commission that he accepted, at the prompting of William Michael Rossetti, for a biography of the recently dead Madox Brown—a work that appeared in 1896 and won considerable approval—may have inclined Ford to the idea of cultivating the role of historian, as in a general way his father had done in his scholarly books. Before 1904, in any event, he reports having pursued research for an unwritten life of Henry VIII; [2] and some historical equipment was required to prepare his large partially antiquarian volume of 1900, *The Cinque Ports,* and his critical study of 1902, *D. G. Rossetti.* To some degree, moreover, he brought the results of historical reading or documentary information to bear in his early approach to the novel; for it was apparently by way of materials in the British Museum that he obtained the factual substance of *Romance,* the novel in which he collaborated with Conrad.[3] During his first years in the country, however, he seems to have been concerned more with verse than fiction, although it is perhaps significant that in 1896 he sought and was granted acquaintance with Henry James at Rye.[4] His lasting admiration for the literary viewpoint and method of James may be seen not only in the critical study of 1913, *Henry James,* but also in nearly everything that Ford wrote concerning the modern novel; and although James eventually dropped him, Ford continued to proclaim his allegiance to the Jamesian tradition. It may, then, be assumed that the decisive event in this period, Ford's meeting with Conrad in 1898, brought together two creative minds sympathetic with respect to literary taste and kinship to James.

The importance that he assigned to his collaboration with Conrad from 1898 to 1903 as a point of departure for his own methods in fiction may be gauged by Ford's remark over a quarter century later: "That it was fortunate for me I am sure, for if I know anything of how to write, almost the whole of that knowledge was acquired then." [5] Yet partly by reason of his numerous reminders in his critical and autobiographical writings of their connection at a time when he was much the younger man, Ford may have helped to foster a legend that he was merely sunning himself in the light of Conrad's genius, whereas it is now evident that he took a full working share in the partnership. Although when he joined with Ford, Conrad had already published three novels, including *The Nigger of the "Narcissus,"* and was shortly to start upon *Heart of Dark-*

ness and *Lord Jim,* he regarded Ford as a practicing writer as well and as one whose knowledge of English style might be distinctly advantageous from a purely business standpoint, so that he stood to benefit by initiating the proposal.[6] Ford, moreover, became more than merely useful in a practical way. With his good mind, which his friend recognized, he furnished Conrad with mental stimulus that the latter needed; and for a number of years beyond the interval of close collaboration and perhaps up to the cooling of their friendship after about 1909, Conrad in his independent work received occasional help of one sort or another from Ford, as appears to have been notably true in the instance of *The Mirror of the Sea* in which Ford's aid demonstrated his customary generosity in assisting the literary projects of others.[7] Before long the collaborational arrangement seemed to promise so well that the partners discussed long range plans for works which, although never written as joint undertakings, did supply Conrad and Ford with ideas or topics which they managed to incorporate in books— such as Ford's Napoleonic novel of 1928, *A Little Less Than Gods*—that they designed separately.

With regard, however, to the actual outcome of the collaboration—the two novels, *The Inheritors,* published in England and the United States in 1901, and *Romance,* published in 1903—the strain upon the joint authors, each temperamentally sensitive in his own fashion, may have scarcely justified itself in terms of material results. Yet if these books have seldom weighed heavily in evaluations of Conrad, they merit closer attention in the record of Ford's development as a novelist. Ford himself conceived and wrote most of *The Inheritors,* with Conrad evidently supervising; and he seems to have provided the first draft of *Romance* as well as to have composed independently a good half of the five parts in the published version.[8] Since he was at the same time in animated discussion with Conrad on joint technical theories, this discipline was crucial to his future course and practice in fiction; and no doubt here he acquired his understanding of Impressionist procedure and his belief in it as the leading experimental movement of the new century. He allowed full value to what he gained from Conrad in mutual interchange, and it appears that both collaborators continued to respect each other on literary grounds. Although Ford's study, *Joseph Conrad: A Personal Remembrance,* provoked some animosities on its publication after Conrad's death in 1924, it must surely seem to readers today a generally appreciative evaluation of that writer.

While in the country Ford passed, then, from a somewhat uncertain trial at expression in a peasant neighborhood to the role of adherent to what seemed to him the most advanced body of fiction writers of the time. Besides James and Conrad he had come to know Stephen Crane and H. G. Wells among a broadening range of acquaintances; and he would willingly have been taken for a participant in a new literary school capable of shaping English taste. Perhaps feeling that he had left apprenticeship for professional status, he and his wife returned to London in 1904, taking a house at Campden Hill that somehow appeared to presage ill luck. For causes that may have been in some measure neurasthenic, Ford's health broke down, a misfortune which not only impeded his work until about 1906 but also led him to seek treatment at various health establishments on the Continent, in Germany in particular. Here, again, another of the many sharp turns in his life introduced him to a milieu—the European spa resorts so much frequented during the early years of the century—which would find its counterpart in the substance of his novels. Readers, for example, of the detailed spa observations in Ford's 1931 volume of reminiscences, *Return to Yesterday,* will discover several hints connecting this experience with some striking features of *The Good Soldier.*

Surprisingly, once more, Ford emerged from this period of depression to enter upon a phase of energetic productivity and unusual public success. In 1905 the appearance of his novel, *The Benefactor,* his first independent fictional work after the Conrad collaboration, helped to cover his lapse into creative debility; and in 1906 an initial short visit to New York, where his name had been associated with *The Inheritors,* resulted in 1907 in *An English Girl,* the only one of his novels so far to attempt extensive use of American character and scene. But more importantly, between 1906 and 1908 he published two works of large scope that brought him favorable recognition of a major kind. One of these, his still admired trilogy of historical novels set in the time of Henry VIII, *The Fifth Queen,* appeared in its successive parts—*The Fifth Queen, Privy Seal,* and *The Fifth Queen Crowned*—in 1906, 1907, and 1908. The other, a trio of related books forming a survey of contemporary English life and character—*The Soul of London* published in 1905, *The Heart of the Country* in 1906, and *The Spirit of the People* in 1907—made evident his capacity for Impressionistic portrayal of a whole society; and as an omnibus volume under the title *England and the English* the same books were published immediately in New York in 1907. Thus on reaching the age of thirty-five Ford had convincingly demonstrated his independence both as novelist and as social observer; and had he elected to remain content as private author, he might well have anticipated a relatively calm future in the Edwardian world of letters. Instead, with customary indifference to placidity, he chose to risk himself in a venture as memorable as it was disastrous to the security which he had for the moment attained.

In 1908 Ford installed himself as editor of what he hoped would be a major literary periodical, the *English Review;* and in December of that year the first number, with contents including James's "The Jolly Corner" and an installment of Conrad's later *A Personal Record,* justified predictions of the review's becoming the most distinguished of its time in England. When eventually in 1909 Ford lost control of the journal through financial mistakes after he had brought out some twelve issues, Arnold Bennett in the *New Age* commended him for a service to English letters, which should indeed be

considered as central among Ford's intentions. Believing as
he did in the public importance of unified art movements and
remembering such older periodicals as *The Yellow Book* and
The Savoy for their association with newer tendencies, Ford
expected to make the *Review* an organ for the most stimulating literary and intellectual currents of its day, as may be
noted in the firm critical tone of the miscellany of articles from
the journal which he published in 1911 as *The Critical Attitude*. In the original plans for the *Review* Ford evidently relied on support from some of his nearest acquaintances. Arthur
Marwood, a Yorkshire squire and mathematician and an admired friend of both Ford and Conrad, provided financial
backing; Conrad, perhaps somewhat reluctantly, supplied advice and promised contributions; and Ford's close political
connection, the Liberal, C. F. G. Masterman, figured as an
approved voice in the department of social opinion. As was
suggested by its first number, the *Review* favored the Jamesian
and Impressionist mode in literature; and during his editorship
Ford saw fit to include a short last collaboration between himself and Conrad, *The Nature of a Crime*, as well as a section
from his own novel, *A Call*—to be published complete in 1910
—an experiment pointing towards *The Good Soldier*.

Yet Ford did not propose to advertise a clique. He wanted
above all the best writing being done; and he obtained it from
authors such as Hardy, Wells, Galsworthy, Bennett, Hudson,
Masefield, and Davies. Likewise foremost in his mind was his
belief in discovering and encouraging young talent, as a consequence of which he acquired credit not only for introducing
in the *Review* the work of the scarcely known D. H. Lawrence
—a benefit that Lawrence was to remember gratefully—but
also for discerning promise in other oncoming writers, among
them P. Wyndham Lewis, Ezra Pound, Norman Douglas, and
H. M. Tomlinson. But remarkable as he proved to be in his
purely editorial functions, Ford showed little capacity for
business management; and after its comparatively short run
under his guidance the *English Review* had to be sold in

order to repair its finances. This discouragement was, however, only a beginning to the difficulties in which Ford now found himself involved. From 1910 through about 1913 he encountered a succession of marital and legal disputes not only embarrassing but also to a great extent humiliating in terms of social disapproval and the disruption of friendships.[9] Despite, however, the expenditure of energy demanded by the *Review,* Ford managed between 1908 and 1910 to publish four novels—*Mr. Apollo, The 'Half Moon,' The Portrait,* and *A Call*—making use of both historical and contemporary themes. Like so many artists of large talent, he had the faculty of being able to survive creatively through intervals of heavy external pressure.

Although it would be difficult to measure exactly the personal consequences of this complicated phase in his career, it seems apparent that it brought Ford to another turning point, in this instance one at which he felt not only markedly at odds with his own immediate past but also impelled to move into an environment in certain ways outside the orbit of late Edwardian convention which he had no cause to reverence. Connected now with Violet Hunt, also of pre-Raphaelite descent and a writer of repute who had contributed to the *English Review,* Ford began to frequent both the fashionable social groups to which Miss Hunt belonged and the company of the younger set of advance guard artists— such as Pound, Wyndham Lewis, and the sculptor Gaudier-Brzeska—whom she welcomed to her house. Entering into the prewar atmosphere of aesthetic controversy and revolt with his customary attraction to the experimental, Ford often took part in the gatherings and parties of those engaged in the issues of Futurism and Vorticism; and quite possibly the growing satirical note in much of his work after 1910 owes something not only to his deepening premonition of the approach of European breakdown but also to the rebellious temper of the young art movements of the day. In any case his 1910 first volume of reminiscences, *Ancient Lights,* takes sardonic views of the late Victorian and pre-Raphaelite world of his boyhood; his 1911 novel, *Ladies Whose Bright Eyes* . . . , presents an anti-romantic conception of medievalism; and his novel of 1913, *Mr. Fleight,* is a brilliantly caustic satire on the shoddiness of contemporary political and cultural values.

By somewhat curious coincidence, too, the years from 1910 to 1915, during a good part of which his private affairs were far from happy, saw Ford's arrival at highest skill in nearly every branch of his art. His *Collected Poems,* representing his interested if occasional cultivation of verse, appeared in 1913. More significantly his first acknowledged masterpiece in the novel, *The Good Soldier,* the result of a long course of fictional experiment, had been completed before its actual publication in 1915, a portion having been accepted for the 1914 first issue of the Vorticist periodical *Blast.* Distinctly pertinent also to Ford's record of work demanding historical equipment and facility are the two books which he wrote on commission after the outbreak of the Great War and published in 1915 in the interests of general Allied propaganda. The title of one, *When Blood is Their Argument: An Analysis of Prussian Culture,* approximately indicates its purpose and scope. In the companion volume, *Between St. Denis and St. George: A Sketch of Three Civilizations,* Ford so impressively advocated the French culture that he admired throughout his life that besides being soon translated in France, the work earned him public gratitude and a measure of official recognition in that country. To the credit of these books, as Ford's biographer Douglas Goldring has pointed out, is their superiority to the usual mass of war propaganda, their judicious and unvindictive tone which leaves them still readable for their own sake.[10] For the particular cultural attitudes that they express, they have bearing, too, on the evolution of Ford's opinions after the war and on the historical and cultural implications of his novels at that time.

At just over forty, then, Ford might in 1915 have viewed with some self-satisfaction the proof of his own literary competence, even though he had still no wide public fame. Perhaps, however, he did not, in the midst of world disorder and the far from tranquil condition of his personal affairs. While over age for military service and at a point in life when Conrad, for example, had left regular sea duty for the writer's desk, Ford determined on a trial of physical action that marked the most abrupt and eventful shift in his entire course. In July, shortly after having applied for a commission, he joined the Welch Regiment in the rank of lieutenant; and until January, 1919, he remained with the army, undergoing periods of front assignment in France and Flanders. So far as may be gathered from his none too explicit direct recollections, his experience was largely that of the ordinary foot soldier— no staff appointment but a succession of varied tasks including, on his own testimony, lecturing to trainees, work with a labor battalion, keeping guard over prisoners. Although not actually wounded, like his brother Oliver, he suffered the disabling effects of shell shock and loss of memory and serious gas injury to his lungs. But his comprehensive account of the war with all that he knew of front line happenings he incorporated in his major creative works of the 1920's, in particular the Tietjens or *Parade's End* novels and the equally well written *No Enemy,* almost an epitome of an intelligent man's reaction to the conflict as a whole. If Ford entered the war perhaps in part with his typical impulse to respond to the main events of his age, he could scarcely have foreseen how deeply it would affect his character and outlook, enlarging his sympathies for the plight of others and implanting a permanent sense of the tenuous division between civilized pattern and barbarism:

> No one could have come through that shattering experience and still view life and mankind with any normal vision. In those days you saw objects that the earlier mind labelled as *houses.* They had been used to seem cubic and solid performances. But we had seen Ploegsteert where it had been

revealed that men's dwellings were thin shells that could be
crushed as walnuts are crushed. Man and even Beast . . .
all things that lived and moved and had volition and life
might at any moment be resolved into a scarlet viscosity
seeping into the earth of torn fields. . . . Nay, it had been
revealed to you that beneath Ordered Life itself was
stretched, the merest film with, beneath it, the abysses of
Chaos. One had come from the frail shelters of the Line to
a world that was more frail than any canvas hut.[11]

Such vision laid its spell upon the mind; and not surprisingly
the years between Ford's enlistment and the early 1920's figure
as the only extended period in his mature writing life with
nothing to show of a creative kind, except a small volume of
1918, *On Heaven and Poems Written on Active Service,* partially made up of some *vers libre* poetry reflecting his solemn
war mood. When at last, however, creative energy returned,
coupled with the literary skill that he had acquired before
1915, it was out of war that Ford would draw major inspiration for a new and hardier phase in his development.

But for the moment, on his putting off uniform in 1919, Ford
seemed intent on personal reconstruction and an even more
decisive break with his prewar existence, a step symbolized by
his change of surname from Hueffer to Ford, under which he
would write for the rest of his life. No longer one with the art
circles of London, he turned for a second time to the country;
and accompanied by Stella Bowen, the young painter whom he
had met in 1918, he settled into the laborer's cottage in Sussex
where he remained through 1920 and 1921. Unlike, however,
his somewhat Morris-influenced conduct in the 1890's—except
that in both cases one detects enmity to coercion—he goes now
to the land itself as a means of subsistence, raising vegetables
by hand and breeding pigs in his role of small producer defy-
ing the war stimulated evils of machinery and mass organiza-
tion. How much social protest, in fact, shared in his small
farming aims may be seen in the quiet polemical strain of his

1929 *No Enemy,* a book commemorating through a form of pastoralism the utopian aspect of this country experiment. From this manner of existence, however, Ford had no wish to exclude the amenities of art and converse with acceptable acquaintances, so that frequent visitors, often Americans apparently directed to the cottage by Ezra Pound, came to enjoy the natural hospitality of Ford and Miss Bowen. Also with his fund of war memories and reflections shaping for utterance, Ford recovered both his desire to write and the ambition to interest a publisher in a standing agreement to handle his future books. Encouraged in the latter hope, he accomplished while in Sussex a 1921 publication of his second volume of reminiscences, *Thus to Revisit;* the composition of a satirical dramatic poem, *Mr. Bosphorus and the Muses,* published in 1923 with woodcuts by Paul Nash; and the completion of his first novel since *The Good Soldier*—a book called *The Marsden Case* which, also published in 1923, deserves attention as a prelude to his fuller treatment of the social catastrophe of the war in the *Parade's End* sequence soon to follow.

With the 1920's, and doubtless largely as an outcome of the state of mind produced by the war, the note of internationalism in Ford's work rises perceptibly, although his long study of English character had still to attain supreme expression in *Parade's End.* As plainly, too, his way of life becomes less attached to any fixed locality, despite the fact that he remained loyal in his affection for France and especially for the Provence that he affirmed as a symbol of trustee to civilized values; and in a sense his Sussex farming, rather than a reassertion of English nationality, appears an effort to lead on wholly neutral earth the imagined existence of a frugal but cultured French provincial landholder. Harsh winters, however, had not favored this attempt; and when in 1922 the offer came of temporary use of a small villa at Cap Ferrat, Ford quickly devised means to transfer to the Continent and, as events developed, to move towards another of the flourishing stages in his career. While stopping at Paris, he noted French

concern over the recent death of Proust; and as he indicated
later in his 1934 fictional autobiography, *It Was the Nightingale*, his consciousness of the vacancy left by Proust as novelist-historian of his time may have helped to urge on Ford's own
growing plan for recording "the public events of a decade" as
this took form in *Parade's End*. By 1923, in any case, the first
novel in the sequence, *Some Do Not*, was advancing well at
Cap Ferrat. Since in this year both Ford and Stella Bowen had
reason to feel creatively optimistic, they journeyed in the fall
to Paris as the center of the most exciting art movements of
the period. So congenial did they find the Montparnasse atmosphere that from 1924 to approximately the end of the decade
they quartered themselves in one or another part of the city
playing their role in the prevailing avant-garde exuberance.

Once again in the midst of a crowd of inspired or would-be
artists and of a climate favorable to aesthetic experiment and
controversy, Ford no doubt felt something of the energy and
hopefulness that he had known in the days of Impressionist
activity around the century's beginning. With his past reputation as a literary figure and with important new work of his
own in progress, he came easily into touch with those vitally
associated with the spirit of the era—writers like Joyce and
Hemingway and members of the young American contingent
in Paris, or painters like Nina Hamnett and Juan Gris; and such
contacts helped to enliven both his personal life and the spurt
of successful productivity that he maintained from the middle
to the end of the 1920's. The time, moreover, encouraged his
always latent impulse to serve the arts publicly; and tempted
to engage in another venture at editorship, he undertook to
found with backing from the distinguished American art
patron, John Quinn, but also at a substantial risk of his own
funds a literary periodical, the *transatlantic review*, representative of the new modernist tendencies. With contributors of
such merit as Hemingway, the magazine itself showed the
effect of Ford's exacting standards; but as in the case of the
English Review, financial troubles caused him to relinquish the

project after its fairly short run up to the close of 1924. Possibly on this occasion Ford had to divert attention from editorship to the exigencies of serious creative work; but the latter so well satisfied him that it may have offered some compensation for the collapse of the *transatlantic,* thus making his disappointment less keen than in the matter of the *English Review.* Certainly, at least, the major event in these years was his completion of the *Parade's End* tetralogy with *Some Do Not* in 1924, *No More Parades* in 1925, *A Man Could Stand Up*—in 1926, and *The Last Post* in 1928. Such a main achievement could well speak in his behalf against detractors who, following Conrad's death in 1924, tried to foster the supposition that Ford had plundered the nest of his former collaborator.

With the end of the Montparnasse gala and the onset of the world depression and the ensuing international crisis of the 1930's, Ford's life entered on its final turn, one that brought him into his closest association with the United States, which he had previously viewed with recurrent interest. In the later years of the 1920's Ford had concluded, with good reason, that America promised a future market for his work; and the latter consideration, in the light of financial loss and increasing age, now weighed seriously. In general his books had been well received in the United States, his latest and most encouraging success being the lively sale of the Tietjens novels; and after about 1926 he made frequent trips to New York, gaining new acquaintances and familiarizing himself with the character of the city. Envisaging this extension of his audience, he tends to address himself consciously in works after the middle 1920's—such as *New York is not America* and his final volume of reminiscences, *Return to Yesterday*—to American interests; and his novels of the 1930's all place American characters in important roles. But at the same time he kept a French anchorage at Cap Brun near Toulon, where he could observe the mingling of various nationalities from which he drew material for his two imposing late novels—*The Rash Act* of 1933 and its sequel of 1934, *Henry for Hugh*. Despite, however, his continuing need to stave off insecurity by lecturing and different kinds of journalism, these last years, during which he watched apprehensively the growth of fascism and the danger of European breakdown in another world war, mark the strongest development of his personal beliefs and the fullest elaboration of his creed of internationalism, frugality, and devotion to the arts as opposed to the forces that he most condemned—aggressive nationalism, mass standardization, and encroaching barbarism in whatever form. For this reason the bulk of his writing at this stage reflects a background of solid conviction less immediately perceptible in his early work and a basic aim to press home the disastrous consequences of further wars. His novels, while exhibiting his customary technical skill, combine alert contemporary observation with an implicit plea for a renewal of traditions essential to civilized relationships. His discursive works—such as *Great Trade Route* in 1937 and *Provence* in 1938—argue, sometimes figuratively, for a freshly designed map of world culture. And in the same intellectual nexus, even books concerned specifically with literature—*The English Novel* of 1929 and, more particularly, *The March of Literature from Confucius to Modern Times* of 1939—postulate his constant faith in the arts as vital to human order and sanity.

Ford's death at Deauville in June, 1939 appears somehow related to the whole tenor of his life in that it occurred with no evident sign that his course had come to a halt. Though his health had been poor, he had just returned from the United States, he had started a new novel concerned with the 1930's, and he had made no gesture of resigning his pen or winding up his affairs. However uncertain, therefore, he may have been at the outset, he knew himself at the end of his career for a confirmed man of letters; and Olivet College, in conferring upon him the honorary doctorate that represented his sole academic trophy, gave perceptive recognition to this fact. Endowed though he was with exceptional literary facility, the

very irregularity of his path from first to last, his evasion of
most ordinary ties of person or place, seems indicative of the
truth that his gift was fundamentally creative and of that kind
which happens to thrive best on freedom of movement and on
the application of renewed mental stimulus rather than on the
support drawn by some artists from comparatively fixed surroundings. One secondary consequence of this mobility was
that from his earliest pre-Raphaelite days Ford, not always to
the advantage of peace of mind, was thrown almost constantly
into relation with persons, from artists to politicians, either
notable or otherwise out of the ordinary, so that one forms the
habit of expecting to see his name somewhere in nearly any
volume of letters or memoirs touching upon the arts during the
first quarter of the century. Closely connected in many respects with this readiness to adopt new habits was his lifelong
allegiance to experiment, to the search for fresh literary
methods and higher standards of prose style, which from today's perspective may certainly be recognized both as a main
cause of his failure to gain wide popularity in his day and as
a reason why he now deserves to be called one of the makers
of the twentieth century English novel. On his own admission,
Ford attempted in times of need to write an occasional pot-
boiler; but perhaps sharing a little the plight of James's Ray
Limbert, he could never quite make the pots boil, as the
present-day reader of such novels may be amused and also
thankful to discover. Because, essentially, his aesthetic aims
were positive, the advancing line of the truly productive artist
traverses the fluctuating chart of Ford's personal history.

Chapter III

The Role of the Novelist

BOYHOOD among the pre-Raphaelites committed Ford to a cult of the artist as an exceptional being, and the writing of a first book before he was eighteen proved him amenable to the surrounding demand for genius. Anticipating a mature conviction, he wrote in a diary at the house of his grandfather, Madox Brown, "Every artist is my fellow-countryman," probably thus expressing both a need springing from his consciousness of mixed descent—so often a complicating factor in his novels—and some feeling of isolation in England within a circle of artists including several, like the Rossettis, of foreign extraction. That this latter circumstance bothered Ford in an Imperial age James may have perceived in noting the dubious half-continental background of Densher in *The Wings of the Dove,* who, supposedly modeled on Ford, suffers this particular handicap to social status. Yet if one side of Ford acknowledged the superiority of the artist, another as strenuously rejected the notion of the artist as art object; and his memory of being compelled as a child to wear one red and one green stocking may account for his later association of these colors with the aestheticism that he ridicules in his 1913 novel, *Mr. Fleight.* Relief for the rebellious side came through impulses to condemn literature as "a mug's game" and to find satisfaction in the Napoleonic sea warfare of Marryat and Cooper, the exploits of Stonewall Jackson, and plans for an army officer's career. But the shock of hearing Holman Hunt endlessly complaining in a voice like a creaking door and Ruskin virtuously hissing like an adder must, if insupportable, have been exciting enough to plant in Ford his lifelong fascination and repugnance for the pre-Raphaelite way of life as well as his equal concern with the nature and aims of the artist.

In repudiating pre-Raphaelitism for the drier classical taste beginning to establish itself in the early twentieth century, Ford acted in part, no doubt, on his quick avant-garde perception that later romanticism was fading with the rise of a new movement. Through the flexible interests of his grandfather, Madox Brown, he had been introduced to the French Impressionist painters, to Stendhal's realism, to *Madame Bovary,* and to the fiction of George Moore, thus preparing himself to transfer allegiance to then radical art creeds. Yet his antipathy to pre-Raphaelitism seems to have been as much native as doctrinal and fostered by some temperamental austerity that enabled him even in childhood to delight in Schopenhauer's *Parerga* and to shrink from the emotional disorderliness of the Rossetti legend:

> And on the night before the planned elopement Mr. and Mrs. Rossetti were in a box at the Opera and Swinburne joined them in a state of intoxication so insupportable that Mrs. Rossetti went home and took an overdose of some opiate. . . .
>
> There were, of course, in Charlotte's account other gloomy and harrowing details of miscarriages and misunderstandings in a lugubriously oil-lamp-lit, indigestion-ridden, gin sodden, damp dripping London of the seventies—than which City none other could be imagined less suited to the sports and loves of lyric balladists of origin whether North Country or Italian. . . . The reports of the inquest—which Charlotte needless to say attended—state clearly that before taking her overdose Mrs. Rossetti had been at the Opera with Mr. Rossetti and Mr. Swinburne . . . and the coroner and jury passed a vote of sympathy for Mr. Rossetti, thus left without anyone to sew on his shirt-buttons. But they say nothing of Mr. Swinburne's intoxication, which you can take or not as you please.[1]

Whether or not the incident was as sordid as Ford makes it seem—and he remarks elsewhere with a trace of ambivalence,

"I was a terribly proper young man"—his account of it registers not only his customary irony in dealing with aesthetic pretense but also his lasting opposition to the pre-Raphaelite attitude towards passion. Even more savagely, and with fictional license, Christopher Tietjens in *Some Do Not* lashes out at an obese, oily Rossetti in a grease-spotted dressing gown standing with ". . . some Mrs. W. Three Stars, gazing into a mirror that reflects their fetid selves and gilt sunfish and drop chandeliers and plates sickening with cold bacon fat and gurgling about passion," [2] the mirror image of self-love and illusion magnifying the disgust of a character in revolt against a prewar society whose sexual ethic, in Ford's opinion, had been colored throughout by pre-Raphaelite influence. Such a conception of the artist, fixed in his mind by the image of Rossetti, may well have been enough to turn the thoughts of the young Ford towards the service career of a soldier or civil servant and to strengthen the decision of his brother, Oliver, likewise gifted, to become a tobacco merchant before taking up literature and writing *The Artistic Temperament*, a novel under the pseudonym of "Jane Wardle," dealing with a painter so afflicted by the weakness named in the title of the book that he causes embarrassment and misfortune by abandoning himself to a Rossettian intoxication with physical beauty.

Whereas these mixed feelings about the pre-Raphaelites, and notably Rossetti, affected Ford's efforts to arrive at a personally acceptable notion of the artist, they involved also the problem of the artist as related to society, on which point Ford shows his readiness to assert and to defend the artist's integrity. Thus in the critical study of Rossetti which he published in 1902 Ford, despite careful observance of his dictum that criticism should apply to the artist's work rather than the personality of the man, speaks out flatly against the harm done Rossetti from the unmerited attack by Buchanan and other supporters of the "fleshly school" indictment:

> It is impossible to say whether he would or would not have had other hallucinations; but it is certain that the horror

of so vile and so unjustifiable an assertion made things infinitely worse and definitely caused Rossetti to think that there was in the world a gigantic conspiracy to hold him up to obloquy. The idea haunted him for a long time; under the horror of it he attempted to commit suicide; it riveted the chloral habit finally upon him and the one thing and the other sapped his life and in their effects gradually ruined his work. The whole affair is one of the most cruel and unnecessary that the history of the arts can show, and one of the most lamentable that in life can be imagined.[3]

Indirectly this passage exhibits Ford's preoccupation with the topic of mental strain and decline, a theme that in many of his novels may owe something to the early memory of Rossetti's plight. But in its immediate bearing, the statement claims justice for any artist exposed to misconception, Rossetti himself offering for the moment a capital example.

Besides taking, then, from his association with pre-Raphaelitism a settled distrust of its assumptions about love, Ford likewise carried away an antipathy to connecting the artist with the artistic temperament. In 1904 he had raised the question in correspondence with Galsworthy; and judging from the latter's reply, Ford had evidently declared himself sick of the word artist and the cant that artists feel more deeply than other people, contending instead that feeling is less prominent in the artist than the "impersonal, analytic, philosophic element."[4] The sharpness of this reaction probably betrays in part Ford's disturbance over the Wilde case, which nagging as it did at the literary world of the early century struck particularly hard at Ford because of his suspicion that art itself had been damaged by public inclination to link pre-Raphaelitism with the Wilde brand of aestheticism in its idea of the artist. As late as 1939, in *The March of Literature*, Ford remarked that Wilde's desire to *épater le bourgeois* ". . . killed for a number of years the art of literature in England" and that Wilde's excesses were merely those of a half artist.[5] In consequence he took pains in much of his discussion of pre-

Raphaelitism to distinguish between true pre-Raphaelites, like Hunt and Millais, and the aesthetic hangers-on of this inner group to whom he assigns the blame for lowering the artist's prestige. Further manifesting his distaste for identification of the artist with the aesthete or bohemian, he formed the habit of thinking of men sometimes numbered among the pre-Raphaelites, such as Madox Brown and Morris, as so far from artists in manner and appearance as to resemble old-fashioned ship's captains with a pre-Victorian Regency air.

Ford's discouragement over the blow dealt the arts by the Wilde scandal, while representative of much opinion at the time, also reveals his belief in the Nineties as a period which might have, from a promising start, given new force to literature and to culture generally. His hopes for the "glorious early nineties" had fastened, shrewdly, on the fortunes of *The Yellow Book* in opening the way for new and really fine work on lines beyond pre-Raphaelitism; and the failure of the magazine meant for him the defeat of an effort to provide artistic orientation for the social scheme and a decline into the vulgarity and jingoism of the end of the decade. In the Boer War, which he deplored as a result of the ill-omened partition of Africa, he discerned the sign of a radical change in the tone of England, "a chasm separating the new world from the old," [6] a contempt for principles in politics and standards in art, and an intensification of war consciousness and war preparation leading to 1914. In addition to quickening his attention to contemporary affairs, this turn in events helped to crystallize his emerging conception of the artist and his purpose in a world now not so much antagonistic to aestheticism as indifferent or contemptuous to the arts in general in the growing worship of power. The times gave Ford reason to weigh more intently the problem of artist and man of action while likewise prompting him to the idea that the arts might be served by a revival of the forces behind the *Yellow Book* enterprise. In the face of popular doctrines that too much study of the arts would make the youth of England effeminate or of tendencies to regard photographs of Venus statuary as indecent, Ford sums up his apprehension with the remark, ". . . it could not be wondered at that I did not feel very English." [7]

Before coming to this conclusion about the deleterious influence upon culture of the spirit induced by the South African War, Ford had made some sporadic attempts to shake off the laxities of aestheticism by exploring forms of active experience in the ordinary sense. He had dabbled in Morris Socialism, which did not satisfy though it left traces on his thought, and had tried country living, a real, if impermanent, attraction. During the Boer War he reports having protested in favor of the African natives, for which he was roughly handled. Kipling stimulated his enthusiasm so far that he wept over stories concerning the deaths of young subalterns and perhaps took interest in Dick Heldar in *The Light That Failed,* the painter who combines art and immersion in the life of war correspondents and soldiers. Briefly, too, he inclined towards the outlook of the Henley circle, writers who did not stand apart from the common herd but ". . . wanted as much as anything to be men—upon the whole quite commonplace men, indulging in orgies of tobacco, whiskey and the other joys of the commercial traveller. About love as they handled it there was nothing mystic; passion justified nothing." [8] But although Ford might find this rebuke to pre-Raphaelite passion congenial, the touch of scorn in the whole estimate indicates his resistance to the vulgarity that he sensed in the Henleyite creed. If the idea that "a man of action was something fine and a man of letters a sort of castrato," [9] offered Ford a resolution to a problem of his own, he could not approve the bluntness of the dichotomy; and in the end he was fastidious enough to decide that ". . . Henley and his friends seemed to me unreasonably boistrous and too loudly cocksure." [10]

On Ford's testimony, perhaps debatable, Henley's main service was to initiate the association between Ford and Conrad which began in the late 1890's. If his reading of Conrad's prose in the manuscript of *Almayer's Folly* brought Ford "the

rarest literary pleasure of my existence" in the discovery of
an English "new, magic, and unsurpassed," [11] his encounter
with Conrad himself seemed to promise a basis of mutual personal accord, despite the ensuing friction between two divergent temperaments. Both were "papists," and both were critical of the direction taken by Imperialism, especially in Africa.
Although Violet Hunt may exaggerate when she says that Ford
imitated Conrad to the point of cultivating in himself one or
another of the latter's phobias,[12] Ford's own remarks in various places in his writings further the supposition that his
estimate of Conrad accorded closely with the image of the
artist that Ford had been seeking. For one thing, Conrad supplied the aptest example of Ford's soon to be established
theory that the writer, to be of any worth, must have lived a
full life of action, the more valuable if it has included participation in war. Similar qualities Ford came to perceive in
Stephen Crane, whose way of life he compared with that of
Henry James in a reflective statement that expresses Ford's
tendency to balance the claims of luxury against those of
privation:

> I wonder which is the better mode of life for a writer—of
> the two modes followed by those two Americans in that old
> corner far away and long ago. There was James with his
> carefully calculated life in a Georgian treasure-house—with
> his lawns and his Ladies and his flowers and his old, mellow,
> brick garden walls and his smooth-running household—
> and all his suavities. And with all his passionate inner life
> for ever concealed so that you would have sworn he had
> never lived at all. . . . And there was Crane, for ever stuffed
> in somewhere as waste paper is stuffed into any old drawer
> —in an Oxted villa; on a Cuban hillside; in a hut in Tin Can,
> Nevada; . . .[13]

The choice was, no doubt, peculiar to a period in which late
Imperialism seemed to have raised the alternatives of material
culture and the rewards of action. But that Ford regarded this

dilemma as somewhat more permanent for the artist appears in his complaint: "For the writer looks at life and does not share it. This is his calamity; this is his curse." [14]

By contrast to the pose of the commercial traveller that Ford had disapproved in the Henley group, Conrad presented himself in the congenial role of the English country gentleman, an attitude that Ford was quite ready to fall in with and to imagine as embodying ". . . the feelings, views of the world and composure of a member of the ruling classes of the days of Lord Palmerston—tempered of course with such eccentricities as go with the spleen of the *milor anglais*." [15] This stand probably helps to explain the mutual attraction of Ford and Conrad to Arthur Marwood, a genuine squire and university man who was to influence the work of both novelists. Ford delighted in the fact that Conrad, while expert in his art, could look anything but a specialized aesthete; and he ascribed to his associate the talents of "a magnificent business man of the imaginative type" [16] and the appearance of never being bookish: "He was frequently taken for a horse fancier. He liked that." [17] Even years later, and towards the end of his own career, Ford insisted on underlining the impression that Conrad was, ". . . the most consummate, the most practical, the most common-sensible and the most absolutely passionate man-of-action become conscious man-of-letters that this writer has ever known, read of or conceived of." [18] To some extent, of course, this verdict carries the stamp of Ford's literary portraiture, Conrad as sitter being represented not factually but as seen imaginatively by a particular painter. Yet the description throws light on Ford's endeavor to escape what he considered the book-fed art of Victorian aestheticism and to create with Conrad a non-literary prose directed to contemporary actualities, even though such prose would carry the authority of Flaubert.

While Ford, consequently, alludes copiously enough to their discussions of fictional technique, his concern is also to portray himself and Conrad as occupied in an alert if detached

fashion with the course of immediate public events—the Boer
War, Fashoda, the doings of men of affairs such as Kitchener,
Northcliffe, Balfour and Chamberlain. Attentive though he is
to Conrad's form and language, he is as much interested in
placing his collaborator in line with a new literary movement
now conceived by Ford as essential to meeting the radical
social and political changes of the later Nineties, so that he is
prone to stress, and possibly over-stress, the political significance, without ulterior political purpose, of Conrad's writing
from the outset:

> But indeed, the political motive is discernible enough even
> in his earlier, Malay-marine excursions. *Almayer* is an ex-
> posure of Dutch exploitations of the spice islands; *The Out-
> post of Progress,* a cynical and dreary exposé of the darker
> sides of imperialism; and *Heart of Darkness,* the most im-
> passioned unveiling of the hidden springs of human hypoc-
> risy, greed, bloodlust—and of course heroism!—that the
> pages of any book have ever recorded.[19]

The poet in Conrad Ford imagined as not impoverished but
rather enriched by alliance with the man of political vision
whose memories extended from the revolutionary atmosphere
of his Polish youth to nearly the whole sweep of the Imperial
movement, which he supported with moderate sympathies.
Naturally enough, therefore, Ford, while recognizing the merits of Conrad's specifically sea narratives, devotes his highest
praise to the Conrad who finally emerged, most himself, in the
"political romances"—*Nostromo, The Secret Agent,* and *Under
Western Eyes*—the latter in Ford's opinion Conrad's greatest
book, "that tremendous masterpiece." [20] In such works, in a
sense, the latent man of action in the artist finds compensation
through imagining complete worlds: typical cities as in *The
Secret Agent,* countries as in *Nostromo* and *Under Western
Eyes*—constructs wherein the reader can ascertain the shapes
and patterns of contemporary existence.

As much as anything, these observations tend to identify

Conrad with the position of the novelist which was becoming substantially that of Ford himself as he outgrew aestheticism: the contemporary historian in fiction. Into this path he could move without difficulty from an interest in history itself, beginning with a boyhood attraction to the Napoleonic legend and the lives of the Greeks and Romans, the latter subject opening to him through an "elephantine and delightfully illustrated work" translated by his father from the German and supplying Ford with the inspiration for a first novel on the young Caesar in the hands of Aegean pirates.[21] This first contact with classical life must have led to his mature admiration for the Greek historians—Xenophon, Herodotus, and Thucydides—whom he credits with a share in the formation of his literary theories [22] and to his acquaintance with the historians of Rome, with whom might be listed Petronius whose *Satyricon* Ford used as a model for certain literary effects. Another of "the greatest pleasures and influences" of his childhood was John Addington Symonds whom he knew not only from the *Renaissance in Italy* but also from other works, such as *Shakespeare's Predecessors in the English Drama.*[23] Although he came to disagree with Symonds' interpretation of the Renaissance, the writer's portrayal of Renaissance atmosphere and even more his general style, representing an era of artist-historians such as Michelet and Carlyle, must have impressed Ford and perhaps suggested to him the possibilities of combining literature and history after the manner of Pater and Vernon Lee. Despite his later and broader reading of history, he seems to have retained something of his boyhood respect for Symonds if only as a contrast to the "horrible commercial scholarship" of Victorian times or the fact-grubbing of the German "Puffendorfiuses" whom he affected to loathe.[24]

Temporarily, therefore, Ford evidently considered the pursuit of history a likely replacement for pre-Raphaelitism; and having put aside the alternatives of soldier or civil servant, he made a start in this occupation. The extensive biography of Madox Brown, which Ford published in 1896, had involved research; and he mentions having studied, both in England and abroad, historical documents of the Tudor period for a projected life of Henry VIII,[25] this ambition finding a different fulfillment later in his trilogy of novels of the early Tudor period, *The Fifth Queen*. In his approach to history Ford reveals his native literary bent in seeking for the "psychology" of certain past times, as when he says, for example, in the dedication to his Stuart novel, *The 'Half Moon,'* that ". . . the psychology of the Old World in the days of Hudson has always been very fascinating to me. It is, as you know, the subject to which I have more than anything devoted my attention: for at that date the Dark Ages were finally breaking up." [26] This kind of study, governed by his literary power of selection, helps to account both for the wealth and precision in detail that enlivens his purely historical novels, in spite of the fact that he placed only moderate value on this type of fiction, and for his ability, beyond the grasp of so many historical novelists, to create an atmosphere entirely foreign to the present.

The same effort to determine the psychological key to the understanding of an age he brought to observations of his own time and the societies—especially English, German, American, and Latin—that he regarded as central to it, so that the practice is likewise essential to his method in the novels on contemporary subjects. Excited by the Dreyfus trial at Rennes, for example, he remarks on having suddenly ". . . the glimpse of extraordinary possibilities of psychology." [27] In the early years of the century he had gained sufficient reputation of a literary-historical kind to obtain commissions for books like *The Cinque Ports* (1900); for impressionistic studies of modern England like *The Soul of London* (1905), *The Heart of the Country* (1906), and *The Spirit of the People* (1907); and, during or after the First World War, for partly didactic treatises on Prussian and French culture. Even so late as his *Provence* (1938) he maintained that he was writing "the history of Our Own Times"; [28] and this historical sense, though his own version of past and present, is a constant factor in virtually all of his novels and one that relates him to the modern literary temper, especially during the first quarter of the century. It was, essentially, not a sense for historical abstraction so much as an artist's sensibility to signs and omens, to shifts in historical weather, like the almost feminine apprehension with which he endows his character, Gringoire, in the postwar *No Enemy* when Gringoire speaks of his feelings in one of the periods of prewar crisis: "It was, therefore, in the southern and central regions of France that, before the war, I had most strongly the feeling—that feeling of affrighted buildings. It came to me one day in a broad French landscape, somewhere, I imagine, just south of Lyons. Perhaps it was in Orange—or possibly in Tarascon. At any rate, it was just after the close of the Agadir incident." [29]

When Ford joined Conrad, it seems to have been with the understanding, among other things, that he would serve the collaboration with a store of usable data. In 1899, for example, Meldrum, a member of the Blackwood firm, mentions Ford in a letter to William Blackwood and adds: "I may say that Conrad is going to work with him on a great novel about the Ana Baptists of which sect Hueffer (who is of the great German publishing family of that name) has great masses of information." [30] Although it may have been no grave misfortune that this big novel never took shape, even if Ford later drew on his Anabaptist information for the *The 'Half Moon,'* Meldrum's comment points to Ford's readiness to employ historical resources just as it does, also, to his study of religious sects and its bearing on the religious issue in so many of his novels. In the collaboration on *Romance,* based on Ford's independent start on a novel to be called *Seraphina,* Ford notes that it was his business to provide the facts of the intrigue in England and Jamaica; [31] and for the earlier collaboration, *The Inheritors,* he supplied the main substance for a novel which, attempting to get in hand some of the principal aspects of contemporary history at the turn of the century, is to some extent a *roman à clef.*

As a major precedent for the blending of literature and history, Ford, as well as Conrad, could refer to the example of the chosen master, Flaubert, who had researched laboriously to produce *La Tentation de Saint-Antoine* and, even more to the purpose, the *Salambô*, which clearly influenced the style of *Romance* and Ford's method in his own novels of the past. While commending everything by Flaubert and subscribing to the usual praise of *Madame Bovary*, Ford tends to view Flaubert as a historian and to return again and again to the work in which the French writer was most obviously the large-scale chronicler of his own time: *L'éducation sentimentale*. Ford's preference for the *Education*, which he often called the greatest novel ever written, rested not only on the artistry of the book but also on his belief in its public importance:

> Nothing was more true than the words of Flaubert, when he said that, if France had read his "Education Sentimentale," she would have been spared the horrors of the Franco-Prussian War. For, during the period before 1870, France had drifted for a time into the same happy-go-lucky frame of mind that has always existed in England. And so exactly did Flaubert depict this frame of mind in this his most monumental book, that could France have set itself seriously to the task of reading and pondering upon it, undoubtedly some tightening up of her national character must have taken place. France, however, amiably ignored the masterpiece, just as, in all probability, England would ignore a similar work did it produce one.[32]

To Ford, the *Education* lifted the novel to a position equal with "an historical event of capital importance"[33] and thus proved that the novelist might outrank the man of action. Of the right of other Continental authors, such as the Goncourts and Zola, to be considered novelist-historians Ford says relatively little, just as he largely ignores Tolstoy in that regard. His reason for conferring the title primarily upon Flaubert and Maupassant evidently lay in his detecting in their form and finish in the working of historical substance precisely those qualities that he wished to associate with the aims of himself and Conrad and whatever other English writers might be attached to the cause.

For a time after becoming acquainted with Conrad, James, and Crane, Ford, who believed in the advantages of cohesive art movements after the French fashion, seems to have persuaded himself that this set of writers living near each other in the south of England might constitute a group with a somewhat similar outlook and basis in literary method. A common enterprise offered the possibility of a revival in the spirit of the new century of the literary front opened by such organs as *The Yellow Book* and Henley's *National Observer*, and Ford moved determinedly to realize this ambition by assuming the editorship of the *English Review* in 1908. That his fellow novelists in the Rye area were not native English he saw as beneficial in making them sharper, less provincial observers not only of the English themselves but also of the international scene, the latter being the proper field for the modern novel and the one wherein Ford placed himself as a writer of books of "international comparison." [34] With a touch of whimsicality he could imagine this group as furnishing the Imperial Englishman with an art comparable to that provided the Imperial Roman by Greek slaves; yet in all seriousness he desired to see, as with Flaubert in the *Education*, a corrective to national slackness through the propagation of a critical attitude of the sort that he later declared central to the purpose of the *English Review*. Like Conrad, he enlarged upon the historical insight to be obtained from Crane, notably with respect to war in *The Red Badge*, and from James, especially in the later work beginning with *The Spoils of Poynton*, which Ford and Conrad favored, wherein James, disillusioned, ". . . devoted himself to the task of portraying the lives of English people who were just people—good people, comfortably off, as a rule." [35] Where Conrad, in his essay on James, praised the latter as "the historian of fine consciences,"

Ford even more explicitly sets James in the category of novel-ist-historian: "His greatness, to put it succinctly, is that of the historian—the historian of one, of two, and possibly of three or more, civilisations." [36]

In asserting the historical function of the novelist, Ford was, of course, responding to the changing climate of taste in the earlier years of the century. With the high tide of Im-perialism—the increase in luxury, the rise in city population, and the over-all growth of complexity in human relationships —the intelligence of the day was becoming analytical and inclined to stock-taking. After the Boer War and the intensifi-cation of international rivalry with its alarms and crises the expansive note of early Imperialism toned down into the more anxious desire to know where England herself stood and might be going, so that the new and strange world for exploration lay not overseas but at home and within the region of "the world's work," to borrow the title of a well-known magazine of the time. In 1909, for example, C. F. G. Masterman, the Liberal politician and a friend whose views of contemporary life Ford respected, contended in his somewhat apprehensive book, *The Condition of England,* which passed through at least six editions, that there was urgent need for "a diagnosis of the hidden life of England," which would ". . . exhibit the temper, mettle, response, character of an island race at a particular period of its supremacy." [37] To such an investiga-tion Masterman held that fiction might well contribute. It had, indeed, done so in novels of the country house, the shop, the slum which could calculate on surprising the reader accus-tomed to a restricted orbit by disclosing the unknown within the supposedly familiar, a strategy employed successfully by Arnold Bennett even in his postwar *Riceyman Steps.* The theory that society, too involved to be depicted as a whole, could best be presented by close study of one or another of its essential, if humbler, units supports an entry by Bennett in his *Journal* in 1907:

I bought Taine's *Voyage en Italie,* and was once again fired to make fuller notes of the impressions of the moment, of *choses vues*. Several good books by him consist of nothing else. I must surely by this time be a trained philosophic observer—fairly exact, and controlled by scientific principles. At the time one can scarcely judge what may be valuable later on. At the present moment I wish, for instance, that some schoolmistress had written down simply her impression of her years of training; I want them for my novel. The whole of life ought to be covered thus by 'impressionists', and a vast mass of new material of facts and sensations collected for use by historians, sociologists and novelists. I really must try to do my share of it more completely than I do.[38]

If, however, Ford sympathized with this mood of historical gravity, it was by no means in accordance with the attitude of the foregoing passage, where Bennett expresses his insatiable curiosity for everything in the way of historical and sociological data. The significance of Ford's own theorizing for subsequent literary developments lies in its fundamental effort to relate the novel to contemporary reality yet to preserve its integrity as an art form, not pleading its right to a place with the sciences but actually asserting its superiority of approach to the imagination. Hence he opposed Wells and insisted, with the authority of Flaubert and the modern French tradition, on the impersonality of the writer and his avoidance of the propaganda that Ford thought the root cause of Galsworthy's failings as an artist.

The energy expended by Ford throughout his life in explaining and defending, sometimes tediously, his view of the nature and value of the novel can be justified by his concern over the future of a literary form which, if large in promise, remained still around the beginning of the century "the Cinderella of Art-Forms" and so in need of firmer public status

and fresh direction. To accomplish this, Ford wanted it released
from the suspicion of triviality sometimes accorded it by English readers in the past and regulated by standards serious
enough to meet the requirements of intelligence, a desirable
schooling being that of the French disciplined sophistication
earlier submitted to by George Moore. Affirming that the novel
stood ready to become ". . . the only vehicle for the thought
of our day" and one by which ". . . you can enquire into every
department of life, you can explore every department of the
world of thought," [39] he sought to guarantee its recognition in
the world of affairs, perhaps even its thoughtful acceptance by
statesmen, by enjoining the novelist to win respect by craftsmanship rather than by the hit-or-miss routine of the inspired
amateur. In his *English Review* days Ford came to the point
of hinting that if novelists stopped muddling through, British
men of action might be inspired to do likewise.

Yet despite overstatement designed to compel assent, such
pronouncements really aim to overcome the true danger of
public resistance to the novel; and since Ford's whole cultural
philosophy, from start to finish, rested on a belief in the connection between the arts and national character, his main
principle was that literature should exist not as a casual or
restricted pleasure but as a source of enlightenment for a widespread audience, which he knew well enough had to be
prodded out of indifference. Hence, despite some retreats as
he grew older, he continued, like Conrad, to affirm substantially that the novelist should find the means, without
aesthetic compromise, to address himself to ordinary active men
in books that ". . . the English gentleman might read in his
library, with the cedar tree on the lawn outside it—or the flag
lieutenant in harbour, during the dog watches." [40] Ford's concern with technique had, therefore, in addition to its formal
end the utilitarian but defensible one of capturing the minds of
readers not only impatient with older methods of narration but
also exposed to the irritant of modern distraction. The enlarged
opportunities of the novelist required increased technical pro-

ficiency to enable him to enforce his indispensable role in contemporary life.

In ascribing broad powers to the novelist, Ford gave proof
of his intent to defend imaginative literature against the weakening of traditional values perceptible at the turn of the century. To blame for this were not only the cheap newspaper,
dating from the South African War, but also the rise of the
specialist and the statistician, whose reduction of experience
to collections of abstract data deprived the ordinary man of a
hold on social continuities forming a consistent picture of the
life of the day. Ford's slogan of "the Impression over the
Statistic" made a case for the vital function of the novelist who
alone, through his gift of direct and imaginative apprehension,
could present a unified vision of the world at large and as fictional historian close the breach between the divided areas of
factual and statistical information, an argument by which Ford
in his plea for imaginative synthesis to transcend abstraction
came close to Koestler's recent stand in *The Sleepwalkers*. In
a life more bewildering through the loss of familiar landmarks,
the novelist may provide the mind beset by accumulations of
fact with some idea of pattern and also aid in restoring contact
between man and man which, in an age of the crowd and of
metropolitan breakdown in understanding by the individual
of the lives of his fellows, Ford thought a main characteristic
and issue of contemporary existence. Because statistics bring
no insight into the nature of private life and its passions, the
novelist alone can record such experience of other men as the
increasingly isolated reader lacks, the writer not moralizing but
simply "rendering" or accurately projecting selected instances
so as to place the reader at a height where he can better observe himself and his neighbors and stimulate his dormant
powers of reflection. Although without the firsthand relationships of the city-state that aided Greek writers toward vivid
expression, the modern novelist can emulate them to the extent
of transcribing eyewitness accounts of typical situations in his
world so faithfully that the reader can arrive at some judgment

of human affairs. As a model of this rendering of a small but highly suggestive episode from the private history of a few ordinary people, *Madame Bovary* remains the archetypal modern novel.

Ford held, then, that the novelist must be above all an Impressionist, a register of his time, or indeed of earlier centuries, not by the laboratory methods of the specialist but by using his temperament and personal insight as measures of experience. Ford rather flaunts the word Impressionist as a label for the movement to which he allied himself with Conrad, Crane, James, and Hudson not only because the term was new and provocative in his earlier years but also because of his conviction that only the individual eye and mind can pass beyond facts to the summarizing view which he thought the compilers of historical textbooks had renounced. Although perhaps influenced by the examples of Pater in *The Renaissance* and of Vernon Lee with her works of brilliant conjecture in *Studies of the Eighteenth Century in Italy* and *Euphorion,* Ford's ideal of the writer was humanistic and related to his liking for the classical tradition in education and art, as this preference became intensified before the advance of science and specialization. In turning to the novelist as the best exponent of a practical historical sense, Ford readily altered his principle of the historian as artist to that of the artist as historian.

Obviously Ford wanted the term Impressionism to denote higher powers of comprehension and creativity in the novelist than Bennett allowed for in his *Journal* entry, where he does not differentiate its aims from those of an official naturalistic realism. Ford, however, did intend a sharp distinction when he noted that Impressionism brought to the prevailing realism new literary techniques, these being calculated to intensify the element of conscious art and thereby to stress incidentally the dominance of the artist over his materials. In this assertion Ford was carrying into the twentieth century the struggle to confirm the importance of the artist but on better and more relevant grounds than those of aesthetic posturing or scorn of the bourgeoisie. While still cherishing a belief in the supremacy of the artist, Ford directs his arguments not to affirming the detachment of the artist from the vulgar but to the far more cogent point of the artist's value to society and, finally, to the positive function of the arts as a whole to the maintenance of civilization. As time went on, and especially in his postwar years, Ford began to see the problem as an issue of industrialism and the machine—invariably capitalized—over against frugality and the arts, the latter virtues being connected in his mind, particularly in later works like *Great Trade Route* and *Provence,* with an image of "Mediterranean" civility as opposed to "Nordic" barbarism. But that he did not in the end foresee a check to industrialism nor its alternative in arts and crafts activity may be gathered from the compromise for the future that he proposed near the close of his life:

> For myself, I look forward to a day when, the automobile being as nearly extinct as is today the railway, men shall live in great or small but intensively cultivated areas. Once or twice a week men shall fly to the power centers, do their three hour shifts, superintending the actions or executing the repairs of the power-supplying machines . . . or their field work in the great grain centers and ranches. The rest of the time they will occupy with the agreeable and unhurried labour of their own soil or with their own benches, chisels, easels, fiddle bows, lasts . . . and with whatever form of night life they shall find agreeable when the day is over. Occasionally even they will take a read in a book.[41]

Ford's hopes for the writer as an influence on the public mind were, however, larger than this in the years when he conceived of the fusion of historian and Impressionist. His idea of what Impressionism might accomplish underwent important changes, too, as he experimented with techniques and studied the work and theories of James and Conrad. In one perspective, considerably modified as he advanced, he viewed Impressionism, much as the Goncourts had done, as a subtle method of representing the shades and complexities of modern feeling by means of a prose instrument more refined than that of abstract and logical statement, more capable of play upon the nerves and senses, especially the visual which had been sharpened by the teachings of Ruskin, Pater and other advocates of trained contemplation of the spectacle of existence. From the later nineteenth century absorption in painting and familiarity with pictorial images, it was an easy step for the Impressionist in writing to direct the eye of the observer to the color of the external environment, making temperament the optical apparatus for the reader. On at least one occasion, in his 1900 book on *The Cinque Ports* furnished with illustrations by Douglas Hyde, Ford's own knowledge of painting enabled him to construct a prose suitable to the topic, as when he turned Winchelsea into a picture with definite associations:

> On the far left there is a mass of green leafage; then a low grey wall, a grey, red-roofed house with its garden cutting up the side of the hill; then the majestic old gate itself— a grey patch, picked out with the green tracery of climbing plants; then a fretted, peaked, and gabled red line of roofs, dominating a profusion of foliage. This—with a grey blue sky above and the sunlight bringing out the red of the roofs —is the Winchelsea that forms the background of Millais's picture of the "Blind Girl." [42]

This style, more ordinary description than the kind of Whistlerian Impressionism that sought to catch the shimmer of rapidly glimpsed details under peculiar conditions of light, Ford confined, happily, to the occasion that called it forth. Impressionistic prose with a Whistler flavor he also subsequently cast off, though he used it at times in early work in the travel or descriptive vein popular before the war. For this manner of Impressionism he seems to have felt little innate sympathy since it registered a spirit of restlessness and strained visual acuity that he thought a shortcoming of modern life by contrast with the past. He understood, however, the adjustment of such a style to the vibration of modernity, ". . . all the little lights that whirl past, in the shadows that flicker, in the tenuous and momentary reflections seen in the polish of carriage panels— the impersonality of it all," [43] and used it at times, as when he represents the flash of crowded events upon the slightly fatigued nerves of the Edwardian pleasuregoer:

> You carry away from it a vague kaleidoscopic picture— lights in clusters, the bare shoulders of women, white flannel on green turf in the sunlight, darkened drawing rooms with nasal voices chanting parodies of prayers, the up and down strokes of fiddle bows, the flicker of fifty couples whirling round before you as with a touch of headache you stand in a doorway, a vague recollection of brilliant anecdote, the fag end of a conversation beneath the palms of a dimmed conservatory, and a fatigue and a feverish idea that if you had missed any one of these unimportant things you would have missed life.[44]

Such Impressionism specializes, above all, in the projection of individual moods, casual moments of reverie when the person feels rapport between his inner state and the external scene— if only a London street viewed from a window—instants not of tragedy but of comprehension:

> He will stand looking down; and a sudden consonance with his mood, of overwhelming and hardly comprehensible joy, of overwhelming and hardly fathomable pain, a sudden significance will be there in the black wet street, in the long wavering reflections on the gleaming paving stones, in the engrossed hurry of the passer-by. It will become, intimately and rightly, the appropriate background for a beginning of— for a farewell from life—for the glow of a communal love as for the dull pain of a malady ending only in death.[45]

Impressions like these, experience "rendered" rather than "told," can, however, when carefully selected, do more than simply convey atmosphere and mood. They can be made to epitomize—perhaps even epiphanize—the essential meaning of places or events and thus arrive at once, through the writer's imaginative apprehension, at the summarizing point that a sequence of abstract data fails to reach. They are, then, the sources, the *quellen,* for the novelist-historian by contrast with the statistics of the sociologist. With such chosen instances the writer may illuminate for the ordinary man larger ranges of experience out of the multiplicity of life and so awaken historical sense or grasp of the definitive "spirit" of a particular time or place. Indicative of Ford's theory are the titles of the three popular books on contemporary England published by him during the first decade of the century and quoted approvingly by Masterman, who supported comprehensive views—works which sought to capture the "soul" of London, the "heart" of the country, the "spirit" of the people. In the first of these, *The Soul of London,* Ford explains his method in this early venture into historical Impressionism:

> A really ideal book of the kind would not contain "writing about" a town: it would throw a personal image of the place on to the paper. It would not contain such a sentence as: "There are in the city of —— 720 firms of hat manufacturers employing 19,000 operatives." Instead there would be a picture of one, or two, or three hat factories, peopled with human beings, where slow and clinging veils of steam waver over vats and over the warm felt on cutters' slabs. And there would be conveyed the idea that all these human beings melt, as it were, into the tide of humanity as all those vapours melt into the overcast skies.[46]

With only a little adjustment, the essential method defined here could be made to apply to books like Conrad's *The Nigger of the "Narcissus"* and Dreiser's *Sister Carrie.*

This theory governs much of Ford's early practice in various kinds of writing; and it also accounts for his openly professed negligence regarding the truth of minor fact as contrasted with his avowed accuracy in framing impressions, for him the lasting

truths of the imagination. And whatever detracts from his right
to the name of historian in the exact sense takes nothing from
his reputation as novelist; for whereas the reader may question
statements in Ford's supposedly informational works, he cannot
help yielding to the display of minute details which gives the
air of truth to Ford's better novels. Actually Ford's mind was
antipathetic to vague impressionism and misty generalization.
It was fundamentally precise, even in the matter of inventing
rather than discovering fact, so that he did not equate his
method with prose reverie. If his liking for a strongly personal
historical manner probably owed something to nineteenth
century precedent, his favorite models were the classical historians, in particular Herodotus whose "matchless projections
of the world of his day" Ford regarded as anticipating "the
technique most usual to the novelist and historian of the present day . . . either the late Joseph Conrad or the living Aldous
Huxley." [47] The quality in the Greek historians that Ford
wished to emulate and that he thought present in the best
English writers from Bunyan and Gibbon to Hudson was the
firsthand rendition of their material which gives to the reader
a feeling of participation, of vicarious experience. This principle, cardinal in Ford's view of the novel, suggests that he
adopted Impressionistic technique not for the purposes of word
painting but in the desire for an idiom as close as possible to
the substance of experience as lived.

To Impressionistic writing Ford ascribed, therefore, a special
intention which removed the implication of subjective lyricism
and exacted from the writer a disciplined choice and shaping
of his materials. Whether embodied in a single passage or a
complete book, an impression was, for one thing, a compressing
and foreshortening of a much broader field of possible data,
such as Gibbon, for example, achieved in his account of the
Siege of Constantinople. In the novel it represents the difference between Tolstoy's expansive and panoramic treatment of
war and Crane's concentrated and suggestive handling of the
same topic in *The Red Badge*. Properly determined and im-

plemented, the impression could be heightened, from a base in action, so as to become symbolic and thus bring home to the reader the central, enduring truth of an aspect of human life. Herein lay the strength of Conrad in his greater stories: in *Youth,* both the narrative of a sea voyage and a lasting record of the universal condition named in its title; or in *The Nigger of the "Narcissus,"* at once a factually complete history of the management and trials of a merchant ship and an image of the whole character of the age of sail in its final days. On similar grounds Ford held in even greater esteem Conrad's middle novels, particularly *The Secret Agent* and *Under Western Eyes,* as virtually condensed histories of the modern world rendered through selected instances of human psychology and passion. In stressing this combination of selective incident with universality, Ford clearly distinguished the aims of Impressionism in his group of English novelists from those of naturalistic realism and the provinciality of its outlook. Although their purposes were similar, Ford less often than Conrad achieved in practice the higher flights of Impressionism; yet works like *The Fifth Queen* trilogy, *The Good Soldier,* and the Tietjens tetralogy so admirably weave together in scene after scene a fabric of immediate fact and symbolic implication that the reader perceives instantly the arduousness and complexity of this technique.

Because of this insistence on selective data with the widest aura of suggestion Ford's novels invariably move in a restricted field, this being evident not only in *The Good Soldier,* almost a nouvelle, but also in the wider sweep of the Tietjens tetralogy, where even if the background covers "the public events of a decade," the foreground drama confines itself to the affairs of a comparatively small number of main characters. Although this effect often relates to the Impressionist device of reducing the scene to the scope of a particular observer's vision, it stems also from Ford's habit of discovering the keys to contemporary history in what he called "cases," startling if sometimes minor occurrences taken for symptoms of

the state of society in general. Perhaps his natural interest in
these matters may be attributed to the circumstances of his
earlier years when scandals like those of Dilke and Parnell
ruffled the surface of Victorian respectability; but his intuitive
and imaginative temperament led him throughout his life to
fix upon such happenings—all the way from sexual misadven-
tures in railway carriages to the embarrassments of statesmen
—as signs of the times. As a rule these were cases within the
legal associations of the term and including a tinge of criminality. At an impressionable age he became lastingly fascinated
by the Dreyfus trial, though almost as much so later by the
execution of Casement and the Hauptmann trial in America;
and this same eye for the significant case, whether of Nietzsche
left alone at Bayreuth or of Edward Ashburnham accused of
assault on a servant girl in *The Good Soldier,* Ford brought to
his relationship with Conrad, conveying to the latter facts for
the piracy trial in *Romance* and for the Greenwich bomb plot
in *The Secret Agent.* As frequently as legal complications
figure in Conrad's work, they are in the very stuff of Ford's
mature novels, either expressly as in *The Marsden Case* or in
overtones of cross-examination as in some of the Tietjens books.
At one time or another Ford's characters are likely to be in or
close to the dock—for divorce, for swindling, for military
offenses, or even for dope peddling as in *Henry for Hugh.*

From Mr. Goldring's biographical evidence regarding Ford's
own legal muddles and contests, one might have cause to suspect in the novelist's private history a ground for his inclination to view such entanglements as threads in the twisted
pattern of modern life. But from the literary standpoint it is
evident that he considered the treatment of cases as belonging, with Dostoevski for precedent, to the canons of the
modern novel. If, however, he went here some distance with
naturalism of the sort that produced *An American Tragedy* and
concerned himself to some extent with the problem of justice,
his particular handling of case material had a technical as
much as an instructional purpose. In aiming to shape the

serious novel for a general audience, he believed in the adoption of devices to ensure readability as at least a primal consideration; and in this respect he pointed to Conrad's tolerance for the workmanlike qualities of Victorian thrillers like *Lady Audley's Secret* and to the use of sensational elements in even so imposing a structure as that of *The Secret Agent,* in Ford's opinion ". . . one of the best—and certainly the most significant—detective stories ever written." [48] This comment shows Ford alert to the problem for contemporary realism of the growing appeal of the detective story; and although in his later years he warned that the novel was dying out in face of the romance of crime, he had certainly been earlier aware of this predicament and had sought its solution by transferring elements from the thriller to the novel proper, thus preparing the way for experiments by younger authors like Graham Greene. Rather, therefore, than opposing the detective story, Ford sometimes declared that his most distinctive techniques —such as time-shift—were taken over from a form really identical with that of all modern novelists. A study of his fiction undoubtedly demonstrates his reliance on the factor of intrigue, the intricate web which might be traced back to Victorian sensationalism but which probably owed more directly in its refinement to the later work of James. If the Jamesian novel that always attracted Ford most deeply was *What Maisie Knew,* a great part of his interest should be attributed to the highly compressed story with its foundation of sordid and elaborate counter-plotting. Moreover, with its opening reference to the Farange divorce litigation, the book stands unique in the Jamesian canon as an example of what Ford would have recognized as a case.

In *Maisie,* furthermore, the case leads perfectly into what Ford, probably enlarging upon a term from James's own critical vocabulary, called an "Affair," another of his prescriptive tenets for the modern novel and a central guide to his own practice. Although he took for granted the novelist's freedom in subject, Ford also held that the novel, especially since

Madame Bovary, had reached a stage where it must deal with
Affairs in order to embody contemporary situations:

> To the theory of Aloofness added itself, by a very natural
> process, the other theory that the story of a novel should be
> the history of an Affair and not the invention of a tale in
> which a central character with an attendant female shall be
> followed through a certain space of time until the book
> comes to a happy end on a note of matrimony or to an un-
> happy end—represented by a death. That latter—the normal
> practice of the earlier novelist and still the normal expedient
> of the novel of commerce and of escape—is again imbecile,
> but again designed to satisfy a very natural human desire
> for finality.[49]

Here, of course, Ford in some measure echoes an accepted
precept of realism in specifying that an Affair contains no
clear-cut ending. In his own work, however, the term embraces
much more than this negative injunction and designates well
the entire form of such a novel, a plexus of individual, sexual,
and social connotations.

Essentially Ford seems to have regarded the Affair as a
situation produced by the character of modern life, one which
has lost the sense of large design and become preoccupied
with small or intimate matters. In a time barren of great figures
in the heroic sense, the actors and their drama are ordinary,
people more or less alike in their ambitions and the parts they
play. Yet if uninspiring in its make-up, by older standards, the
Affair is the novelist's only means of reproducing the odd or
strange complications or predicaments that belong inalterably
to the present; and for her recognition of this difference from
the spirit of the past, Ford praised Ethel Colburn Mayne as
a "portrayer of the fine shades of civilized contacts" and as a
"real historian of this our fugitive day":

> For no one will today assert that his life is really an
> affair of bashings of skulls, plots, campaigns, piracies, Wall
> Street panics, debauches, or the ignoble rewards of virtue.

And no one will deny that his life is really a matter of "affairs"; of minute hourly embarrassments; of sympathetic or unsympathetic personal contacts; of little-marked successes and failures, of queer jealousies, of muted terminations —a tenuous, fluttering, and engrossing fabric. And intangible! [50]

Occasionally among earlier writers Ford detected foreshadowings of the Affair: Dickens, for example, in *Great Expectations*, ". . . the muted book of a man for whom most of the savor has left life" and wherein "the hero is no hero and the heroine, no heroine." [51] Likewise Hardy, almost wicked in his failure to squeeze his subject to the utmost in impressionist fashion, had in his story "On the Western Circuit" everything requisite to an admirable Affair in the situation of the barrister who seduces and then marries an illiterate servant girl in the belief that she has written the love letters actually composed by her mistress. Hardy's mistake was to have broken off where the real Affair ought to have begun—when the man faces the consequences of his error. As a Shakespearean prototype for the Affair Ford referred to *Othello,* the tragedy closest to modern specifications in its compressed plot turning on domestic passion and intrigue.

But to Ford the Affair really emerges only from modern circumstances. In the drama he saw its nearest companion in the plays of Granville-Barker where if the rather dull characters talk like "inverted Nonconformist ministers," they are, nevertheless, in their very lack of brilliance, closer to real life than those of Shaw. Yet the completely conscious master of the Affair in English was always the James of the later phase, who had drawn an unbiased picture of contemporary life through his "stories about worries and perturbations," his note of the nightmare rather than the murder, his choice of "selected instances of long chains of embarrassments." [52] His ". . . utterly refined world where it was always five o'clock" captured the essence and tone of the modern condition:

His characters will talk about rain, about the opera, about
the moral aspects of the selling of Old Masters to the New
Republic, and these conversations will convey to your mind
that the quiet talkers are living in an atmosphere of horror,
of bankruptcy, of passion hopeless as the Dies Irae. That is
the supreme trick of art today, since that is how we really
talk about the musical glasses whilst our lives crumble to
pieces around us. Shakespeare did that once or twice—as
when Desdemona gossips about her mother's maid called
Barbara whilst she is under the very shadow of death; but
there is hardly any other novelist that has done it.[53]

This brilliant critical glimpse, though it leaves a great deal of
James to be accounted for, illuminates both the temperament
of Ford himself and the manner in which his methods nurtured
themselves upon those of James. The foregoing passage is, in
general, a better description of the handling of dialogue by
Ford than by James; and despite their sharing of techniques,
Ford is more Jamesian in sympathy than in spirit and his Affair
cut closer to his own requirements than to Jamesian design.
Yet in his desire for subtle effects he was nearer to James
than was Conrad. Ford shrewdly maintained that Conrad had
in him a strain of the Elizabethan, and during their collaboration his more vigorous talent expressed itself in his appeals to
Ford to "give." Despite the latter's determination to enroll
both James and Conrad squarely in the Impressionist group,
the Affair as Ford defined it was probably never quite congenial to Conrad, as might be argued from his somewhat
lumbering try at the form in *Chance.*

Of these three novelists, in fact, Ford remained most faithful
to the letter of his own critical principle, the treatment of "a
little episode—a small 'affair' affecting a little circle of people
—exactly as it would have happened." [54] No single novel by
Ford seriously departs from this rule; and if *The Good Soldier*
most perfectly exemplifies the mode in its fullest development,
Ford strives for the same intensity and complexity in his other

works as well, even at times with some tax upon the reader's credulity. Yet this compactness is indispensable to the staging of an Affair which is less the fulfillment of an extended action in time than the knotting together of a criss-cross of intricate relationships. Like James, Ford dealt by preference with upper-class "good people," not only because this was the stratum of society exhibiting most plainly the strains of late Victorian conflict but also because it was here that he could display the "muted progressions" by which the aspect of an Affair ". . . will change incredibly whilst the characters do no more than sit in arm-chairs or open bookcases." [55]

By means of the Affair, consequently, the novelist-historian goes beyond the statistician in opening to the ordinary man the otherwise closed book of the private lives of his fellow beings. As a link in the weakening system of personal communication, the novel requires in addition to techniques for compelling attention a language suited to its needs. With his natural aptitude for languages, especially French and German, and his belief in the growing international character of literature to be written for ". . . Man, Woman, New Yorker, inhabitant of Tokio, a seller of groceries behind a counter in Athens," [56] Ford stressed the right control of the word as an instrument for preserving the values of civilization: ". . . the exact use of words seems to me the most important thing in the world. We are, in the end, governed so much more by words than by deeds." [57] The issue becomes imperative as rapid change tends to a coarsening of the language sense, evidence of which startled Ford on a visit to Gettysburg in his later years:

> For as to the latter city I never formed but one not lugu-brious thought—which is that on each side of one fork of its main cross-roads is a public convenience that the coarse French would call *pissoir* but which the City Fathers have had labelled in enormous letters: MEN'S COMFORTER and WOMEN'S COMFORTER. Only Philadelphians could have conceived of a sort of prescience that can almost knock

you down when it first confronts you. I know that other
cities apply the name of Paraclete to such institutions but
I know of no other that so prominently takes the name of the
Holy Ghost—but perhaps not in vain.[58]

In allying himself with Impressionism and its French sympathies, Ford also placed himself in the general modern movement for the repair of the English literary language to be
carried forward in poetry by Pound and the Imagists, whose
work he approved. Although he drew no strict line between
prose and verse, there is little doubt that in practice, and because of the advance of fiction with the decline of poetry after
the Nineties, he staked his real hopes upon prose, which he
sometimes affirmed to be the more exquisite medium for recording the finer shades and contrasts of contemporary experience. Whereas he lauded Christina Rossetti, tolerated por-
tions of Browning and Meredith, and read with pleasure Hardy
and Doughty, his objections to the bulk of Victorian poetry
followed the customary modern classical line of attack: the
growing divorce of language from life resulting from dependence on literary sources and a bookish idiom.

The time, in short, called for a return to language founded
on the vernacular and a strenuous cultivation of the *mot juste*,
an effort in which prose might still succeed where poetry had
failed to engross a public audience. Sharing Conrad's belief
that English was not naturally a good vehicle for prose, Ford
and his collaborator held endless discussions which tested
English words and cadences against French or other resources
of the extensive vocabularies of the two writers. The result was
their aim to achieve a "keyed down" style related to the common spoken language and securing effects by simple words.
On this account, according to Ford, Conrad decided against
"The horror! The Horror!" as the phrase to end *Heart of
Darkness*, the accentuation and shade of meaning of the
English word being different from the French "L'horreur" and
so too melodramatic and rhetorical for the final stroke.[59] The

rule of the collaborators was to ban anything literary or
affected which might detract from the limpid flow of the story:

> Our most constant preoccupation, then, was to avoid words
> that stuck out of sentences either by their brilliant un-
> usualness or their "amazing aptness." For either sort of
> word arrests the attention of a reader, and thus "hangs up"
> both the meaning and the cadence of a phrase. We wanted
> the Reader to forget the Writer—to forget that he was
> reading. We wished him to be hypnotised into thinking that
> he was living what he read—or, at least, into the conviction
> that he was listening to a simple and in no way brilliant
> narrator who was telling—not writing—a true story.[60]

Ford states here almost the key doctrine for the Impressionism
of himself and Conrad: to provoke in sedentary readers the
feeling of participating vicariously in active human affairs.
The theory led Conrad to the invention of Marlow, and Ford
gradually to the rendition of Affairs by oral narrative.

In spite, however, of their agreement on general aims, Ford
approached the problem of style somewhat differently from
Conrad. Though both sought new form for the novel, Ford
maintained that Conrad advanced more positively in mastery
of architectonics whereas Ford himself pursued more intently
the search for a non-literary vocabulary suited to "the simple
expression of fine shades." [61] Instinctively, and perhaps as a
further reaction against the genius cult of his boyhood, he
seems to have cared more for a "muted" style as an antidote
to fine writing and hence tried, independently of his collaborator, ". . . to evolve for myself a vernacular of an extreme
quietness that would suggest someone of some refinement talking in a low voice near the ear of someone he liked a good
deal." [62] Lacking artificiality, speech of this kind should also
employ, as a rule, as few words as possible and strive to ap-
proximate the tone of "non-literariness" which Ford admired in
Jane Austen and Trollope and thought that the later James
had achieved by study of the conversational habits of certain

aristocratic circles. Ford's sureness of ear enabled him to progress towards this norm of a spoken style in a manner entirely his own in his work from *The Good Soldier* on, despite occasional charges of imitation probably resulting from his admitted sensitiveness to the rhythms of other writers and to the stylistic facility which he exhibited in his historical novels that catch the flavor of sixteenth-century chronicle or of Boswell with little trace of Wardour Street. In his low-pitched and colloquial style he reflects his ideal of the artist as man of letters, less the student of books than the man who has lived a full life and who writes much as he speaks. Ford's classical model was Homer rather than Vergil; and in English he liked the companionable tone of Walton. The image of the ordinary man conversing quietly with his neighbors carries likewise a semblance of restored communication between individuals: "I write rather as a man who shall go along a road and see some sheep over the hedge who were not doing well . . . And I shall go to the farmer and suggest his throwing a little sorghum cake on the meadow morning and evening. The cake would increase the nitrates in the dung; and the improved dung would help the grass in the meadow . . . And so on . . . Talking like that." [63]

Other writers were, of course, talking something like this— in their own ways Yeats and Frost—and so also subscribing to the return to the personal voice. Yet it is difficult not to associate Ford's choice with the operation of individual bias, in particular his early preference for the man of action over the aesthete. His youth, moreover, had been spent among notable talkers, like Madox Brown, though perhaps he found such talk a little too highly keyed. Possibly more to his taste was the manner of Conrad, whom Ford reports as reminiscing in a disconnected narrative formed of anecdotes and "pictures":

Half of it came in a shyish way, for biography, half in pictures, the result of stray anecdotes. Thus if one or other of us happened to be nervous from overwork and we talked

of nerves Conrad would say: "By Jove, after I came out of
the Ospedale Italiano and went into the City to draw some
pay, I was so frightened at the racket in the Underground
that I had to lie down on the floor of the compartment.
Nerves all to pieces. . . ."[64]

Even though this report may be an impressionistic rendering
of how Conrad might have talked, it is, more importantly, a
good sample of Ford's prose in its maturity, a conversational
style founded on a structure of anecdote. In Ford's opinion,
". . . readability, as far as I have observed it in its effects
upon myself, has seemed always to resolve itself into relating
anecdotes and drawing morals from those anecdotes." [65] As an
aid to communication the anecdote afforded an impressionistic
substitute for the statistic and a means for fixing in an instant
the individuating trait of a scene or person. Believing that a
writer's erudition was valuable only insofar as it could illuminate life and bring "an immense range of human illustration" to its possessor, Ford observed the principle of carrying
the reader from anecdote to anecdote, such illustrations, in
keeping with Ford's dislike of the over-emphatic, being apt
rather than startling and, at their best, always memorable.
These often occur in his portraits of writers which are not so
much essays in literary analysis as a kind of "composite photograph" of a man and his work. Thus Ford's memories of
W. H. Hudson gather about his recollections of a correspondence with Hudson on the treatment of birds in captivity, Ford
having let loose in his London room a number of exotic birds
on the theory that watching their flight would ease his recovery from a nervous breakdown:

> At that he came to see me and stumped up the stairs to in-
> spect my bedroom. He looked for a long time at the birds
> which were perfectly lively. Then he recommended me to
> have some large mirrors set into the walls with perches in
> front of them. And to hang about bright silvered balls from

Christmas trees, and scarlet ribbons. Birds, he said, loved
all bright objects, and the mirrors gave them the illusion,
with their reflected images, that they were in great crowds
of birds. Then he said, "Humph," and stumped down the
stairs and never to me mentioned the subject of birds in
captivity again.[66]

Here Ford quite intentionally presents Hudson almost as a
character in a novel, since in Ford's view all writing is to some
degree imaginative and the more so the better. Anecdote, consequently, supplies the novelist-historian, too, with material
for illustration, so that Ford's own novels frequently consist of
a tissue of anecdotes, a leading example being *A Man Could
Stand Up* with its war-front impressions sifting through the
mind of Christopher Tietjens on the day of an expected German attack:

He saw the doctor—plainly! It was one of the plainest
things he could see of this whole show. . . . The doctor, a
slight figure, vault on to the parapet, like a vaulting horse
for height; stand up in the early morning sun. . . . Blind
to the world, but humming *Father O'Flynn*. And stroll in the
sun-light, a swagger cane of all things in the world, under
his arms, right straight over to the German trench. . . .
Then throw his cap down into the trench. And walk back!
Delicately avoiding the strands in the cut apron of wire that
he had to walk through! [67]

This passage, from a novel in which Ford was at full development as fictional historian, well represents an active man's
speech salted occasionally with the slang that Ford held essential to the expression of certain new shades. The style, moreover, has the consistency that Ford admired in James of the
period of *The Wings of the Dove* and *The Golden Bowl*,
where the reflecting centers of character find voice only rarely
through conventional dialogue but instead through the cun-

ningly disguised narrative of James himself. In the same way it is Ford who, in his mature work, talks and illustrates though by means of appropriate masks.

Through his conception of the Affair as a distinct form together with a style adapted to the mood of contemporary life, Ford not only discovered his special position as an artist who is likewise a historical observer but also took an important step in attempting both to define aims for the novel in the present century and to assert emphatically the cultural indispensability of serious fiction. His achievement was, therefore, different in kind from that of James or Conrad, whose path he followed to his own ends, in that he separated less rigorously than they the artist-writer from the public apologist for his craft; and in this respect he may have foreseen more distinctly than the men he chose for literary associates the problems lying ahead for the novelist. In a certain light all of Ford's work, the novels as much as the occasional writing, is a manifesto against an age of unstable social and aesthetic standards; and when this is borne in mind, many of the peculiarities of his novels—in particular their characteristic ironies—better explain themselves. On the whole, the Affair is a tense balance between artistic scrupulosity and historical scepticism, for which reason its inner mechanics deserve further attention.

Chapter IV

The Elements of the Affair

THE DISLIKE of rhetoric and pomposity which marks his prose style may, by a frequent and calculated off-handedness in statement, curb recognition of the fact that Ford was one of the most stimulating analysts of the craft of writing, his knowledge that of the professional insider. Among critics and practicing writers, experts of this sort are comparatively rare; and to his interest in advancing the cause of the modern novel should be attributed a good part of his willingness to disclose items of literary shop that Conrad, for example, ordinarily excluded from his rather lofty pronouncements on the nature of art. Besides, however, being unmethodical as a rule and often displaying the partisan bias which makes them doubly provocative, Ford's remarks on craftsmanship usually appear in the form of intuitive and curtailed flashes of insight, frequently inspired in a studio fashion by glances at specific features of the work of another writer, so that a reader, while given the pleasurable sense of acquaintance with art in the making, also has to exert some effort to relate and interpret the variety of technical asides that Ford scatters through numerous books.

Whereas this habit may encourage the assumption that Ford was primarily a technician, any coherent study of his creative work must recognize the bearing, which he did not sufficiently bother to explain, of sheerly procedural rules on the construction of the Affair—technique thus being subservient to dominant form as in any other novelist of repute—as well as his custom of giving anecdotal guise to abstract statements of a theoretical kind. When defining, for instance, the general purpose of Impressionism, he represents the matter casually as a sleight of hand performance: "If the reader will give a box

of matches to a friend and then begin to talk really enthrall-
ingly, he will be able to take the box from his friend's hands
without his friend being in the least conscious that the matches
have gone. . . . It is a trick worth performing—the tongue
deceiving the eye. . . ." [1]

Although in its context this anecdote may seem a little too
pat, it does fling a light answer to those opponents who had
accused the Impressionists of trying to hypnotise the public
while slanting the reply so as to convey the point that the
writer's situation requires of him the use of highly conscious
techniques, Ford in this respect taking a main hand in in-
augurating the modern concern with formal and technical control. Whereas by natural inclination he valued the expert over
the amateur, his view of the change in public attitude towards
literature since earlier Victorian days—the increase in metropolitan readers less given to patience and reflection, though
perhaps quick in mental response—prompted him to regard
the novelist as needing methods subtler, or at least more
flexible, than those employed in the past if he is to carry weight
with a large audience, the latter purpose being ultimate in
Ford's conviction. In declaring towards the end of his career
that the technique of writing is "a matter of raising and holding attention of bodies of men," [2] for which accomplishment he
commended Samuel Richardson, Ford maintained that the
novelist should study closely the methods of his predecessors
and distinguish the possibilities of his art from those of other
literary modes. Ford cited Conrad for anticipating Joyce in his
lifelong and minute knowledge of writers preceding him; and
in his own sometimes erratic but lively canters over the field
of literary history, Ford ranges back to Chaucer as an example
of one of the earliest authors to perceive the connection between
literature and the individual reader and forward to Conrad
and James as men almost overly conscientious about their
art.

For all of his belief in the writer's obligation to address a
large public, Ford was not, however, during his lifetime a

popular novelist in the ordinary sense; and although at present, by the familiar process of posthumous recognition, he appears to be attracting a wider following, it seems likely that his appreciators will continue to be those most capable of his own dispassionate regard for skilled workmanship as in itself a pleasure. Although his technical principles do constantly further the aims of the Affair as a whole and admirably attain their purpose of ensuring the hold of the novel upon the reader, they are to a great extent personal to Ford just as the Affair, in its own right, conforms to his attitude towards contemporary experience and requires acceptance in that light. Moreover the Affair, in his view, is a version of life in accord with truth as measured by the writer's temperament, in which respect Ford conceded neither to the pretended objectivity of the naturalistic *tranche de vie* nor to the advocates of social optimism as these stood, especially, before the Great War.

In affirming the now orthodox opinion that subject, whether in painting or literature, matters less than treatment and concerns no one but the artist himself, he was again defending the artist's integrity; yet with reference to himself he so strictly claimed the privilege as to make it seem at times that he almost wilfully sacrificed fortunate choice of topic for an idiosyncratic conception of the nature of truth, and on this account he more often than either Conrad or James begs the indulgence of the reader. Ford's respect for James would hardly have extended to the latter's reserves on the subject of *Madame Bovary*, since to Ford Flaubert's novel was a prime example of the Affair; yet on the whole James seems to have been shrewder than Ford in observing the importance of the novelist's eye for subject simply from the standpoint of literary effectiveness and in proving the fact in practice by hitting upon such fortunate germs as, for instance, those for *The Aspern Papers* or *The Spoils of Poynton*. The Affair, to Ford, was not a story; and it is interesting to note that through most of his untiring discourse on James's art the remarks seldom touch on that side of it nearest to story, as this pertains to subject.

Instead James emerges as a master of the Affair, represented notably by *What Maisie Knew,* and of technical resource, the aspect especially fascinating to Ford being James's increasing ability to secure an effect with little or nothing in the way of material. If in this Ford takes a characteristically un-Victorian position, he likewise reveals what is to be recognized so often in his comments on general fictional technique—his own attitude with respect to method.

Since Ford conceived the Affair as a necessary departure from the portrayal of enterprises of great or heroic scope and instead as a rendering of private embarrassments and muted conflicts, he wished, as he claimed Conrad did also, to rid it of the "strong situation" that he saw as belonging to the older novel. Similarly, and because of the narrowing of human relationships, he ascribed to it a natural limitation in range, even though by an accompanying intensity it may, like *Othello,* become as exciting as an epic. If intricate enough in its pattern of events, no subject need be considered small, though it must be rightly selected and, in Impressionist parlance, squeezed to the limit:

> Your "subject" might be no more than a child catching frogs in a swamp or the emotions of a nervous woman in a thunderstorm, but all the history of the world has gone to putting child or woman where they are and up to either subject you might lead with an epic as thrilling in its end as that of "Othello" or an episode as poignant with absolute relief as came to the world on the eleventh of November 1918. You have at your disposal heredity, environment, the concatenation of the effects of the one damn thing after another that life is—and Destiny who is blind and august.[3]

This attraction to a closely bound stage, apparent in nearly all of his novels, seems to have been as much an outcome of instinct as of theory. In his early study of Rossetti, for example, he drew attention to the painting of "Dr. Johnson at the Mitre" for its tight grouping of the figures in the tavern box:

The whole suggestion of the eighteenth century, of the Mitre and of Boswell's "Life"; of the faint touch of architecture which then meant chimney-pots and sky-line seen through windows of a peculiar "look,"—all these are caught along with the Doctor's great, uplifted finger, and great, planted foot; his tea and Boswell's leer and toddy. It only exemplifies Rossetti's desire for a peculiar smallness of space, that he should have selected a coffee-room box into which to literally cramp his figures.[4]

Besides touching on Ford's appreciation of the eighteenth century, a feature of so many of his novels, the passage also conveys, in its careful listing of details in the painting, something of his preference for fine and precise literary brush work. Restricting the frame of the action allowed for density in verbal texture, for such almost medieval profusion of detail as fills out novels like *The Fifth Queen* trilogy and *Ladies Whose Bright Eyes*. Perhaps taking a hint from Ford, Conrad likewise caught the trick of using compressed space for dramatic effect in major climactic scenes in *Under Western Eyes* and *Chance*, though he applied the device to single episodes rather than to the whole of a novel.

But, more important, the condensed outline of the Affair made for realization of an ideal of form upheld by both Ford and Conrad: that of the strictest unity through which a novel becomes ". . . one embroilment, one set of embarrassments, one human coil, one psychological progression."[5] Even though both writers used digression expertly to conceal their art, they maintained that a novel should be designed so that every word would contribute to the total effect, the full significance being held in suspense until the final line. In Conrad the key example of this doctrine is *Heart of Darkness* where, as he himself explained, the concluding interview between Marlow and Kurtz's Intended ". . . locks in—as it were—the whole 3000 words of narrative description into one suggestive view of a whole phase of life, . . ."[6] and the better novels of Ford show his adoption of the same rule. With the progression went, likewise, a steady increase in narrative tempo, a mounting breathlessness as the pace grew swifter up to "the inevitable logic of the end," a procedure described by Ford under the borrowed French term *progression d'effet,* a useful addition to critical vocabulary and the best possible summing up of the rising tension at the end of such novels as *Chance* and *The Good Soldier.*

The sway of these principles of compact form, economy of means, and *progression d'effet* over the Impressionist novel of Ford and Conrad raises some question of the relationship between sheer technique and the conception of experience produced by the Affair. In an obvious way a method intended to grip the reader and hold him absorbed to the last page served a purely utilitarian aim grounded in the belief that the modern novelist risks losing the reader without the lure of heightened tempo. Yet the devices proposed by Ford are also functional, in that they correspond with his views on contemporary life. A good example of such combined purpose is the technique which Ford called "justification," meaning that every element in a novel must justify its presence and so win the reader's rational conviction. On this reasoning a character, for instance, cannot be launched convincingly until nearly everything in his background has been established—in particular the facts of his birth and family history. Poorly handled, this can be one of the clumsiest of Impressionist devices, and is so frequently in the earlier work of Ford. Yet Conrad regularly employed it in ways that demonstrated its indispensability in various circumstances, as when in *Under Western Eyes* Razumov's illegitimacy and concealed relationship with his father, Prince K——, account importantly for the young man's motives. Where Conrad, however, ordinarily makes sparing use of justifying detail for larger ends, Ford often seems to revel in it for its own sake, especially when his tracking down of genealogical information—a stubborn feature in even his mature novels—comes to appear a tiresome eccentricity. But that this is not merely whim becomes evident when understood as the equivalent of Ford's sense of the complexity of modern experience wherein the private history of the individual endures the burden and confusion of the past, in which awareness Ford stands close to Faulkner.

With *progression d'effet*, moreover, justification measurably promotes in a novel, by contrast to the short story which Ford seldom practiced, the over-all effect of inevitability that both Ford and Conrad thought essential to long fiction. When securely planted with technical care, the element of inevitability becomes indistinguishable from a sense of fate or destiny, the "grim semblance of an implacable outside Providence" [7] that Ford praised in *Germinie Lacerteux* and *Madame Bovary,* novels in which he discerned the same technical formulas as those adopted by the English Impressionists. Whether or not he meant here by "semblance" merely "illusion" of Providence, his remark suggests that the appearance of fatality, strong in Conrad and in a somewhat different way in Ford, might well be attributed to technical provision as much as to the personal conviction of the writer. Again, however, it is difficult in practice to separate the two alternatives. A chief reason given by Ford in proclaiming the modernity of the Affair was that it appealed to an adult willingness to face life as it is, as a rigorous system of cause and effect involving suffering rather than the fulfillment of personal hopes and, as in Flaubert's "Coeur Simple," favoring the virtues of disillusionment, resignation, and fortitude.[8] In this light inevitability in fiction incorporated the movement of experience as Ford perceived it.

Such a reading of inevitability probably differed from that of Conrad, or at least in Ford's view of Conrad's outlook. On Ford's testimony Conrad possessed a settled belief in "an august and inscrutable Destiny" quite apart from considerations of technique, although thought and expression meet in a tale like *Youth* where an ironical destiny casts a smudge of oily vapor across the serenity of the sky as a lesson to youth on the nature of the cosmos:

> But Conrad was obsessed by the idea of a Destiny omnipresent behind things: of a Deity that was august, blind, inscrutable, just and above all passionless, that has decreed that the outside things, the sea, the sky, the earth, love, merchandising, the winds, shall make youth seem tenderly ridiculous and all the other ages of men gloomy, imbecile, thwarted—and possibly heroic.[9]

In Ford's world of the Affair the universe does not so readily offer signs of its intentions; and perhaps the greater modernity of Ford's spirit shows through his comment that although life may ultimately contain design supposing one were able to discern it, we actually experience it as a sequence of unforeseen accidents, of "one damn thing after another." [10] Possibly for this reason his novels play upon mischance rather than outright fatality and often contain a large measure of coincidence, which he freely acknowledged and ascribed to the frequency of such happenings in his own life. Fatalism intellectually conceived does not figure prominently in his opinions, and perhaps on this account the action in his novels comes less often than in some of Conrad's to the brink of melodrama.

As will be noted in subsequent chapters of the present study, Ford in the Affair created a form which would represent by ironic means the incompatibility of high tragedy and the temper of modern life, thus minimizing the role of positive fate. In doing so, however, he evidenced his personal sympathy with the tragic spirit as he had encountered it in the Greek dramatists, especially Euripides whose *Alcestis* he had translated. He likewise commended the motif of inevitability in more modern works, such as the *Celestina* of the Spaniard Rojas, a drama that Ford saw as anticipating the *progression d'effet* in its advance "with remorseless and always hastening footsteps from beginning to end" and its effect of destiny, ". . . almost as central a figure as it is in Aeschylus." [11] Particularly revealing, too, of his high regard for Richardson as opposed to Fielding, with respect to the former's early innovations in the technique of the Affair, is Ford's claim that Richardson had observed the rule of inevitability and sobriety in the face of experience and so produced in Clarissa a figure ". . . moulded on the great lines of the tragedy of the Greeks." [12]

What such comments seem most to reveal is Ford's attraction to works exemplifying not so much a theory of fate in the abstract as his own idea of the classical note that he sought for in his writing: remorseless treatment of fact and avoidance of sentimentalism, "the spirit of complete and remorseless observation of effects and cause." [13] Hence although his characters and Ford himself at times speak of the inflictions of Fate or of the queer jokes of Providence, it is usually with the modern, or early modern, bewildered desire to grope for any sort of imposing name to simplify or rationalize the mishaps due to contemporary social habits or faults within the individual himself. In Ford fatality is of human or historical making and proceeds inevitably from causes, however remote. Thus fate enters into the atmosphere of his novels but not as an agent from outside the scene. Human error, consequently, cannot be eliminated, though its effects may be traced without lapse from dignity into the vice of pity. The right tone in a serious novel should be one of austerity, so that glimpses of horror may occur but the ending itself remain unharrowing.

Where the rule of inevitability may, then, be brought into relation with Ford's view of experience, another of his main principles, that the novel should everywhere aim at surprise, seems more obviously concerned with technique alone. In reiterating the point that surprise gives charm to art, Ford says nothing very new; but his constant use of the device in the design of his fiction may awaken the reader's suspicion that here, if anywhere, the Impressionist effort at engrossment deep enough to permit the stealing of the match box comes close to deliberate trickery. In part, no doubt, Ford em-

phasized surprise in order to remedy what he thought had
been a fault in too many nineteenth-century novels, their
failure to keep ahead of the reader's prevision of their course
and outcome; and scarcely any of Ford's books can be charged
with this error. His reader does enjoy the satisfaction of
frequent contact with the unexpected through Ford's calculated avoidance of the obvious in every step of the story, from
the choice of the original situation and its opening down to the
shaping of individual scenes. Besides affecting structure, surprise, too, may be imparted to the pattern of language, again
a matter that he blamed the Victorians for too often neglecting,
as in the case of Darwin and his "chloroform style." [14] However muted and limpid a good style ought to be, it could
still be enlivened by a succession of tiny, unobservable surprises of the kind to be found in Conrad:

> If you write: "His range of subject was very wide and his
> conversation very varied and unusual; he could rouse you
> with his perorations or lull you with his periods; therefore
> his conversation met with great appreciation and he made
> several fast friends"—you will not find the world very apt
> to be engrossed by what you have set down. The results
> will be different if you put it: "He had the power to charm
> or frighten rudimentary souls into an aggravated witch-
> dance; he could also fill the small souls of the pilgrims with
> bitter misgivings: he had one devoted friend at least, and
> he had conquered one soul in the world that was neither
> rudimentary nor tainted with self-seeking.[15]

Although the passage is one of Ford's impressionistic renderings of fact, it embodies much the same point as that in his
homelier statement that because of the superiority of contrast
over orderly classification, the catalogue of a farm sale attracts
greater interest than that of a hardware store.

Another of Ford's methods for obtaining surprise was to
adjust the reader's vision to an angle more unconventional than

the frontal view of a particular scene, a device which suggests
parallels with cinematic techniques. But although he certainly
studied the movie, at least by the time of his postwar novels,
Ford also appears to have tapped the resources of painting,
having been familiar early with that branch of the arts. In his
previously mentioned book on Rossetti he pauses to inspect
features that seemed to him unusual in the contents of pictures
like "Dr. Johnson at the Mitre" and "How they met themselves"; and in the same study he calls attention in Rossetti's
"Lucrezia" to a device of pre-Raphaelite origin that he himself
was able to borrow later:

> In the *Lucrezia*, in the mirror near the left shoulder of
> the sumptuous woman is shown Lucrezia's husband, Duke
> Alfonso of Biscaglia, whom she has just poisoned and "who
> is being walked up and down the room by Pope Alexander
> IV., in order to settle the poison in his system." This device
> of narrating in a mirror the happenings in the part of the
> room occupied by the spectator—of thus completing the
> anecdote—was a trick much beloved by both Rossetti and
> Madox Brown. The latter had already adopted it in his
> *Take your son, sir*. In the *Lucrezia*, its use, dramatically
> speaking, is singularly effective and indeed admirable.[16]

This kind of anecdote in painting Ford found adaptable to the
novel; and often as the mirror appears in his work, its use in
the second unit of the Tietjens tetralogy, *No More Parades*,
is the one that recalls most directly the example from Rossetti.
In this episode Sylvia Tietjens, herself a sumptuous woman, sits
partly nude before the glass of her hotel dressing-table, her
husband thus being able to glimpse in the mirror the door at
the other side of the room as it opens to admit Sylvia's former
lover.[17]

Instead of surprise, which is likely to bear too heavy a con-
notation of shock technique, Ford might have been better
equipped had he been able to employ a word to make evident
that he intended to bring the surprising incident into relation

with his view of experience as a series of unforeseen accidents. Perhaps a term meaning something closer to what is now understood as the absurd would have made his intention clearer. He did, however, disclose his awareness that the unexpected belongs to life itself by remarking on ". . . that element of queer surprise that life actually gives to all its affairs," [18] a statement in which he was also maintaining that a genuine Impressionism, by contrast with an older and more logical realism, should endeavor to incorporate this element as one of its main concerns. Just how much he gained directly from Conrad in support of this theory is difficult to say; but he was surely alert to Conrad's use of abrupt and seemingly inexplicable digressions to produce an effect of irrationality, as when, for example, in *The Secret Agent* the terrified spy, Verloc, breaks into the interrogation to which the cynical Vladimir has subjected him by going to a window at the foreign embassy to demonstrate the range of his voice.[19]

Although in Ford the kind of Dostoevskian tone which Conrad imparted to occurrences like the foregoing is much less prominent, the design of his novels often seeks to trace the course of the unpredictable and thus awaken the reader's sense of experience at close hand. In this respect the use of the unconventional visual angle in the scene, above mentioned, in *No More Parades* is more than technical ingenuity, since it helps to convey the impression of illogicality in a war atmosphere. Similarly, when Ford begins a novel on one of his favorite notes of shock, he does not rest with the confidence of having gripped the reader but goes on to justify the initial premise. A notable example of this is his novel of 1913, *Mr. Fleight*, which opens with an apparently incredible reference to an Englishman's strangling of a groom at Newport, Rhode Island. As the story continues, however, in a mode of satire on contemporary indifference to violence, the opening falls into place as a keynote preparing the way for recurrent episodes marking the absurdities of an effete society, an instance being

the setting up of a dentist's chair among the clothes lines of a
back yard—an inventive stroke worthy of Graham Greene:

> Having brought in the chair, the workmen retired, and re-
> turned with a quantity of metal objects, long tubes and
> large metal cases containing storage batteries. These they
> proceeded to set up beside the monstrous and grotesque
> red chair in the back yard, which was already amply oc-
> cupied by packing cases, loose straw, and the washing,
> which was hanging out to dry.[20]

Surprise, therefore, is indigenous to the Affair as an Impressionist transcript of life, which substitutes a kind of abrupt
spotlighting of some area in the flow of experience for the
story governed by the providential logic of the author or the
will of a central character. And since the Affair deals with
". . . the turning world of averagely sensual, averagely kindly,
averagely cruel, averagely honest, averagely imbecile human
beings," [21] it concerns less the carrying through of an action
than the disturbance or realignment of a set of already existing
relationships, a progression inward to the center of an existing
web. In the tortuous conditions of modern life, the attempt to
initiate action is precarious, since the individual cannot measure the ramifications of the net encircling him and likely to
make him victim rather than victor. For this reason the Impressionists avoided the strong situation and dwelt upon the
mishaps or unpredictable results of action. Certainly James had
initiated this development in the labyrinthine patterns of his
later work from *The Spoils of Poynton* through *The Golden
Bowl,* books all eminently Affairs to Ford and illustrating a
tightening and refinement of human contacts rather than the
moral education of intelligent "reflectors" whose real purpose
is to act as lens for the reader. In an Impressionist perspective
Ford would see, perhaps more than James himself, that the
situation of "trapped spectators" like Fleda Vetch or Milly
Theale is merely an extension of the normal in modern circum-

stances where the individual is trapped from the outset by the complexities of social convention. Whereas, therefore, one may have a premonition of doom in the forces surrounding him, as actor in an Affair he will feel this as a shadow over a series of meaningless episodes and accept his fate, for example, while playing golf:

> From what one of the other men replies you become aware that all these men know that to-morrow there will be an end of you; the sense of that immense catastrophe broods all over the green and sunlit landscape. You take your mashie and make the approach shot of your life whilst you are joking about the other fellow's necktie, and he says that if you play like that on the second of next month you will certainly take the club medal, though he knows, and you know, and they all know you know, that by the second of next month not a soul there will talk to you or play with you. So you finish the match three up and after walk into the club house and pick up an illustrated paper.[22]

Ford's ancedote, which while ostensibly summing up the method of James so perceptively seizes upon the typical in contemporary conduct, draws attention to two peculiarities of modern life that the Affair attempts to reproduce—the habit of suppressing unpleasant truth and the use of speech to conceal thought. Although both are traits of civilized existence, they obtained particularly in polite late Victorian society, as Mr. Eliot's Prufrock convincingly demonstrates. Since modern culture preserves the amenities by muffling the emotional outcry, actual violence tends to occur only beneath the surface of a world whose conflicts are chiefly mental; and whereas it may erupt, society conspires to silence or ignore its reverberations. At one level James treats this theme in the high comedy milieu of *The Golden Bowl,* where incredible diplomacy succeeds in dissolving the ugliness that would offend an almost Oriental system of courtesies; and at the opposite end of the social scale Conrad in *The Secret Agent* observes the spirit of the Affair by

subordinating the Greenwich dynamite incident to the sequence of psychological explosions creating a shambles which
higher authority deftly hides from public notice. Ford himself
tended to associate the habit of concealment with English
upper-class reserve, so dominant a feature in *The Good Soldier*
and the Tietjens novels; and it is possible that the semi-expatri-
ate position that he attributed to himself, James, and Conrad
did make such writers especially sensitive to the implications
of this custom. But in its larger aim the Affair, as a disclosure of
intimate contemporary history, sought to take the reader beyond the surface of convention and to make him conscious of
underlying truth as well as the possibilities of havoc in a society
outwardly so comfortably organized. In one light, Conrad accomplished this in *Heart of Darkness* where the horror confessed in Kurtz's dying whisper takes firmer hold upon the
reader's consciousness as counterpoint to Marlow's ultimate
Victorian lie for the protection of the gentler sex.

The fact, then, that conversation, in modern circumstances,
really circumvents frank exchange of thought led the Impressionists to doubt the validity of passages of direct dialogue
unless deliberately formalized, as in *The Awkward Age.* Here
once more James offered a precedent in moving in later books
like *The Golden Bowl* towards a language of the ultra sophisticated who communicate by radical short cuts or by a tacit reading of gestures and glances, as when Mrs. Assingham grasps
the message of the shadows crossing the eyes of Prince
Amerigo. Although Ford and Conrad rarely attempted to
match these refinements of a fictional domain more exclusive
than their own, Ford's comments make clear how often their
discussions of technique turned to the problem of conversation. Although both writers experimented with variations on
the theory that the English only speak thoughts of the greatest
simplicity, they seem to have agreed that speech covers the
depths of real thought or provides an escape from internal
tensions, words acting largely as distress signals. This principle
accounts for the irrelevance so often present in the talk of

Conrad characters when under extreme emotional pressure and for Ford's regular practice of distinguishing between the planes of polite speech and of thought removed from the immediate scene, a memorable example being the long episode in the Tietjens's London flat in *Some Do Not* when on the day before Tietjens returns to the front he and Sylvia converse to defend themselves against undercurrents of conflicting emotion. Although in his postwar work Ford sometimes used a type of stream-of-consciousness, he may have preferred instead a method compelling the reader to focus intently upon what fell between the lines of supposedly open discourse.

One advantage of the Impressionist re-examination of dialogue and its function was to promote regard for the novel as an independent form, a rhythmic unity rather than a patchwork of narrative, description, and conversation. In drawing a clear line between drama and novel, sometimes to the apparent disadvantage of the former,[23] Ford intended not merely to stress their obvious divergence in technique but also to put forward the novelist's claim to a distinct province and special opportunities. In his own fully mature work, beginning with *The Good Soldier*, Ford followed James in devising a novel to be read, one that cannot be acted or filmed and in which the portion of actual dialogue is minimal. Where it occurs, it supplies a particular effect; but it is otherwise subordinate to the movement of the novel as a single psychological progression clothed by a style in itself so much the story that any effort to sever the two would be futile. By this means Ford endowed the novel with the same integrity that it possesses in Joyce, Virginia Woolf, and Faulkner.

The Impressionists, in fact, studied carefully what might be done with the printed page for an astute reader who becomes, to an extent seldom achieved before or since, an active part in a fictional game; and such accomplishments as *The Golden Bowl*, *The Secret Agent*, and *The Good Soldier* are, in great measure, intellectual constructs in a literary mathematics demanding the reader's complete mental engagement, though no special erudition. In this endeavor the Impressionists counted on a reader familiar with the printed word and capable of response to the lightest stimuli, so that even language itself might be pared below the limits of traditional statement. To Ford and Conrad the problem of language was partly one of discovering means to eliminate language, to reduce the number of words on the page, not only because long handling has tended to rob words of their edge but also because a loosening of the fabric of statement opens the way to a closer perception of reality. By this route, from the belief that meaning can now be transmitted with fewer words, the Impressionists arrived at one of their most characteristic and subtle techniques, that of the omission of entire scenes, even such apparently crucial ones as would be developed at length by other novelists. Although to find the reason for such exclusions, each must be studied for itself and in relation to the whole work in which it appears, a main idea governing the device was that the Affair ruled out strong situations and, as a corollary, that if the steps to a scene were marked clearly enough, the reader's imagination could be trusted to supply the details of the resulting action. Thus Ford invents the following illustration to describe Conrad's probable treatment of a crime:

> For having minutely described the purchase of the dagger, Mr. Conrad will go on to render for us the journey of the murderer in a four-wheeler through a thick fog. We shall be conducted to the door of a house where the crime was to be committed, the rust of the knocker would be felt, not seen, because of the thickness of the fog. The door would open upon a black hall and there the episode would end. The point would be that Mr. Conrad would by this time so entirely have identified us with the spirit of the expedition that we should take up the tale for ourselves.[24]

Verification of Ford's point comes from *The Secret Agent* where Conrad omits a direct account of the central bomb incident yet so sharply visualizes contributing details—the figures of the

participants, the varnish can for the explosive, and the mangled
remains of the victim—that the event comes to life precisely
because it has not been embodied in words. James employed
the same device in *The Ambassadors* and *The Wings of the
Dove*, the latter notable for its omission of a last interview
between Milly and Densher, as did Ford in major works like
The Fifth Queen and the Tietjens tetralogy as well as in his
Napoleonic novel *A Little Less than Gods* where, for reasons to
be explained later, he completely excluded from a tale of the
Hundred Days any description of the Waterloo battle as
though he might have read and taken to heart Percy Lubbock's
censure of *War and Peace*.

Like the majority of the other Impressionist techniques advocated by Ford, the art of omission helped serve the end of
inducing the reader to participate imaginatively in the action
of the Affair and thus intensify his sense of vicarious experience in happenings significant for contemporary history. But
as Ford noted also, to accomplish the aim of making the reader
feel present at the scene of a novel is very difficult, especially
when this procedure involves the exclusion of the author in his
traditional role of story teller or commentator. To the latter
rule, however, the Impressionists gave particular weight not
only because they wished to make their methods prevail over
those of earlier Victorian fiction but also because their general
theory that life does not tell stories but makes impressions on
the brain dispensed with the former middleman author. Although familiar enough today, this change in practice, while
to the advantage of the one volume novel as a self-contained
structure, did institute a fairly abrupt reorientation for the
reader confronting work divested as far as possible of customary literary controls and substituting the illusion of firsthand
experience. From the latter standpoint the Affair should begin
more or less *in medias res,* the reader, as in life, finding his
bearings gradually and coming to know a character, for example, only after an extended series of encounters. For this
system of presenting character, Ford acknowledged a debt to

Herodotus, whose habit was to introduce his characters, leave them for a time, then return to them so as to provide a sense of renewed acquaintance; [25] but the less technical inspiration derived from the idea that in contemporary circumstances the individual discloses himself only reluctantly and bit by bit. In keeping with the nature of the Affair itself, the truth of character lies beneath the surface and, the individual life being primarily secret, emerges perhaps chiefly in moments of crisis, as Conrad had shown in works like *Typhoon, The Secret Sharer,* and *Under Western Eyes.* Like James and Conrad, moreover, Ford often emphasized the discrepancy between a person's outer appearance, or beauty in the usual meaning, and the hidden and frequently discreditable truths of the "dark forest" of the heart,[26] so that any knowledge of one's fellows is in itself a train of surprises:

> You meet an English gentleman at your golf club. He is beefy, full of health, the model of the boy from an English Public School of the finest type. You discover, gradually, that he is hopelessly neurasthenic, dishonest in matters of small change, but unexpectedly self-sacrificing, a dreadful liar but a most painfully careful student of lepidoptera and, finally, from the public prints, a bigamist who was once, under another name, hammered on the Stock Exchange. . . .[27]

In this way, essentially, the reader comes to know Conrad's Lord Jim or Ford's Captain Ashburnham by a technique that approximates experience, the Affair being no longer a straightforward narrative of a fictional hero.

When presented in the foregoing manner, character develops in accordance with the fundamental Impressionist principle of "rendering" rather than "telling," which in all phases of an Affair is an effort to project character and scene directly upon the senses, and mainly the visual equipment, of the reader, so that his evidence is entirely concrete. As the term Impressionism implies, knowledge involves contact, without intermediation, between subject and object; and in trying to follow this theory, Ford and Conrad faced the handicaps as well as the rewards of a complex narrative method. Although dismissing the omniscient author removed the burden of psychological analysis and the necessity of "going behind" character to interpret motive, the gain in objectivity might also call, to command full assent, for a machinery as elaborate as that in *Lord Jim*. To Ford as fictional historian, however, the risk seemed worth taking since the Impressionist procedure of relating experience to a particular observer, as Conrad did with Marlow, was analogous to a return to the kind of eyewitness proof that Ford admired in the classical historians by contrast with modern textbook abstractions. In striving, therefore, for this effect of immediacy—which he obtained even in his historical novels by seeking to identify himself, like Flaubert in *Salambô*, with the point of view of a past age—Ford helped to advance an important trend in fiction from *The Good Soldier* through *The Great Gatsby* and *Absalom, Absalom!*

Partly, then, on technical grounds and partly, no doubt, in deference to historical relativism, Ford abandoned the nineteenth century panoramic vision and referred events to the viewpoint of the individual onlooker, so that in the Tietjens tetralogy, for example, the Great War is simultaneously that of General Campion or of Christopher Tietjens and, on the home front, of Sylvia Tietjens or of Valentine Wannop. While this limitation in range probably reflected to some extent a modern suspicion of historical generalization as conducive to propaganda, it also corresponds with the individual's consciousness of being involved with historical phenomena that are omnipresent but irreducible to simple logic. In this respect the replacement of the panoramic conception, at least with reference to the novel, cannot be said to destroy the reader's feeling of the larger movement of history; for although, for example, in *The Old Wives' Tale* Bennett refers most of the siege of Paris to what Sophia Baines sees of it, this is not to remove the significance of the event but rather to call attention to the pressure of historical necessity upon the individual striving to exist, on which account the Franco-Prussian War remains as sinister in Bennett as it is in Zola's *La Débâcle* or the World War in *A Farewell to Arms*. For main inspiration Ford looked chiefly, however, to the work that he considered the archetypal modern novel-history, Flaubert's *L'éducation sentimentale*, in which the central character, Frederick Moreau, stands as principal witness to the public affairs of a decade. In the later sections of the book the disjointed impressions of the Paris street fighting of 1848, where Frederick looks on as if at a show,[28] placed at Ford's disposal as ready a model for his own historical reporting, especially in the war front sections of the Tietjens tetralogy, as did Crane's *The Red Badge of Courage*. The ironies of Flaubert's novel, with its muted treatment of history brought to the level of ordinary or ineffectual lives flowing on to no perceptible end, gave it exactly the quality that Ford associated with the Affair.

In its resemblance to chronicle, however, the *Education* did lack the intensity and sharp psychological focus that Ford desired; and in this respect *What Maisie Knew*, wherein the closed ring of the child's consciousness frames the external action, came nearer to his ultimate requirements. Although the influence of this novel upon Ford's techniques up through their consummation in *The Good Soldier* was unquestionably important, the predicament of Maisie interested Ford as much as James's method. Whether or not he read the situation as more sinister than James intended, Ford regarded the novel as a solid segment of contemporary history with impressionistic overtones in the general theme of innocence and evil. Here, too, he recognized the significant step taken by James in making his central intelligence more than simply a perceptive spectator; for the nature of Maisie's consciousness really colors the action by furnishing a glass through which the reader observes the figures in the background intrigue. James's brilliant experiment in limiting his material to what Maisie actually sees as a "register of impressions"[29] conformed almost perfectly to Ford's standard of objective and visual rendering, even though for the reader's sake James had to violate consistency by filling gaps in the child's experience. Yet although he did not go so far towards subjectivism as did Joyce and Faulkner later, he does imply by the touch of the fantastic in the adult characters and by noting that Maisie's ". . . little world was phantasmagoric —strange shadows dancing on a sheet" [30] that the child not only wonders but also fears and doubts in her exposure to the warring passions around her. Always alert to the complicating issues of money and sex that James made prominent, Ford very likely interpreted the novel strongly in the light of his notion of the Affair as a matter of "worries and perturbations" and found in the book all of the fertile stimulus to his own practice that he attributes to it.

The tinge of fear imparted by James to Maisie's vision also corresponds with the Impressionist recognition that the observer's view of his surroundings is mingled with personal emotions of one sort or another. Civilized conditions suppress rather than allay primitive feelings, among which fear tends most stubbornly to afflict the mind. This restrained terror of the ultra-civilized, often the product of withheld knowledge, James understood well, as may be seen in his close study in *The Golden Bowl* of the state of nerves of Mrs. Assingham when she grasps completely the approaching crisis for the Ververs [31] or his stress on the mood of apprehension in the closing scenes of *The Wings of the Dove.* Crane and Conrad likewise followed this practice of bringing emotion to bear upon the senses in works like *The Red Badge of Courage, The Secret Agent,* and *Chance;* but of these novelists Ford showed himself most persistently concerned with the modern climate of anxiety. Persuaded that contemporary nerves and senses are constituted differently from those of the Victorians,[32] he quite early became attentive to the "mental maladies fostered by the spirit of the age" [33] and in his novels increasingly identified the Affair with situations involving such maladies.

To some extent his preoccupation with mental suffering was doubtless a factor in his own temperament; but he was also acting as historian of his age in noting its subjection to the strain of worry, which moved him by its everyday recurrence. He shivered over the financial troubles of the clergyman in Trollope's *Framley Parsonage* [34] and the worries of Richardson's Pamela; but even more in *Clarissa* he felt that ". . . with Clarissa the agony of the mind of the reader becomes one of the great major agonies of the world." [35] Ford's prediction in 1900 that the noise due to increasing mechanization might one day prove more than the human brain could endure [36] bore ironical fruit in the Great War when, with gunfire shaking the earth in the first Somme battle, Ford himself prayed in pitch blackness for the saving of his reason.[37] Hence largely by natural endowment he could create his personal variations on the theme of fear and so become notable in earlier modern fiction for his emphasis on psychic strain and disaster, topics at that time somewhat less familiar than they are at present. Significantly, he added to the theory of impressionistic rendering his own definition: ". . . Impressions are sensations that impinge and leave scars on the consciousness . . ." [38]

Perhaps in part as a technical expedient to engross the reader, Ford sought through his awareness of the nature of contemporary mentality the formula for a novel that would proceed under conditions of tense emotional or psychological pressure and thus provide an alternative to the older strong situation in its leaning to melodramatic incident. Here again some of his early observations on pre-Raphaelite painting seem to show signs of a developing interest of this kind, since he tends to single out works in which the subject depicts a moment of psychological drama. In the "Ferdinand" of Millais, for example, he remarks on the ". . . single figure under the influence of a strong emotion" like ". . . a man tortured by vague hauntings"; [39] and he maintains that Rossetti's real gift lay in rendering convincingly ". . . moments of passion that he had really seen." [40] For illustration he took Rossetti's "The Laboratory" and explained that in its Browning-inspired subject "the passionate woman and passionless alchemist" are "human beings in a moment of stress" and the whole atmosphere "one of illicit passion in a closed place"—[41] the latter being a kind of situation often employed by Ford in his novels. In such painting he may have detected anticipations of his own literary method in which emotional tension colors visual activity in a manner sometimes reminiscent of Rossetti's poem "The Woodspurge" where under the shock of "perfect grief" the poet's eye discovers that "The woodspurge has a cup of three." That Ford, together with Conrad, was experimenting with such effects in the collaboration, *Romance*, appears in a number of scenes, among them one in which the hero, John Kemp, momentarily overcome by "paralyzing hopelessness," stares about the ship carrying him to Havana:

> And I noticed, also, small things without importance—the hirsute aspect of a sailor; the end of a rope trailing overhead; and Castro, so different from everybody else on board that his appearance seemed to create a profound solitude round him, lounging before the cabin door as if engaged in a deep conspiracy all by himself. I heard voices talking loudly behind me, too. I noted them distinctly, but with perfect indifference.[42]

Similarly in the fifth and final section of *Romance*, for which Ford took responsibility, the climactic episode of Kemp's trial for piracy at the Old Bailey offered special opportunity to render lived experience at a point of highest pressure. Ford's account of the mental state of dread and fierce resistance while Kemp in the dock is pleading for his life before prejudiced judges is crude but psychologically defensible:

> I had my eyes fixed on the face of the young girl upon the bench. Her eyes were fixed, fascinated, upon my hand. I tried to move it, and found that it was stuck upon the spike on which I had jammed it. I moved it carelessly away and only felt a little pain, as if from a pin-prick; but the blood was dripping on to the floor, pat, pat.[43]

Although the spiked hand compels a little too obviously the reader's vicarious participation in Kemp's ordeal, the incident looks forward to renderings of mental tension in such mature work by Ford as *The Good Soldier* and the Tietjens tetralogy.

Ford's treatment of visual experience is too essential an element in his work to be regarded solely from a technical point of view. His repeated examples of vision altered or distorted seem to refer back to a basic theory not only of the nature of modern man's specialized constitution but also of the disturbance to mental or sensory functioning caused by the multiplying forces of distraction in contemporary existence. What the individual sees or comprehends depends always upon the kind or number of tribulations besetting him, and he is only rarely in a condition sufficiently detached to see things as they are or for themselves. This point enters into the narrative fragment, *The Nature of a Crime,* in which Ford collaborated with Conrad apparently around 1908. Having decided to solve his personal predicament by suicide, the narrator, a man of business, achieves for a moment, in the thought that he is already dead, something like the Dostoevskian epileptic clarity of sight:

> And out on the pavement it was most curious what had befallen the world. I had lost all interest: but it had become fascinating, vivid. I had not, you see, any senses left, but my eyesight and hearing. Vivid: that is the word. I watched a newsboy throw his paper down an area, and it appeared wonderfully interesting to discover that *that* was how one's papers got into the house. I watched a milkman go up some doorsteps to put a can of milk beside a boot-scraper and I was wonderfully interested to see a black cat follow him. They were the clearest moments I have ever spent upon the earth—those when I was dead. They were so clear because nothing else weighed upon my attention but just those little things. It was an extraordinary, a luxuriant feeling. That, I imagine, must have been how Adam and Eve felt before they had eaten of the fruit of knowledge.[44]

As the last sentence implies, the contemporary, mentally absorbed man is generally incapable of such purity of vision; and in consequence he receives impressions intermittently and ordinarily under such stress of nervous excitation that his perceptions, like Rossetti's in "The Woodspurge," leave scars upon consciousness. From this principle Ford evolved his conception and technique of memory as formed largely upon moments of excited apprehension, a method approached tentatively in the early novel *The Inheritors* but finally mastered in *The Good Soldier*. To a work that he had every reason to know well, *The Wings of the Dove,* Ford probably owed suggestions for his own procedure; for in his great study of fear and strained nerves in Densher, caught in the ambiguous game with the dying Milly and wandering alone in the "dark labyrinthine alleys" of Venice, James indicates the fixation of impressions upon the memory as Densher's eye fastens upon the strips of paper on the shutters of the rooms where he had closed his bargain with Kate Croy:

> The humor of those days came back to him for an hour, and what further befell in this interval, to be brief, was that, emerging on a traghetto in sight of the house in question, he recognized on the green shutters of his old, of his young windows the strips of white pasted papers that figure in Venice as an invitation to tenants. This was in the course of his very first walk apart, a walk replete with impressions to which he responded with force . . . he saw that even after years he couldn't lose his way—crowned with his stare across the water at the little white papers.[45]

If in the impingement of objects upon his sight, Densher in his "ramble" about Venice a little resembles Bloom in Dublin, the method here is even closer to the one adopted by Ford in the connection established between Densher's overwrought emotions and the hyperacuity of his response to particular impressions. His glance at the white papers, with their hint of secret diplomacy, is a subconscious compulsion foretelling his ultimate fate.

What Densher observes, therefore, relates, even more de-

terminedly than with James's Maisie, to his subjective condition; and this practice of making the observer a measure of his
surroundings entered into the technique of both Conrad and
Ford, often with a refined interest, as in *The Good Soldier,* in
the contrast between an observer's peculiar temperament and
the material which it must confront and interpret. More than
James, however, Ford tended towards internalization in the
novel by moving from progressive chronological sequence in
narrative to an order determined by the mind itself as pressures
upon it dictate the course of impressions. This accords in part
with the principle of rendering:

> Life does not say to you: In 1914 my next door neighbour,
> Mr. Slack, erected a greenhouse and painted it with Cox's
> green aluminum paint . . . If you think about the matter
> you will remember, in various unordered pictures, how one
> day Mr. Slack appeared in his garden and contemplated the
> wall of his house. You will then try to remember the year of
> that occurrence and you will fix it as August 1914 because
> having had the foresight to bear the municipal stock of the
> city of Liège you were able to afford a first-class season
> ticket for the first time in your life. You will remember Mr.
> Slack—then much thinner because it was before he found
> out where to buy that cheap Burgundy of which he has since
> drunk an inordinate quantity though whisky you think would
> be much better for him! [46]

Although Conrad had employed non-chronological patterns,
especially in *The Secret Agent* and *Under Western Eyes,* Ford
gave his own form of plausibility to disarrangement of conventional sequence by assigning the shuffling of impressions to the
play of the mind under stress or while remembering, processes
released from the forward movement of time and so amenable
to the operation of "time-shift" in any direction. To some extent
the cultivation of this device enabled him to dispose of the
troublesome time problem of some of his earlier novels, the
inadequate illusion of time lapse or flow between incidents in

traditional narrative. In *The Good Soldier* he successfully removed the handicap by making time a property of memory and also with this freer pattern allowed himself more opportunity for surprise. Yet the technique gains its authority ultimately from his convictions regarding the nature of mind and memory.

As exemplified, therefore, in his own best and later work in fiction, Ford's assortment of guiding principles demonstrates its relevance everywhere to the form of the Affair, his transcript of the pattern of life in his time. On the basis alone of his speculations on method he should certainly count as one of the valuable literary theorists of the century and, after James, as one of the most adept and imaginative; yet he did not, in the end, value technique as an aim in itself or consider any system of rules absolute or inalterable despite his faith in the general Impressionist position. Although he declared that criticism should concern itself with methods and nothing else and practiced this doctrine in an illuminating way, he did so partly as a repudiation of what he considered Victorian inspirational commentary on an exacting craft and not with the idea that the significance of the novel stops at that point. As an artist he admitted that all formal standards are to be created and demolished at the need of the writer; and whereas throughout his career Ford remained faithful to his essential precepts, his novels show his readiness not only for technical modification but also for personal adaptability to fresh experience.

Chapter V

The Burden of the Past: Historical Fiction

SINCE Ford wished all of his literary work to represent his position of historian of his time, it may seem at first arbitrary to set apart from the rest of his fiction the novels dealing with the past and to put these at the beginning of a study of his creative production. In their basic form the purely historical novels differ very little from those on contemporary themes; except for the accident of setting, they are essentially Affairs, impressions of the general character of a period, and disclose in their construction the same ruling principles of craftsmanship that Ford applied elsewhere. He himself, moreover, rather encouraged the impulse to treat summarily this branch of his work not only by his disparagement of the historical novel in general, which he called even at its best ". . . nothing more than a *tour de force*, a fake more or less genuine in inspiration and workmanship, but none the less a fake," [1] but also by his usual tendency to belittle his own efforts in this line, as when he speaks of having written the novels "listlessly and a little disdainfully." [2] Although the latter statement is undoubtedly misleading, it does reflect a cautionary attitude towards a type of fiction in which the temptation to exploit technical ingenuity for its own sake Ford quickly recognized. As a modernist, furthermore, he probably desired to renounce a form too closely associated both with the romantic taste of the nineteenth century and with the atmosphere of his boyhood when "the historic picture was very much in the air." [3] Although Douglas Goldring, while rightly estimating the excellence of the trilogy, somewhat misrepresents the tone of *The Fifth Queen*, the chief of Ford's historical romances, by remarking that the novels embody "Madox Brown's vision of the colour and romance of medieval England," his suggestion

91

that the work gave Ford opportunity to purge himself of the lingering influences of the aesthetic movement is perhaps a hint at one truth underlying Ford's mistrust of this fictional genre.[4]

For several reasons, however, including the actual record of Ford's productivity in this vein, some consideration of the historical novels is a necessary preliminary to a rounded view of his art and personal outlook. A good seven of his books—excluding *The Young Lovell* (of 1913), which appears to be a romance for juveniles—occupy the conventional category of historical fiction; and when these are segregated and ranked by topic, they may be seen to cover a formidable range in time, each century from the fourteenth to the twentieth having a novel devoted to it so as to establish a line of approach to his treatment of the contemporary scene. These works, moreover, are no more haphazard in conception than in temporal order, nearly all possessing a design so elaborate as to belie sharply Ford's confession of listlessness in composing them. Contrary to his pretensions, his native qualifications for this form of writing went far beyond the ordinary. His early liking for history itself and admiration for the kind of artist-historian that seemed to him represented by the Greeks and Plutarch as well as by the imaginative writers of the century of Burckhardt and Symonds, together with his own later familiarity with original period documents, provided him with incentive and equipment for the production of novels worth far greater respect than the costume romances so often passing for creditable historical fiction. Because he devoted to these novels of the past the same care for precision and imaginative credibility that he brought to the rest of his work, their accuracy in atmospheric detail and original historical sense fit them for the mature reader; and even though they are necessarily only Impressionist renderings of remote periods, they attempt consistency in the impression conveyed and so are never sheerly fanciful reconstructions. Like Nietzsche, whose philosophy he knew, Ford objected to schoolmasterish writing of history; and in this light his fiction stands related to his whole serious purpose of accustoming the reader to an enlarged historical perspective.

The novels, in fact, are too somber, too intolerant of a careless optimism, to consort well with the popular term "romance" which custom perhaps obliged Ford to attach to them; for much of their interest lies in his refusal to treat historical fiction as a means of escape and in his insistence on recognizing the evils of the past as a record of the cruelties and ambitions of men always fallible and essentially unchanging despite alterations in government and manners. Largely because he felt that it had lost touch with the harshness of common fact and falsely glamorized the past, he censured the greater part of nineteenth century historical fiction as escapist and particularly condemned sentimental conceptions of medievalism, the illusion of which had removed English poets in the Seventies and Eighties from the gloom of their surroundings and set them singing of ". . . Launcelot and Guinevere, Merlin and Vivien, ballads of staffs and scrips, of music and moonlight." [5] Scott he reproved for ignorance of method and a guilelessness incomprehensible to grown men; yet he was harder still on the Victorians whose writers he thought too thickly padded against the discomforts of active life to produce anything but watery imitations of the historical novel. On the positive side, however, he praised those writers whose standards he considered deserving of emulation. Among these he placed Manzoni, whose *I Promessi Sposi* he had evidently studied with care and profit,[6] and Stendhal, whom he commended for "the light of sinister reality that plays on all his scenes" and for making the Fabrice of *La Chartreuse de Parme*—a novel with bearings on Ford's practice—as real a character as Julien Sorel.[7] A more evident debt was, however, to Flaubert's *Salambô*, which besides meeting Ford's demands in the way of conscious artistry also afforded, in its strange but unitary vision of ancient Carthage, a close parallel to his ideal of a novel which would consist in a unified impression of the nature of a particular age while keeping the features of that age entirely distinct from those of the present.

This aesthetic and, by Ford's measure, impressionistic aspect of *Salambô* is perhaps too obviously slighted by Georg Lukács in his *Der Historische Roman,* one of the more illuminating studies of historical fiction. To Lukács, from a Marxist position, *Salambô* is a turning point in the decline of the European historical novel after its "classical" phase from Scott through Balzac, an example of the novel's becoming more exotic and remote in its central action from the common life of a whole people. Although granting the stylistic virtues of *Salambô*, Lukács, in agreement with Saint-Beuve, accuses Flaubert of casting the work as a violent reaction against the trivialities of his own time and of investing the main characters with psychologies entirely foreign to the period they are supposed to represent—the orientalized Salambô, for instance, being at heart a sister to Emma Bovary and thus a replica of hysterical young women of the modern great cities.[8] A reading of *Salambô* itself, however, without regard for the special problems of Flaubert's motives or of Carthaginian psychology, favors the supposition that the work may not be the sort of historical novel that Lukács tries to make it appear but rather something nearer the free creation of an independent world perhaps not altogether remote from what Conrad attempted in *The Secret Agent* and *Nostromo* or even Joyce in *Ulysses.* More pertinent, however, are the implications from Lukács' thesis as they would apply to the novels of Ford or to resemblances between the aims of Ford and of Flaubert.

Although it seems likely that, had the critic examined it, Ford's work would have been exposed to many of the same objections that Lukács brings against *Salambô,* it presents exceptions enough to cause embarrassment to the theory of decline in historical fiction in the later nineteenth century, Lukács' contention depending strongly on the idea of a post-Hegelian denial of the reality of history as process and an ensuing subjectivism in the novel. To some extent Ford's work does con-

tinue in the *Salambô* tradition but chiefly in matters of style
and atmospheric effect, points discussed during the collaboration on *Romance* when, according to Ford, Conrad had expected ". . . a drama of Cuban pirates, immense and gloomy,
like *Salambô,* with a reddish illumination, passing as it were
upon a distant stage," [9] a statement describing fairly well, in
fact, what *Romance* eventually became. With respect to character, moreover, Ford stands open to the censure of Lukács on
the subject of transferring modern psychology to the past; for
in contrasting himself with the popular romancer, Maurice
Hewlett, whose *Queen's Quair* of 1904 entered into rivalry with
Ford's *Fifth Queen,* Ford admitted freely having imparted
modern psychologies to his characters whereas Hewlett took
great pains ". . . to keep his characters well within their historic *cadres* in the matter of psychology. I think he loved the
Middle Ages better than I. I was more interested in humanity." [10] In this decision Ford probably looked to Stendhal and
desired to substitute the refinements of realistic psychologizing
for the simpler physical action of romance, his reasons for so
doing being integral to his whole historical outlook as well as
to his view of romance as a literary problem.

What Ford's example tends to show is an over-simplification
in Lukács' claim for *Salambô* as an archetype in a subsequent
movement of historical fiction towards unreality; for although
Ford's work is Flaubertian in tone and craftsmanship, it is not
so with respect to the attitude towards history which Lukács
imputes to Flaubert in charging the latter with having invented
a violent past to affront a tamer present. Whether or not
Lukács is correct, so sharp a juxtaposition is not present in
Ford, despite the fact that he expresses regret for the disappearance of certain kinds of eagles and trumpets and also
grapples prominently with the theme of action and its failure.
As has been noted, he distrusted the trend of the contemporary
world toward science, industrialization, and mass culture; yet
at the same time he saw no glamor in the past and, as a pro-
fessing historian, rejected this spirit in the novel. Although he

could turn somewhat nostalgically to the arts of former times,
as when in 1900 in *The Cinque Ports* he deplored the restoration of churches, he surveyed the human chronicle as

> . . . history which is the history of men. Rioting through the
> long tale you perceived every kind of falsehood, every kind
> of treachery; every kind of murder, every kind of greed. It
> did not matter whether it was the Biblical Hebrews triumph-
> ing, in the name of Jehovah, by every kind of fraud, guile,
> deceit or treachery. . . . You perceived Richard III murder
> his nephews; you perceived Henry of Windsor murder wives,
> murder protestants, murder Catholics, in the name of God;
> you perceived the Church of England founded on a king's
> desire for adultery. . . . Every unthinkable wrong you will
> perceive to flourish and to be justified in the pages of His-
> tory.[11]

Quite early in life, Ford maintains, he had adopted the attitude
of *homo homini lupus;* and this is, after all, perhaps the real
basis of his idea of history as a record of persistent evil.

As a fictional historian, however, his opinions are more concrete; and in his novels he attempts to foster historical sense
and a notion of continuity that will be plausible in the light of
his own beliefs. For this reason his novels, though they have
some affinity with *Salambô* in being imaginative impressions of
the character of various periods, differ in their effort to provide
the reader not merely with a vivid aesthetic experience but
with a defensible account of the culture of societies closer to
the present than Carthage and hence more familiar. From the
fact that the novels, in keeping with Impressionist principle,
depart from romantic story and offer instead a coherent image
of a phase of culture including arts and manners as well as
government and politics, they appear both a late offshoot of
the dramatic historical writing of the nineteenth century and
a product of Ford's acquaintance with the exponents of cultural
history such as Burckhardt and Nietzsche. Unlike the single
instance of *Salambô*, moreover, the novels are sufficient in num-

ber to demonstrate the presence behind them of a recognizable attitude, even though they need not be regarded as a series. Viewed as a group, they are impressions of stages in the history of the modern world from the Tudor era depicted in *The Fifth Queen* down through the earlier nineteenth century; and all exhibit under different lights traits of modernism that Ford emphasized in his novels of contemporary life. By his reckoning the modern world and its habits of thought came into being with the Reformation breach in unified faith and, in England, with Henry VIII's dissolution of the monasteries and the ensuing conflict for material power; and whereas on realistic evidence Ford assigned no superior virtues to medieval society in itself, he tended to attribute to medievalism an unworldly spirit which respected chivalric values not only foreign to modernism but also its major lack. Like other writers of his time and persuasion Ford, in short, had a clearer sense of the shortcomings of modern life than of the ideal to which it might conform; and his literary career, particularly towards the end, reveals a continuing personal effort to define and embody such a unifying image. His historical novels, however, adhere to the record of developing modernism as he surveyed it sceptically and also reveal his endeavor to endow it with pattern, as in his unorthodox speculations on phases of English rule according to "pre-Tudor," "Tudor-Stuart," and "post-Stuart" divisions each marked by the dominance of individuals of a special "type." [12]

As a step towards the acquisition of methods and of the unromantic tone subsequently featured in the historical novels, Ford's five-year collaboration with Conrad on *Romance* (1903) merits more consideration than it usually receives, perhaps because the title of the book is too easily taken at face value and without the ironical turn that the authors intended to give it. Although not, properly speaking, a historical novel but a tale of adventure in which the young hero, John Kemp, involves himself in early nineteenth century political turmoil around Jamaica and ends by narrowly escaping execution for piracy, *Romance* contains elements of history weighty enough to set it apart from the type of Stevensonian romance that it was probably meant to rival and to rid it finally of any hope of real juvenile appeal. In writing to Blackwood that the topic, though "grubbed out of the British Museum" by Ford, was authentic in all of its details of political feeling in Jamaica,[13] Conrad apparently wished to call attention not merely to Ford's recourse to documents bearing on the actual piracy trial of a man named Aaron Smith for Ford's original draft of the novel but more significantly to the book's conforming to the Impressionist canon that a subject ought to grow out of a germ supplied by life itself and thus carry a note of authenticity to a general audience. Conrad's hint of a political overtone also suggests a measure of topicality capable of recognition by a curious reader. Kemp's final struggle in the Admiralty Court to establish his innocence before heavily prejudiced authority parallels slightly the Dreyfus trial, which interested both Ford and Conrad; and the Irish villain, O'Brien, invented by the two authors, a figure of some depth with the grandiose ambition of heading Jamaican piracy in a war against the English, may be read as a reflection of Ford's concern with the contemporary problem of Ireland's move towards independence. Complicated by his descent from Irish kings and his renegade Catholicism, a trait bringing him near the orbit of Graham Greene, O'Brien, like many of the ostensibly subordinate characters in the novel, has far greater body than the hero, John Kemp; and O'Brien's denationalized status contributes a kind of anti-Imperialistic flavor which may have emanated from the private Impressionist creed of the collaborators.

Although in its way an exciting enough tale, *Romance* suffers from the fault of over-writing, since it was so much a proving ground for the evolving technical theories of Conrad and Ford. In demanding that the novel be as "written" as *Salambô*, Conrad got what he wanted and more; for in spite of brilliant passages, especially a number from Conrad's hand in the Fourth Part, the prose has a deliberate and marmoreal quality, with a tendency in places to almost hallucinatory atmosphere, which suggests an uncomfortable proximity to Flaubert's Carthaginian landscape. The cadenced sentences on the town of Rio Medio, for example, induce an effect of artifice while conveying the sense of immobility and decay:

> The general effect of the place was of vitality exhausted, of a body calcined, of romance turned into stone. The still air, the hot sunshine, the white beach curving around the deserted sheet of water, the sombre green of the hills, had the motionlessness of things petrified, the vividness of things painted, the sadness of things abandoned, desecrated.[14]

From the groundwork of style, resemblances to *Salambô* extend to elements of situation and design. In the third part of the novel, for instance, set in Rio Medio, the declining magnificence of the grandee Riegos encircled by a nest of pirates recalls Flaubert's picture of the Barcas threatened by the swarming mercenaries. Moreover, the contrast of races in *Salambô* compares with the racial variations of English, Spanish, Irish, and Jamaicans in *Romance,* which in this respect perhaps anticipates *Nostromo,* an arrangement in keeping with Conrad's view, pertaining directly to the English-Spanish love affair, that romantic feeling arises partly from ". . . the contact with a different race and a different temperament." [15]

More important, however, to the whole effect of *Romance* than such technical resemblances to Flaubert's work is the approximation to Flaubertian irony in the developing contrast between romantic illusion and the hardships of immediate experience, a result obtained partly by relegating the adventures to the reminiscences of an old man upon his youth and thus suggesting that romance is chiefly a property of memory. The story, moreover, exhibits the strongest marks of *progression d'effet,* the aim, according to Ford, being ". . . to give one more, and one more, and again one more turn to the screw that sent the rather listless John Kemp towards an inevitable gallows." [16] The action, consequently, acquires from the outset a pervading tone of fate, as the young hero's initial expectations of high adventure fade with the accidents and mischances that lead him toward his solitary ordeal in the hostile courtroom. Throughout the story premonitions of his ultimate disillusionment fall along his path: on his outgoing passage from England he sights the flagship on which he is destined to return as an accused pirate; and on witnessing the hanging of a group of pirates at Kingston and hearing one of them protest his innocence, he observes the whiteness of his hands which anticipates the spiked and bleeding hand that he will later display in the Admiralty dock. The *progression* technique undoubtedly belongs with the conception of life infusing the novel which, as in Conrad's *Lord Jim,* points to the insufficiency of the romantic ideal in its ironic and abstract summation in the title of the book. Looking back on his youthful self, the old Kemp reflects: "It was, I suppose, what I demanded of Fate—to be gently wafted into the position of a hero of romance, without rough hands at my throat. It is what we all ask, I suppose; and we get it sometimes in ten-minute snatches." [17] Rounding out this sentiment are Ford's own final words for the novel— "suffering is the lot of man."

Although the last statement typifies Ford's customary view of the human situation, *Romance* as a whole does not well represent his manner as historical novelist, a fact to be laid to the account of the collaboration. Whereas with Conrad Ford undoubtedly gained in command of technical resources, *Romance* is Conradesque to a point lending support to Ford's later remarks on his submissive part in the relationship.[18] By his description the first draft of the novel, which he had written under the title of *Seraphina* and submitted to Conrad's inspection, aimed at imitating "a very faded manuscript of a Greek play" and at a style in which "every sentence had a dying fall and every paragraph faded out." [19] But evidently such delicacy yielded to Conrad's demand for heavier orchestration, this explaining in part the strained air of the finished work. In certain respects Ford's hand is subtler than Conrad's, especially in the delineation of evil which Conrad tends to handle with a moral

or philosophical emphasis but Ford, nearer James in this regard, with a more acute sense of personal depravity often
implicitly sexual and hence, perhaps, Victorian. Of Ford's leaning to Richardson in the sounding of sexual entanglements,
Romance shows almost nothing, just as it reveals little of Ford's
naturally oblique and muted style, so that for all of its technical
sophistication the novel looks more plainly an adventure tale
than Ford's independent accomplishment in his first major
work, *The Fifth Queen* trilogy, dominated by the complex
woman character of Katharine Howard. Yet with the earlier
novel *The Fifth Queen* shares at least a sceptical view of experience; and despite some aestheticism in manner it is no
tapestry of color and romance but a somber record of passion
and intrigue based on positive, if debatable, historical convictions.

Like most of Ford's better work the fabric of the triology is
too close, the workmanship too minute, to be systematically
analyzed. But together the three novels combine in a single
impression, based on Ford's study of the reign and character
of Henry VIII, of the early Tudor period as one in which the
medieval spirit of chivalry and faith dies out against the new
forces of modernism—an age of deceit, Machiavellism in politics, relativism in morals and belief, luxury rather than deeds.
It is a world in which men are solitary, human fidelity a fatal
error, because of the general practice of intrigue. The New
Learning exemplified by Nicholas Udal, the lascivious scholar
and playwright, has replaced the Plutarchian nobility of character which Ford seems to have associated with medievalism.
Standing for the medieval attitude is Henry's Catholic queen,
Katharine Howard, whose headstrong passion and Plutarchian
idealism make her victim of a cynical society and whose form
of beauty ". . . fair and reddish hair, and eyes that had a glint
of almond green" [20] relates her to the "rufous" type that Ford
imagined dominant before the Tudor age.[21] To complete the
contrast between ". . . the old faith and the new learning, between empirical, charming conceptions of an irrational world

and the modern theoretic way of looking at life," [22] Ford sets against Katharine Howard the statesman, Thomas Cromwell, the spoiler of monasteries, disciple of Machiavelli with an army of spies, and actual ruler of an England torn by religious feuds and governed only in name by the neurotic and irresolute Henry, to Ford the unhappiest of England's kings.

Although in close perspective the trilogy centers in the tragedy, or martyrdom, of Katharine, who in the end virtually elects to die in defiance of moral calumny, it is the age itself which victimizes everywhere by its maze of treachery concretely symbolized at the conclusion of *The Fifth Queen* by the "black range" of palace corridors through which the terrified Katharine runs to encounter Henry, captive as much as herself of a realm of nightmare. With a suggestion of Fortune's wheel Cromwell falls as Katharine rises, while later Katharine declines with Cranmer's accession to power. Yet Katharine's personal fate seems ordained from the beginning when on her first appearance her mule stumbles at the threshold of the royal palace, even though she moves to an end which, in keeping with a main Ford precept, is not harrowing since the trilogy concludes not with her execution but rather with her courageous speech to the shamefaced Henry:

> And so, now I am cast for death, and I am very glad of it. For, if I had not so ensured and made it fated, I might later have wavered. For I am a weak woman, and strong men have taken dishonorable means to escape death when it came near. Now I am assured of death, and know that no means of yours can save me, nor no prayers nor yielding of mine.[23]

Just as the whole scene illustrates Ford's preference for muted effects, so also Katharine's final address to the king and council gains authenticity by its echoes of classical rhetoric and the cadences of Tudor chronicle. The whole trilogy is, in fact, relatively free of the abuse of Wardour Street; and the occasional archaic terms—"manchet," "scandarach"—are precise and without ready synonyms.

Ford instills his sense of period less by antiquarian detail than through atmosphere, so that the novels symbolize a moral or spiritual condition rather than narrate political action. Despite its luxury the Tudor world is overcast by twilight or darkness and bathed in a cold and watery air. Snail tracks slime the castle walls behind the costly hangings; and under the Cromwellian diplomacy of fear illness reveals itself in Cromwell's own persistent earaches, Henry's ulcer, and the "wasting complaint" that afflicts the embittered Mary, condemned for bastardy as the daughter of Katharine of Aragon. And as clearly as the atmosphere anticipates the symbolic landscapes of Greene and other later fiction, so also it draws something from *Salambô* and from Conrad's *Youth* and *Heart of Darkness*. At the opening of the trilogy the black night pierced by torches and bonfires while Cromwell rows in his barge to Greenwich sets the mood for the entire first novel:

> The Lord Privy Seal was beneath a tall cresset in the stern of his barge, looking across the night and the winter river. They were rowing from Rochester to the palace at Greenwich, where the court was awaiting Anne of Cleves. The flare of the King's barge a quarter of a mile ahead moved in a glaring patch of lights and their reflections, as though it were some portent creeping in a blaze across the sky. There was nothing else visible in the world but the darkness and a dusky tinge of red where a wave caught the flare of light further out.[24]

The ominous coloring that mingles the flames of a state procession with the fires of Smithfield and perhaps foreshadows Katharine's ultimate martyrdom borrows a note from *Salambô*. But the portent blazing across the sky also connects with Ford's interpretation of Conrad's symbolic pall of smoke against the azure heaven in *Youth*.

For atmospheric purposes, too, Ford in *The Fifth Queen* resorted to the *Satyricon* of Petronius, a work used by him frequently thereafter. One episode in particular—that of Gito leading the guests through the streets after the banquet—captured Ford's imagination:

> I must confess that, after twenty years or so, there had remained in my mind the impression that the passage that followed was one of the really fine descriptive pieces in the world. I had in my mind a picture of a pitch-black Rome, of immensely high houses, narrow and maze-like alleys, and the guests shouting confusedly and lost in the shadows. I had imagined that it had some of the depth and some of the quality of Maupassant's nightmare called "La Nuit." But it is a matter of very dry epithets. . . . Nevertheless it is marvellous language, if you come to look at it. The guests at last find their way home by means of chalk-marks, for all the world like blazed trees, that Gito has made on the outward way. It is a picture of manners.[25]

The incident specified in this passage, another insight into Impressionist handling of sources, finds a parallel in *The Fifth Queen* where guests returning by night from Gardiner's revels are pelted with chalk by boys on housetops:

> There was a swishing repeated three times and then thuds and twists of white on heads and shoulders just before her. Undistinguishable yells of mockery dwindled down from high above, and a skylight shone at an immense elevation illuminating a faint square of casement that might have been in the heavens. The apprentices had thrown down paper bags of powdered chalk. The men who had been struck, and several others who had been maltreated on former nights, or who resented this continued 'prentice scandal began a frightful outcry at the door of the house. More bags came bursting down and foul water; the yells and battlecries rolled, in the narrow space under the housefronts

that nearly kissed each other high over head, and the crowd, brought to a standstill, surged and packed against the walls.[26]

Ford, however, made more than superficial use of the *Satyricon*. For one thing he read it to identify himself with the viewpoint of characters like Katharine Howard and Nicholas Udal and to imagine how circumstances might appear to them after they had become familiar with such a Latin text. But more than this he controverts the later nineteenth century confidence in the Renaissance by making the *Satyricon* the counterpart of a degenerating Tudor world paganized by the New Learning.

As chiefly a "picture of manners," therefore, *The Fifth Queen* establishes the pattern for nearly all of Ford's later historical novels in its interweaving of art, morals, and diplomacy in a unified impression of a selected period. Throughout the trilogy are copious details of English Renaissance taste, usually classical or Italianate, in dress, gardening, furniture, stage decoration; but in keeping with the central intent of the novels the splendor tarnishes in the air of moral corruption. Icy shadows surround peacock-shaped trees, and cold wind forces the pagan deities in the wall hangings to writhe menacingly. Cromwell, the man of his age in his equal devotion to his art treasures and to the precepts of Machiavelli, emits an aura of treachery that renders squalid all of the luxury of his Greenwich rooms. Similarly representative of the time, though in learning rather than power, the Magister Udal makes his first appearance loaded with volumes of Tully and Plautus but also wearing a silver medallion stamped with figures of Cupid and Venus which he values less for itself than as barter for lechery, as another kind of counter in the universal play of intrigue. The medallion is not a chance image but one of a variety of slanting lights cast by Ford on the debasing of aesthetic values in a mercenary and luxurious age. Even against her will the "fair and upright beauty" of Katharine Howard makes her a desirable commodity; and in the ironical ending of the first novel she buys her protection from Henry, only her illusion of the just monarch, not on the strength of her plea but on that of a wordless revelation of physical worth: "Her fair face worked convulsively, her lips moved, and her hand, falling away from her brows, showed her hair that had golden glints." [27]

As with others of his historical novels, the trilogy shows Ford's reliance upon painting as a source of atmospheric detail. In 1905, the year of the appearance of *The Fifth Queen*, the first novel of the three, Ford published his study of Holbein which advances much the same notion of the antithesis of medieval to modern that enters into the design of the trilogy. In Ford's cool appraisal, Holbein represents the emerging modern spirit: "He was the painter of men and cities, and inasmuch as modern life is a matter of men and cities, he was the first painter of modern life." [28] In support of this, Ford cited Holbein's portrayal of "indoor statesmen" no longer distinguishable from great merchants as a sign of the painter's complete identification with the Renaissance. By contrast Dürer was the artist of outgoing medievalism; and whereas in Holbein's portraits the eyes are ". . . half closed, sceptical, challenging, and disbelieving," those in the work of Dürer the mystic, "the last fruit of a twilight of the gods," reveal that they ". . . dream, accept, or believe in the things they see." [29] Where Holbein, moreover, was indifferent to nature, Dürer painted lords who ride hunting and displayed the love of outdoor life that Ford, much like Vernon Lee in her *Euphorion*, associated with medievalism.

In keeping, then, with this opinion of Holbein, Ford represents the great men of the Tudor world of *The Fifth Queen*, from Henry down, as ponderous, sedentary schemers. It seems likely, therefore, that he made literary capital of the method that he used for studying Holbein's work, that of spreading on the floor a set of reproductions of the painter's Windsor sketches for his portraits of Henry's court and comparing these to detect common features going to form a kind of "composite photograph." [30] Although Ford does not, of course, attempt a mechanical copy of the portraits, the main characters in the trilogy are sufficiently like Holbein models to add this distinguishing note to the atmosphere. The result, moreover, is not simply novelty but a matter of functional importance; for in their early modernism of bearing and feature, the Holbein people, as Ford maintains, are prototypes for average individuals of the present day:

> If you glance rapidly along the series of sketches at Windsor you will be astounded to see how exactly they resemble the faces you will pass in the Windsor streets. If you compare them with, say, Lely's portraits of a later court, the characteristic becomes even more marked, since Lely's men and women died a century or so later than Holbein's—and have yet been dead so much longer. He got out of his time—as he got *into* our time—with a completeness that few painters have achieved—hardly even Velasquez or Rembrandt.[31]

On these premises the atmosphere of *The Fifth Queen* can mingle notes more or less authentically Tudor with those suggestive of the mundanity of contemporary existence to produce an overall impression of a modernism extending from past to present. If the mood of the trilogy is static, this is partly because its Holbein world is one of bulky indoor men who accomplish their ends by calculation and the mere lifting of a finger; yet it also follows that the structure of the novels should conform to the Jamesian scenic pattern, since Tudor England at the aristocratic level parallels the Jamesian society where, in Ford's description, changes occur ". . . whilst the characters do no more than sit in arm-chairs or open bookcases." A scheme of this kind enabled Ford to achieve his favorite low keys and muted effects and to exclude the strong situation that he disliked, so that there are, for example, no direct reports of major happenings such as Cromwell's arrest or Katharine's death at the block, tableaux of the kind dear to the nineteenth century historical painter. Instead, Ford obtains memorable effects in scenes of restrained emotion like that in the second novel, *Privy Seal,* where the rejected Anne of Cleves gives audience to her successor, Katharine Howard:

> The silver and the bright light of the sun swathed these two women's figures, so that Katharine seemed to hear the flutter against the window-glass of a brown butterfly that, having sheltered in the hall all winter, now sought to take a part in the new brightness of the world. Katharine kept her knees, her eyes upon the floor; the Queen, motionless and soft, let her eyes rest upon Katharine's hand.
>
> The butterfly sought another window; the Queen spoke at last.
>
> "You seek my queenship"; and in her still voice there was neither passion, nor pity, nor question, nor resignation.
>
> Katharine raised her eyes: they saw the imprisoned butterfly, but she found no words.
>
> "You have more courage than I," the Queen said.
>
> Suddenly she made a single gesture with her hands, as if she swept something from her lap: some invisible dust—and that was all.[32]

Such rendered episodes contribute to making the whole trilogy an Affair in the Jamesian tradition with people moving quietly under the shadow of doom. Even the completely depraved—like the spies Throckmorton and Lascelles—are low-voiced and smiling enough for a drawing room, so that Ford's tale of having used James himself as a model for Henry VIII may convey obliquely more than a surface glimpse at intention.

Between the trilogy and *What Maisie Knew,* the book by James that nearly always most mattered to Ford, there are, in fact, detectable analogies, in particular a resemblance between the trapped situation of the uninitiated Katharine and that of James's child ". . . moving amongst elemental passions that are veiled." [33] Perhaps more than chance prompted Ford to endow Throckmorton, Cromwell's chief spy, with the rich golden beard of Beale Farange in *Maisie;* for Throckmorton, who

warns Katharine that her career will be short unless she fights
the Tudor world with its own weapons of deceit, is the character most at ease in that world's evil. By contrast to the
Holbein court that she enters after her childhood in her father's
small castle in the north, Katharine, with her combined traits
of physical vitality and of dreaminess fostered by her reading
of ancient books on human virtue, is alone in her likeness to the
medieval figures of Dürer. Ford seems to have intended, also,
to connect her with the irrational factor that he attributed to
medievalism by involving her from the beginning with her
cousin, Thomas Culpepper, whose unrestrained passion is a
determining element in her fate, partly because, like her own
idealism, it is out of place in a society ruled by guile: "A hundred years ago kings made war with blows. Now it is done
with black velvets or the lack of black velvets." [34] With a
violence somewhat reminiscent of Matho's savage passion for
Salambô, Culpepper is ready to kill on emotional impulse, as
he does on his first appearance with Katharine in the London
street scuffle which occurs when she enters the city: "A man
in green at the mule's head, on the other side, sprang like a wild
cat under the beast's neck. His face blazed white, his teeth
shone like a dog's, he screamed and stuck his dagger through
the butcher's throat." [35]

Although the relationship of Katharine and Culpepper introduces the theme of direct action and its consequences which
comes to figure importantly in Ford's novels, both historical
and contemporary, the presence of Culpepper in the trilogy
and his final error of forcing his entry into the king's bedroom
helps to make Katharine's downfall inevitable. If Katharine
does not consciously respond to his blundering passion, her
growing enmity to the ways of the Tudor court puts her, even
against her will, upon his side; and her refusal to save herself
by the accepted practice of betrayal affirms her fidelity to that
tradition in her past of which Culpepper is an extreme manifestation even while it establishes her guilt in the logic of the
world. In all probability Katharine dies a Christian martyr;

yet her final rebuke to Henry and his courtiers includes an admission of leniency towards the dead Culpepper: "I die a Queen, but I would rather have died the wife of my cousin Culpepper or of any other simple lout that loved me as he did, without regard, without thought and without falter." [36] These words touch on a slight strain of ambiguity in her motives which, without blurring her character or making uncertain her innocence of adultery, leaves her not only in the company of James's Maisie but also of Richardson's Clarissa, in Ford's eyes a tragic heroine.

Although Conrad hoped that *The Fifth Queen* might be the swan song of historical fiction, though he thought the work in itself amazing,[37] the trilogy provides a convenient point of approach to a study of Ford with regard both to his habit of mind and to his resourcefulness in method. In the latter respect his blend in the trilogy of the Jamesian scenic divisions with the Stendhalian compressed historical stage of *La Chartreuse de Parme* removes *The Fifth Queen* from associations with conventional romance and gives it more of the tone and pattern of mature psychological fiction. The centering of the action largely within the Tudor court so that this forestage epitomizes, in Stendhal's fashion, a broader background of general history likewise deserves notice in regard to doubts like those of Lukács; for even if Ford, who is hardly a novelist of the proletariat, glances only occasionally at the Tudor lower classes and thus seems to overlook what to Lukács is fundamental to the best historical fiction, he does so not simply to exclude reference to common life but rather in order to stress his own point of the national disunity caused by the governing policy of opportunism and deceit. In the light of the unified design sustained through the work nearest to the Tietjens tetralogy in length, *The Fifth Queen* emerges successfully from the elaborate scaffolding employed by Ford in its construction and so demonstrates superiority in plan over *The 'Half Moon,'* his novel of 1909 which attempts to contain too broad a field within a narrow frame. Leaving the sixteenth century, Ford

in *The 'Half Moon'* offers an impression of the spirit of the
Stuart world of James I as a period of overseas enterprise which
coupled the continuing dissolution of European faith into
sectarian conflicts with the expansion of trade and settlement
in the New World as conducted by navigators like Henry
Hudson, the chief historical personage in the book. Representing, therefore, an age one century beyond that of *The Fifth
Queen*, *The 'Half Moon'* takes on a more international com-
plexion as its focus swings from England, to Holland, to America; and Ford's principal technical innovation is an effort towards the end to suggest simultaneous action by alternating
episodes in England with others on Hudson's voyage into icy
American waters, a procedure conducive to *progression d'effet*
as well as to the elaboration of a fundamental irony not unlike
that effected by Waugh in the concluding sections of *A Handful of Dust*. This exposure of the hollow utopianism of mere
spatial conquest perhaps thrusts indirectly at the Imperialism
of Ford's own day.

Although once again Ford manages to evoke a special period
atmosphere, it is less consistent and readily comprehensible
than that in *The Fifth Queen*. His characteristic method of
cultural suggestion is, however, to be seen in the following
picture of a torchlight procession in Amsterdam which may
owe something to the night scene in the *Satyricon* or to the
color of seventeenth century masque:

But when Edward Coleman came out from the lawyer's
house it was nearly pitch dark; there was a procession with
many torches just close at his right hand, but upon the glow-
ing water of the canal there was no boat below the quay.
He stood at the edge to let the procession pass. First, appearing of portentous size in the frame of darkness, with two
torches above a huge umbrella held high over his head,
marched a great, brown-faced man with fierce eyes and a
long grey moustache; round his shoulders was a pelisse of
ermine; green robes dropped to his feet; a great turban of

white fur was around his head, and, high up, an aigret swayed above a huge ruby-jewel. Behind him walked a Moor all in white, holding forward the umbrella with a strained and anxious attitude; and behind came many men in straight black cloaks with high, black, sugarloaf hats and with white collars that caught the light. This was the ambassador from the Soldan of Berby, who was being escorted back to his lodgings by the Dutch notables.[38]

Although the description catches notes from seventeenth century art, perhaps that of Rembrandt, the device functions less integrally than Ford's transference of Holbein portraiture to *The Fifth Queen;* and the sheerly pictorial element in *The 'Half Moon'* tends to overburden narrative and character. More obtrusive, too, than in the trilogy is the basing of speech upon period chronicle, even if the logic of permitting a character like Hudson to talk like a page from Hakluyt or Purchas fits with the substance of the novel:

"Sir, . . . former Ages have been called Ages of Gold, of Brass, of Iron; or Ages of Horace, of Tully, of Aristotle, as the bookmen will tell you. But I think the future ages shall speak of this as the Age of Pilots. For, for sure, the great men that be masters of my craft and mystery shall have great honours shown to them that for princes, kings and commonwealths, discover realms, islands, empires, continents, harbours, passages, anchorages or straits, and do give to the Alexanders of their day new regions to conquer or to the republics that at present exist, the lands upon which to set up colonies and commonwealths.[39]

The fact, however, that Hudson talks like a book—as Ford himself could for a joke—and not with the personal dignity of Katharine Howard at the close of *The Fifth Queen* satirizes by the inflated rhetoric the fraudulent character of the navigator himself. Hudson, ". . . a man of great girth, heavy upon his feet, with a square and curly beard of an iron grey and deep-set eyes of a shining black," [40] is a recognizable descendant of the Tudor, and modern, types of *The Fifth Queen*—an inactive navigator who scorns mere sailors and who rules his ship by guile and trickery. With his public bombast he has mastered the new art of handling crowds, which Ford thought characteristic of the twentieth century, and thus stands as a forerunner of the Joseph Chamberlain brand of Imperialism which Ford detested.

In spite, however, of its too literary style, the novel presents frequent examples of Ford's peculiar ability to endow a period with his own kind of historical sense and to give imaginative shape to a world of James I and Bacon, of Jonson and Stuart drama, of demonology and religious controversy. The final impression is sinister, but in a different way from that of *The Fifth Queen*. The age in *The 'Half Moon'* is brisker, further still from medievalism than that of Henry VIII; and its corruption proceeds more from the arrogant will of men like Hudson than from Machiavellian intrigue, a probable reason why Ford dropped the Jamesian scenic method in the Jacobean novel. Again, however, he finds opportunity to exhibit his talent for scenting evil, as in the scene which describes King James in the company of his favorites:

He had a hooked nose, that crooked over to one side, a little moustachio that turned upwards, and little, tired, beady bright eyes that had many wrinkles beneath them. His voice was monotonous and haughty and, at the same time querulous. . . They moved from the great window all in a mass, with slow pacings as if they were a machine pushed forward from behind. Five of them were dark and wore chin-beards that fell down upon their ruffs, and they maintained airs of great gravity and were clothed in black. But the sixth was a fair youth with high eyebrows; he tittered often, and was habited in a suit of red, very slender about the waist and sewn all over, right down to his red stockings and shoes with large pearls. Later on he leaned over the King's shoulder and

made faces at Anne Jeal, kissing his fingertips and rubbing
the jacket above his heart till the pearls came unsewn and
slipped on to the dark floor.[41]

Even so brief an impression implies much regarding a society
notorious for the Overbury murder, a case which Ford may
have had in mind in introducing his theme of a man destroyed
slowly by the passion of a woman trafficking in the black arts,
though he perhaps counted likewise on familiarity with sorcery
in readers acquainted with Michelet and Huysmans. But even
though the theme consorts well with the Stuart legend of
demonology, Ford's larger intention in his story of the revenge
taken by Anne Jeal, a young girl of Spanish descent, upon
Edward Coleman, the youthful Rye shipmaster and voyager
with Hudson, was to place further emphasis upon the decay of
the Old Faith in England. Hence in *The 'Half Moon'* by contrast with *The Fifth Queen* Ford pays fairly minute attention
to the existence and customs of dissenting religious sects, like
the Dutch "Knipperdollincks" in the port of Rye, thus revealing
his continuing interest in unorthodox forms of belief as well as
his probable employment of some of the materials to have been
used with Conrad in their projected Anabaptist novel.

In his dedication to *The 'Half Moon'* Ford speaks of his
fascination with ". . . the psychology of the Old World in the
days of Hudson" and adds that ". . . what is inspiring about
a voyage or a world is the passion that gave rise to the one and
the other." Proceeding impressionistically, therefore, Ford tries
with his foreground situation of Anne Jeal's destructive passion
for Coleman to offer a compressed statement of the psychological forces at work in an era of disintegrating faith and terri-
torial expansion, so that the interwoven themes of sorcery and
New World voyaging suggest that the same underlying state
of mind drives Anne to satisfaction in the practice of black arts
and Hudson to seek fame in egotistical exploits of navigation.
Both characters express the breakdown of faith into sterile will
to power and demand for new excitements; and each in his

own way exercises this will to destroy Coleman, a man with no ambition except that of restoring a little of the fading strength of his native town of Rye. Skilfully, therefore, Ford closes the novel by interlocking his main themes: Coleman's death in an American forest occurring at the moment when he has become most completely victim of Hudson's ruthless will to fame and of Anne's perverse desire that she satisfies by transfixing with an Indian knife the wax puppet of Coleman that she has used to bring him ill luck.

As is sometimes true of Ford, *The 'Half Moon'* gives better proof of his intelligence and inventive resource than of his ability at proportion in the ordinary sense. By contrast with *The Fifth Queen,* the novel suffers from an excess of material to the detriment of style for its own sake, perhaps always the danger when Ford aims at too compact an impression, though in this respect *The 'Half Moon'* is hardly an exception to the rest of his creative work. Once, however, the reader establishes proper focus, it is clear not only that the novel puts the trapped Edward Coleman in much the same position as that of Katharine Howard but also that the central situation is in some measure suggestive of that in *The Good Soldier* and in the Tietjens tetralogy insofar as Anne Jeal's fanatical impulse to torture Coleman crudely anticipates the attitude of Sylvia Tietjens towards her husband. Ford hints at the sexual-religious complications in Anne's motives but tends to distract attention towards her pursuit of black magic, an issue kept subordinate in Sylvia Tietjens, and thus throws her into apparent relationship with such a character as Rossetti's Sister Helen. But in reality Ford's deeper aim was evidently to explore through Anne and Coleman the problem of sexual attraction made fashionable in the earlier years of the century by Otto Weininger in his *Sex and Character,* a book that Ford would have known by the time of his writing *The 'Half Moon,'* if his statement may be trusted.[42] In this respect the novel may have seemed bolder in its time than it does today; but again, as in *The Fifth Queen,* Ford assigns traits of modernism to any age following the medieval disruption of faith and so, in a sense, puts history second to the mysteries of the heart.

With a probable eye to historical fact but also for further emphasis on religious division and power seeking, Ford's cultural impressions of the Tudor and Jacobean periods contain no reference to the practice of the visual arts, whereas his eighteenth century novel of 1910, *The Portrait,* with the Hogarth-like painter Hitchcock for a leading character, uses architecture and painting as main expressions of taste and manners. By contrast to the murky atmosphere of *The 'Half Moon,'* the prevailing tone is that of wit and elegance in part reflecting Ford's growing attraction to what he considered the eighteenth century clarity of mind. Quite early he speaks of ". . . that remarkable and only half appreciated eighteenth century of ours" as a source of ". . . the first shoots of nearly all our present-day findings"; [43] and he continued to refer approvingly to the person of Johnson, the prose of Boswell and Gibbon, and the art of Hogarth. His general impression of the society of the time reveals, nevertheless, his customary irony with respect to the extremes of luxury and misery, perhaps implicitly inherited from the Tudor disunity; and while he avoids calling up associations with what he regarded as the coarseness of Fielding and Goldsmith and tends rather to the sophisticated view of the Goncourts, he dwells a little satirically upon the cultivation of artifice and upon the dilettante wager to discover the model for Hitchcock's portrait "Celia in Her Arbour" which provides a controlling theme. Hence the impression at times becomes that of a Beardsley illustration for Pope:

Mr. Bettesworth found Lady Eshetsford still at her toilet, in a flowing bedgown of white and silver and pink, her dark hair as yet unpowdered. She was much gayer, she spoke in a voice more natural, her motions were more sinuous, her hands more free. She sat to a Chinese table of greenish-yellow olive-wood, from the center of which there rose a tall

mirror framed in silver. Let into the table-top were twelve
small cells containing a profusion of little articles, patch
boxes in French porcelain, powder-dredgers in English sil-
verware, pomanders in silver gilt, and a number of little
golden keys. Lady Eshetsford was just dismissing a small
milliner with a huge band-box. Tutt, with her demure face
and downcast eyes, stood behind the mirror, and obedient
and silent, Maria was at her guardian's side.[44]

Such passages, furnishing ornate décor, show Ford as still
affecting some of the painterly mannerisms of the earlier historical novels and attempting to combine these with an illusion
of Boswellian speech for the characters, so that *The Portrait,*
as its title suggests, seems to aim at achieving a kind of composite portrait in the eighteenth century style.

The novel is, however, more subtly organized than a glance
over its polished surface might disclose. As in *The Fifth Queen*
Ford relies on period detail and ornament to evoke a sense of
history; but, apparently inspired in part by the architecture of
Vanbrugh, he concentrates, in a brilliant illusion of Georgian
style, chiefly on domestic building for his clue to the spirit
of the age and to the values which it set above the painting of
a native genius like Hitchcock. Thus the extended descriptions
of country houses indicate that behind these elaborate façades
are not only the remains of earlier layers of history but also
traces of the evil necessarily attendant upon such accumulations of luxury. Thus of Lady Eshetsford's Ashford Manor-
House with its porticos, lawns, and classical temple Ford notes
that the Vanbrugh improvements have been added to an older
building ". . . erected by Francis Eshetsford, the founder of the
family, a notorious informer, diplomat, and spoiler of monasteries of Henry VIII's time." [45] Likewise the rear of the house
owes its existence to ancestral complicity in the modern habit
of intrigue:

This had been added to the oldest portion of the house by
Philip Eshetsford, who had materially aided Lord Burleigh

in his successful counterplots against the Jesuits, and in bringing about the execution of Mary Queen of Scots. It consisted of three wings, the two outer ones being the larger, of red brick, and thus forming in outline the letter "E," the initial of the Queen's name. Of dark red brick, with long, low, diamond-paned windows that crumbled in their leads and reflected what sun they got at odd angles, the rear portion of Ashford Manor-house was an unconscionable tangle of small rooms . . . secret passages and pantries.[46]

Behind, and also below, the outward magnificence lie the "contrived corridors" leading down from Tudor history and continuing the labyrinthine passageways that terrified Katharine Howard. The unobtrusive architectural symbolism thus exemplifies not only the deviousness of eighteenth century sophistication but also the connection within history of luxury and evil, Ford here touching on much the same problem as that confronted by James in *The Turn of the Screw* or by Yeats and Eliot in their poetry.

Most significant in *The Portrait* is not, therefore, the ending of the slender theme in which young Mr. Bettesworth discovers in Lady Eshetsford the original of the Celia in Hitchcock's portrait but his sudden exposure, during his quest, to the underworld whose existence he has never suspected in his life of connoisseurship and devotion to the pleasures of his manor-house library. Like Katharine Howard and Edward Coleman in *The 'Half Moon,'* Bettesworth must experience the horror below the civilized glory when, falsely arrested through the malice of a rival, he is cast into a cell of common felons. As a generally serious and rather unfortunate man Bettesworth feels that he has been gripped by forces hitherto unknown to him and made witness to sights as hideous as those from hell. Such an initiation, in some ways like that of Marlow in *Heart of Darkness*, takes from him any romantic belief in his own privileged status and any impulse to self-satisfaction in his eventual winning of Lady Eshetsford. Thus in the light of his

handling of a dual vision of luxury and vice, Ford perhaps
alludes to a perplexity of his own time in treating his portrait
symbolism so as to suggest implications the reverse of those
in Wilde's *Dorian Gray*, Bettesworth attaining to the real
woman that he seeks only after having passed beyond the contemplation of art to a perception of genuine evil. In doing this
he perhaps arrives at full comprehension of the nature of
Hitchcock's art which has been concealed by the blanking out
of the woman's face on the canvas; for Hitchcock appears an
enigmatic figure, cautious and secretive, with "a mind very full
of the secrets of his art." [47] As he had done with Holbein for
The Fifth Queen, Ford here ingeniously makes the work of
Hogarth the measure of historical conditions in his age in their
extremes of high and low life; for the prison scene, in which a
Methodist moralizes on a dying prostitute while sermonizing
Bettesworth on the evils of the country, is in key with "The
Harlot's Progress":

> "For here, but that the fair seemliness of the surface is
> neither visible nor in evidence, you have an epitome of all
> this land. In this harlot, with the death-rattle in her throat,
> having been beaten at the cart-tail and lying in filth, you
> have personified the cruel lusts of all the land, which, in
> spite of all premonitions, persist unto death itself, amidst foul
> stenches and filthy garbage, unto eternal torture. And in this
> other woman you see those who go scratching upon this
> turning earth for the bare portion of a beggar, and to raise
> a roof of rushes over their heads. Until at the last gasp,
> with their sides caved in and their bodies naked you find
> them thus humbled in the dregs of this world." [48]

A dual meaning thus seems to attach to the title of *The
Portrait;* for while using the art of Hogarth to intensify the
period impression, the novel offers a form of commentary upon
that art.

In its final effect, therefore, *The Portrait* sets an underworld
of evil against the elegance of eighteenth century aristocracy

in an antithesis relevant perhaps less to the past than to Ford's
own day of cushioned security thus given literary shock treatment by a method similar to that in work by James and Conrad.
In *The Portrait* the creative artist, Hitchcock, has no real connection with aristocratic society but, not being a gentleman,
occupies a rather menial position apart from it. Yet his productive force stands counter to the inherited luxury—the
Poynton spoils—of the established order; and by following the
trail of the painter's art from the fashionably posed girl without features in the portrait, Bettesworth passes beyond the
complacent face of society to its Hogarthian recesses of evil.
Hence in the end, by Ford's conception, the ruling values of
this world are the same acquisitiveness and power that domi-
nate in the earlier novels.

Ford's general aim in his historical fiction up through *The
Portrait* of stationing the reader at a point from which to view
modern history, including by implication the present, from a
supposedly medieval outlook, becomes modified in 1911 in
Ladies Whose Bright Eyes through the stratagem of transport-
ing a modern man back to the medieval surroundings of the
fourteenth century and so juxtaposing directly past and immediate present. Although properly sub-titled a romance in its
ingredients of strangeness, love, and happy ending, the book
has something in common with Wellsian fantasy, examples
of which both Ford and Conrad admired, as well as with Mark
Twain's *A Connecticut Yankee,* though Ford had disparaged
the latter work for "preaching down chivalric ideals to the tune
of nineteenth century morality" [49] and evidently intended to
correct this mistake. Thus in making its hero Sorrell, a modern
publisher, a visitor to a world different from his own, the novel
contains a note of satire; yet the device is not altogether for
the purpose of demeaning the twentieth century but rather
aims in an Impressionist manner at enabling the reader to
participate vicariously in a way of life foreign to him and so
obtain a genuine conception of the medieval spirit. Even
though its structural frame is not, therefore, quite that of historical fiction, the novel displays Ford's imaginative treatment

of history in the fourteenth century episodes which form the greater part of the book; and the general method resembles that of *The Fifth Queen* insofar as Sorrell functions like Katharine Howard in supplying a mental or temperamental lens for viewing an unfamiliar landscape. Having suffered a head injury in an accident to the boat train in which he is hurtling to London at the excessive speed demanded by the modern time obsession, Sorrell loses contact with his old self lying unconscious in a hospital and enters the self of a Greek slave wandering on foot in fourteenth-century Salisbury Plain. Temporarily, therefore, his role is that of "dispassionate spectator"; and his state of shocked and intensified vision continues until he becomes absorbed into the story as an actor.

Despite the element of romance, *Ladies Whose Bright Eyes* seems founded upon premises similar to those in Ford's other historical novels in that a complacent and materialistic modern outlook meets its opposite in a life governed by a medieval code. At the outset, in his post-Reformation habit of thought and his shifting career from engineering to publishing, Sorrell is the latest descendant of men like Thomas Cromwell and Henry Hudson. Disturbed at the sight of a nun in the train with him shortly before the accident, he thinks for a moment of the Middle Ages as merely another opportunity for the exercise of power:

> And suddenly it came into his head to think what a bully time he might have if he could be thrown right back into the Middle Ages. What would not he be able to do with those ignorant and superstitious people! He would invent for them the railway train, the electric telegraph, the flying machine, the motor-car, and the machine-gun. Above all, the machine-gun. He would be the mightiest man in the world: he would have power, absolute and enormous power. He could take anything: he could do anything. No king could withstand him.[50]

Ford's version of the fourteenth century, however, presents Sorrell, and through him the reader, with nothing of what has been anticipated. Contrary to his Imperialistic illusions, Sorrell's first contact with the past, as his eye fixes upon bodies swinging from gibbets, settles upon him a feeling of bewilderment and danger. Rather than ignorance and superstition, the characteristics of medieval life that confront him as he adapts to it include sophistication and cruelty different in kind but not in degree from such habits in contemporary life; the people are cunning, quarrelsome, and rapacious, and the age itself lies in the shadow of the murder of Edward II. At times the atmosphere seems to reflect Ford's comment elsewhere on "the appalling dullness of medieval life," and his aim was evidently to create a medieval picture with no vestiges of pre-Raphaelite mystical or occult associations. Perhaps for this reason Ford admits episodes of sheer violence and of love as physical passion in no way tempered by religious emotions belonging to another sphere. Yet in common with *The Fifth Queen* he tends to distinguish the medieval from the modern temper in the readiness of the former to outspoken thought and direct response to passionate impulse whether in love or anger. Acquaintance with these traits, as well as with medieval acceptance of pleasure as good in itself, converts Sorrell to a point where, on his return to the twentieth century, he wishes to restore some of these past values to modern existence. His transformation, however, into an active figure in riding boots superintending a country estate with a house of fourteenth century stonework—a little like Stephen Crane playing at medievalism in England—demonstrates Ford's inability at this time to envision clearly a satisfactory image by which to project his growing attraction to a personal ideal somehow associated with medieval aspirations.

Ford's remark in his Dedication to Violet Hunt that the writing of books was for the time being giving him little pleasure perhaps explains why *Ladies Whose Bright Eyes* seems today, except in places, one of his duller works, its plot devices awkward and trite in a way unusual in his practice. The apparent popularity of the book with young writing circles shortly before the Great War may have owed something to its unsentimental treatment of the medieval scene in accordance with the rising influence of Pound; but the apparatus of shifting between present and past remains forced and cumbersome. Yet the novel is significant in Ford's literary career as a step towards the formulation of what ultimately became, in his late work, the outline of an individual ethic founded upon a private vision of Provence as incorporating virtues of craftsmanship, gaiety, and personal grace of the sort possessed in a simpler combination by the Lady Dionissia in *Ladies Whose Bright Eyes*. Sorrell's head injury which effects his transmigration into the Greek slave may have been employed as a means for registering psychic experience on the model of Kipling in "The Finest Story in the World"; but in his novels of the 1930's, *The Rash Act* and *Henry for Hugh,* Ford uses much the same device of the accidental wound to place his central character not in a hypothetical past but in a much more complex modern recreation of a Provençal community.

What most obviously runs counter to Ford's theories in *Ladies Whose Bright Eyes* is, however, the moralizing conclusion on the nature of the good life that Sorrell tries to adopt; and the difference between this romance and work strictly impressionistic may be seen in a contrast with Ford's last truly historical novel, *A Little Less Than Gods*, published years later in 1928. In this strange but exciting story of the Hundred Days Ford employs nearly every main Impressionist device to create by a method of foreshortening the scope of the period surrounding Napoleon's escape from Elba and his ultimate defeat. Although this topic and the appearance of the novel just three years after the posthumous publication of Conrad's unfinished *Suspense* with its similar Napoleonic background provoked some indignation, especially in Mrs. Conrad,[51] on the score of Ford's making capital of the reputation of his former collaborator, it seems difficult to consider Ford guilty of more than an unfortunate choice in timing; for a comparison of Conrad's book with Ford's reveals too marked a difference in emphasis and tone to justify a charge of Ford's attempting to offer a continuation of the incomplete *Suspense.* Part of the truth appears to have been that during their active collaboration Conrad and Ford, both keenly interested in the Napoleonic legend, had talked of a joint novel of the post-Elba situation with Marshal Ney for a main character, Conrad himself taking over the task after Ford had gone to war.[52] But however Conrad intended to develop and conclude *Suspense,* the fragment, with its air of mystery and foreboding, does not resemble Ford's approach in a novel quite independent and linked with his customary historical outlook, despite the fact that both books, each in its own fashion, use Impressionist methods. What most sharply distinguishes *A Little Less Than Gods* is its topical bearing on post-World War I circumstances, a fact that relates it more closely than *Suspense* to the wave of general war literature in the later 1920's.

What perhaps most irked Mrs. Conrad was not, however, a suspicion that Ford had stolen plot material from *Suspense* but rather the turn given in *A Little Less Than Gods* to one element in the story forming a near parallel to a strand in Conrad's novel. Ford's lovers—the young Englishman, George Feilding, who accompanies Napoleon on the latter's final exploit, and Hélène de Frèjus, the French wife of an international banker—recall in some measure Conrad's Cosmo Latham and Adèle d'Armand, especially in the fact that both pairs of characters stand in an ambiguous but dependent relationship to a paternal English aristocrat. Whether or not Ford concluded from reading *Suspense* that Conrad meant to introduce an incestuous complication between Cosmo and Adèle, a not entirely unwarranted guess at the outcome of certain leads in *Suspense,* he did maintain in his 1928 introduction to Conrad's early abandoned tale, *The Sisters,* that Conrad had long desired to treat incestuous passion and in his late security ventured definitely on the theme in his last work. Whatever the truth of this assertion, Ford in his novel makes the discovery of incestuous links between Feilding and Hélène, who are both children of Feilding's squire father, an episode of central importance, thus perhaps fostering the supposition that he had wilfully misrepresented Conrad's own purpose. An analysis of *A Little Less Than Gods* shows clearly, however, that the incest motif is too essential to Ford's effect to be merely an extraneous factor. For one thing the long withholding of the truth of Hélène's parentage establishes a tense *progression d'effet* leading to the scene in Paris where the lovers separate finally in complete knowledge both of their own misfortune and of the extinction of Napoleonic glory. In this scene, as passionate as anything written by Ford, the influence is not from *Suspense* but from Conrad's *Under Western Eyes* and in particular from the episode of Razumov's confession to Natalia Haldin, an incident praised by Ford for its "aching passion" and actually duplicated in the small but memorable item of the black veil dropped by Hélène de Frèjus.[53] The air of political corruption in *Under Western Eyes* could be suitably echoed in *A Little Less Than Gods;* and the frequent reminiscences of Conrad's novel include a notable modeling by Ford of his Paris salon of Madame de Krudener, the intriguing occultist Egeria of the Tsar of Russia,[54] on the drawing-room of the corpse-like Madame de S—— in *Under Western Eyes.*

The incest theme is, therefore, a vital part of the whole atmosphere of Ford's highly complicated novel, an atmosphere designed to produce the impression of a period of hectic romantic emotion culminating in the tarnishing splendor of the Napoleonic defeat at Waterloo. The incestuous tangle in the lives of the foreground characters reflects a background of Byronic extravagance, of the reckless gambling of an Imperial adventurer himself suspected of bastard origin. In keeping, moreover, with Ford's usual historical pattern, the story is one of progressive disillusionment with power, both Feilding and Hélène passing, like Katharine Howard, from a naïve confidence in a great man with Henry Hudson's gift for dominating crowds to the bitterness of knowing themselves implicated in the sordid aftermath of the Napoleonic fiasco. From his own

experience of the Great War and the lost generation mood of
the 1920's Ford wrote here his own judgment on nineteenth
century great man theories of history. Much of the indifference of Jake Barnes to the faded wreath below the Ney statue
in *The Sun Also Rises* may be detected in the scorn of Hélène
de Frèjus for the wealthy Assheton Smith, a main participant
in the Bonaparte adventure:

> "So that, in the end," Hélène said, "we are all of us puppets
> in the game of this nabob, whose money is his sole means of
> illustriousness and whose heart is as dry and thin as last
> year's leaf!"
>
> "Why," Gatti answered, "are we not all in the end the
> puppets of the Gods?"
>
> "Ay, but the men at whose hands we suffer are a little less
> than Gods!" she answered bitterly.
>
> He conceded that, in their separate roles, Michel Ney, the
> Baron de Frèjus, Mr. Assheton Smith—and the greatest of
> all!—were a little less than Gods.[55]

Hélène's remark on the perverting influence of money throws
light on a main issue in Ford's work, though one more dominant in a postwar and distinctly modern historical novel like
A Little Less Than Gods than in the earlier *The Fifth Queen*,
despite the revealing glints of gold in the hair of Katharine
Howard. Her belief that money paid by bankers to hire Wellington's troops and not military valor has been the real cause
for Napoleon's defeat aids in extinguishing Hélène's generous
feelings about chivalrous behavior and also motivates her re-
nunciation of the fortune willed her by her husband, Baron
de Fréjus, the international financier. Her attitude, moreover,
contributes to the irony of Ford's plot as it turns on mistaken
identity between de Fréjus and the soldier, Marshal Ney.
Although the doubling motif runs through all of Ford's later
fiction following *A Little Less Than Gods*, it acquires special
meaning in the latter context in that de Fréjus, the modern type
of speculator, achieves personal heroism by doubling for Ney

and dying before a firing squad, whereas the former public
hero, Ney, escapes ignominiously to America in women's
clothes. The banker's tall hat, rolling away as he falls dead,[56]
seems to signify the replacement of the Imperial eagles by the
era of bourgeois values with its martyr in de Fréjus whose
body, spread like a cross, commemorates a new epoch banal
even in its attitude to death.

To cap his central irony, Ford took the radical step of
rendering the Hundred Days while omitting a direct account
of its climax at Waterloo. Whereas this daring example of the
excluded scene follows both the Impressionist principle of
recording history only through eyewitnesses and the procedures
of Conrad in middle novels, like *The Secret Agent,* upon which
Ford modeled the structure of *A Little Less Than Gods,* the
stratagem is too boldly marked to be accounted simply technical bravura. By constructing the novel in two divisions—
the first leading from Elba to Waterloo and reflecting Napoleon's confidence, the other depicting the dreary settling of
claims after the battle—Ford left a break at the center which
is not quite bridged by later short flashbacks of the armies
taking position, even though the continuing record of the
private concerns of Hélène and Feilding preserves the unity of
the story viewed as an Affair. Yet the absence of a panoramic
canvas of Waterloo not only concedes to modern, and specifically postwar, disenchantment with the historical event in itself but also makes the presence of the gap doubly significant.
By the procedure that he had noted in Conrad, Ford intimates
what the outcome of the Napoleonic venture will be by placing
weight on preliminary details such as those observed by
George Feilding as he rides into Cannes with Napoleon and
his troops soon after the Emperor's landing in France:

It was intolerably thrilling in the narrow main-street that
ran through the town—the *Marseillaise* . . . There were
even shops, tradesmen who stood at the doors; women with
kerchiefs waved from upper windows that were on a level

with the faces of those that rode. . . . Wine merchants, oil merchants, fish merchants, taverners, tin-smiths! It was queer to see the everyday accompaniments of life through a haze of glory. A couple of young girls who were carrying sheaves of roses started to see the troops. Then they tore blossoms and buds from the stems and cast them beneath the feet of Napoleon's charger. One plucked an iris with two buds from a jar on a butcher's slab and threw it at George Feilding. It struck him on the shoulder and he found that that was glory.[57]

But as Feilding will only later come to know with Hélène, the glory of shopkeepers' applause and tossed flowers has no force against the gold-laden powers of Wellington and the intrigue which undermines both the Imperial dream and the passion between Hélène and Feilding. Because of the financial advantage of the Allies the outcome of Waterloo is already as much a foregone conclusion as the execution of Katharine Howard; and the omission of the battle scene is itself a comment on the disappearance of medieval chivalry with armies in open contest, and, indirectly perhaps also, on the absence of World War writing of epic scope. Instead, therefore, of an over-all vision of the engagement of masses, Ford employs the subtler Impressionist technique of selective foreshadowing as he touches on glimpses of the fading Imperial star seen through the returned Napoleon's triumphant progress towards Paris:

. . . they had nearly a dozen little drummer-boys; the fifes laughed and neighed, all the horses curvetting a little and moving sideways except the Emperor's. The light grew: what looked like tree-stumps amongst the vines appeared as early peasants, petrified, watching with the dung-forks laden with dung and suspended. They had near two hundred cavalry, dismounted; but a dozen had their shining bugles with the embroidered bugle-cloths depending; and the small details of the hill-tops became visible to the sound of their long, mournful, silver preludes. It was to the sound of the *Marseil-*

laise that the red sun came up before them. The peasants and children came running down towards the road, leaping boulders, their arms in the air, springing over irrigation streams: innumerable children! [58]

The Impressionist statement is exact: in the modern world glory is stuff for children, though it is still glorious in the freshness of dawn. Once again it is the indoor statesman—Wellington with his account book in Paris like the Tudor Thomas Cromwell in his stone chambers—who rules "the grey and piebald world" of the nineteenth century "new race of nabobs and financiers" that derives from the sixteenth century clan of spies like Throckmorton and Lascelles. Cold passion like that between the parents of George Feilding determines fate in the shape of incest.

Although in qualities of style *A Little Less Than Gods* belongs with Ford's later fiction rather than with the early century historical novels, which tend to possess a slight antiquarian flavor, its attitude to history is sufficiently like that of *The Fifth Queen* to suggest a rounding out of an unpremeditated modern chronicle unique in the historical fiction of the present age. Like the earlier books, the Napoleonic novel reveals a sceptical outlook on the course of history as a record chiefly of human evil, so that the same ironies underlie Katharine Howard's effort to restore an old faith in Henry's court as in Bonaparte's plan to regain an empire. Yet where Ford shows no confidence in historical progress, though he accepts the reality of history that Lukács blames modern novelists for denying, he does display sympathy with the lost cause in and for itself and with individual character too given to a medieval spontaneity and generosity to escape victimage by modern circumstance. Thus in *A Little Less Than Gods* Ford may expose the personal hypocrisy and cupidity of Napoleon yet look tolerantly on the valorous illusion surrounding his defeat so long as this represents vestiges of the medievalism that has perished in modern conditions. In this respect his historical novels remain essentially fictions, products of his own bias and intuition, but also convey a sharper and better informed historical sense of their own than do the common run of romances of the past. Ford's view of history is, moreover, fundamental to his attitude in dealing with contemporary topics and so to be assumed in interpreting the novels under consideration in the following chapters. Perhaps in spite of their complexity and their relation to the Affair as a governing form, the historical books did prove easier to Ford because of his literary equipment and the greater freedom in invention which recreating the past allowed him. It is evident, in any case, that he was longer in mastering and ordering the materials of contemporary experience.

Chapter VI

The Approach to Form: Early Novels

ABOUT the ten or so novels of contemporary life that he wrote before the Great War and prior to *The Good Soldier* Ford said hardly anything in the way of criticism, and his curt references are like those to the historical books in their attitude of reproval. When he tends, however, to dismiss most of these novels as offhand or even potboiling productions, he entirely conceals the fact that, with the exception of possibly two or three, most of them show a concentrated attempt to arrive at a form of the Affair suited to his conception of society in his time. On at least two occasions, in *A Call* (1910) and *Mr. Fleight* (1913), it appears certain that he came close to his eventual accomplishment in *The Good Soldier,* falling short mainly through inadequate means, so that in retrospect his earlier work probably seemed to him negligible when compared with the masterpiece which supplanted in his esteem all that he had done on the road to *The Good Soldier.* Yet in addition to his indifference to work below his own standard of perfection—and some of the earlier novels fail chiefly by that measure—other considerations may have entered into his subsequent reticence towards his early fiction. Among these might be counted his dissatisfaction with late Victorian society, a feeling based not only on intellectual and "sentimental Tory" conviction that English culture had deteriorated following the South African War but also perhaps on a variety of private frustrations—illness, marital and legal quarrels, lost hopes in the *English Review.* Even though his distaste for the commoner trends in Edwardian optimism gave to his better work in this phase a satirical edge and cogency too often missing in the melioristic writing of novelists like Wells and Galsworthy, his frequent strength in social and historical perception tends

131

to be offset by streaks of petulance that vent only personal ex-
asperation and that give way after his war experience to a pro-
founder concern with a world of suffering and crisis on a scale
distinct from the Edwardian problems of luxury and dissolving
tradition that Ford dwelt upon in his early novels, at times
perhaps with some degree of forced interest. Patronizing as he
was in theory to historical fiction, he may still have felt a certain ease in that genre because treating the past conduced to
a Flaubertian detachment in which the *mot juste* might flourish
for its own sake. Contemporary life, to the contrary, demanded
an adjustment of form to material in many ways repugnant,
for which reason Ford could well regard *The Good Soldier* as a
single triumph in a form absolute enough to transcend crudities
of substance and to result in the mirror within mirror effect
detected by Mark Schorer.

From a present standpoint, therefore, consideration of Ford's
early novels should examine both the evolving form of the
Affair and the emergence of themes that underwent development throughout his career, which despite interruptions shows
a continuous pattern. Beyond these central issues, other elements in the fiction require of the reader something of the
same exercise of historical imagination that he would give to
such contemporaries of Ford as Bennett and Wells; for in addition to his chosen role of novelist-historian Ford was at this
time Edwardian enough to be preoccupied with questions of
politics, feminism, Irish home rule, and the multiplication of
religious and psychic phenomena. Yet his place in the Edwardian literary scene deserves better notice not only because
of his opposition to the popular assumptions and complacencies
of the age but also because his Impressionist aims made purely
temporal questions subordinate to an effort to render what
seemed to him the essential forces involved in the disharmonies
of late Victorianism. By reason of this attempt at a fictional
synthesis of main historical data several of the early novels
possess independent interest over and above their accidents of
setting and date, restrictions which Ford, moreover, sought

methods to escape. To this end his resistance to provincialism, a trait that he attributed likewise to James and Conrad, proved useful in leading to his customary stand as an observer and critic outside national, and specifically English, allegiances and to his cultivation of a type of novel which, though influenced by the internationalistic bent in James, advanced further towards urban and cosmopolitan situations and the employment of characters of American or foreign extraction with their own equipment of psychology and motivation. As a result his novels at this stage tend to create the effect of an Imperial, almost late Roman, world of fragmented powers and traditions which has little in common with the views of his English contemporaries though it corresponds at times with the outlook in the later work of Conrad or the earlier poetry of Eliot. Taking this route carried Ford inevitably in the direction of satire and, allowing for his Impressionistic bias, towards the manipulation of ideas. It might, in fact, be reasonably maintained that he was potentially, and sometimes actually, the most talented novelist of ideas among English writers, perhaps excepting Forster, in the years immediately preceding the Great War.

Evidence of Ford's choice of ground as an unprovincial recorder of the English scene appears already in his first novel, *The Shifting of the Fire*, published in 1892; and although the book displays the immaturities to be expected of an author of nineteen, it repays study in showing that Ford had begun to find a manner of his own well before the collaboration with Conrad. In keeping with the mood of the 1890's, the novel has an aesthetic coloring of shadows and firelight and a modish French note or two, as when for no particular reason a character airs his acquaintance with "Daudet the Frenchman"; and the fact, not typical of the mature Ford, that one of the principal characters, Edith Rylands, is an artist, a concert violinist misunderstood by a rich merchant father, demonstrates Ford's as yet uncertain grasp of the issue of art and materialism that would be handled more shrewdly in his later fiction. Yet elements in the novel are authentic to Ford, among them the dreary and sodden winter landscape, marked at one place by the ruins of a monastery, which aims rather clumsily at an atmosphere of a decaying past to set against a story of modern error and misfortune. In spite, furthermore, of the English setting, the characters seem a little detached from any postive social center; and Ford somewhat timorously attempts an international complication by introducing his first American, a girl from New York whom he eventually has to dodge by declaring her more English than Yankee. More importantly, however, the central male character, Clement Hallebone, Edith Rylands' lover, occupies an ambiguous position as member of a shipping firm, doctor, professor of chemistry, and devotee of the arts including "The Music of the Future" as though Ford has tried, perhaps under some autobiographical compulsion, to invent a comprehensive solution to the problem of relating the active man to the art appreciator. To manage this difficulty, Ford makes one of his first essays in "justification" by providing Hallebone with a past reaching back to Holbein, "the painter of Queen Elizabeth's time," and thus accounting for Hallebone's surname. Though he anticipates here one of his common later devices, Ford less explicitly divulges the full reason for the tracking of Hallebone's ancestry, though this was probably in part to stress the complications in modern psychology. Particularly interesting in this regard is Ford's comment on Hallebone's behavior under emotional strain, a clear forecast of views of English temperament in the later novels:

> It is not in the English nature to express its passions with dignity, though in individuals the power varies. Perhaps it is that in foreign natives their emotions are more superficial, and therefore show themselves with greater hability, and seem more fit. Be that as it may, an Englishman in high tragedy, or even in the heat of joy, seems out of place and angular, and Hallebone under the sudden shock, could do nothing better than rave and swear—blaspheming, abusing everything and everybody, animate and inanimate.[1]

Despite the callowness of this observation, which is at odds
with the more penetrating study of English character in *The
Good Soldier* and the Tietjens tetralogy, it does plainly exhibit
Ford's early preoccupation with the nature of the modern
temperament and its potential for tragedy.

Most significant, however, in *The Shifting of the Fire* is
Ford's concern with the theme of passion due to attain full
complexity in his mature work. Details of the plot mechanism
are clumsy and show traces of his reading of Wilkie Collins or
other Victorian novelists of sensation, though the basic predicament is ugly enough to be humanly plausible. On the
failure and bankruptcy of his shipping firm, Hallebone re-
leases Edith Rylands from her engagement, whereupon the
inexperienced girl marries the *nouveau-riche* septuagenarian,
Kasker-Ryves, with the vague idea of obtaining money to
help her lover. This step—in which Edith at first conceals the
marriage from Hallebone and her love from her elderly husband—causes misery for everyone concerned: illness in Edith,
despair in Hallebone, jealousy and desire for revenge in
Kasker-Ryves whose convenient death is all that ensures a
drably happy ending. Although the plots of Kasker-Ryves to
goad Edith to death by tales of his youthful sins are gro-
tesquely melodramatic, his senile fury completes a pattern of
sexual frustrations almost as snarled as that in *The Good
Soldier* with which the earlier novel has one detail in common: a vial of poison, which, like Florence Dowell's "heart"
medicine, will cause death indistinguishable from apoplexy.
Ford would not again make the error of endowing an English
character with Kasker-Ryves's Italianate capacity for open
revenge, which besides being out of tone with the muted
effect of the true Affair is incompatible with the modern habit
of bridling strong emotion and letting it act only subter-
raneously.

Notable, however, with regard to Ford's subsequent development is that he begins by ridding passion of sentimental or, in
his view, pre-Raphaelite sanctions. Although the harsh temper
of the novel may owe something to Ford's memory of Rossetti's

picture drawn from Browning's "The Laboratory," with its subject of young woman and old man bartering in lechery and poison, the strict logic that illicit or compromised passion results in torment comes to the fore when Edith, originally sympathetic to pre-Raphaelite ideals, confesses that her marriage has been so like hell that for her to have really entered the latter state would have been only ". . . a shifting of the fire from within my soul to without" [2]—a remark that ironically twists the title of the book from its first association with Hallebone's romantic illusion of Edith's beauty seen in the shifting firelight to its last with Edith's acknowledgment of suffering. In the course of the story various accidents intrude to thwart the romantic expectations of the lovers; and if these happenings appear to overload the element of fate, they are actually in keeping with Ford's constant conviction that life as a remorseless train of cause and effect always moves contrary to unwarranted optimism. Even at the end, as fate begins to relent, Ford stations a raven in a tree to eye the human characters with cautious scepticism.

Ford's stringent account of the consequences of passion also includes partial recognition of the force of passionate motive when opposed to conventional restraint, perhaps an outgrowth of his acquaintance with Schopenhauer and Wagner. Although the novel presents a closed situation in which Ford has not yet arrived at sufficient maturity to comprehend passion as counterbalanced by formidable social or cultural restrictions, his initial predicament, in which Hallebone chooses honor and the payment of his debts instead of the enjoyment of Edith's love, does open the way to an inescapable conflict between passion and conscience. Whereas Ford does not offer an opinion on the rightness of this decision—although Edith's friend near the close of the story accuses Hallebone of vanity—he proceeds definitely to bring his main characters to an awareness that neither honor nor simple morality can check passion fully aroused and destructive of ethical platitudes. Once Hallebone must bear completely with the outcome of his denial, he dis-

covers to his horror that he desires Edith no less for suspecting
her of poisoning Kasker-Ryves:

> And he was in hell, and not a hell like M. Renan's ideal
> place of future abode, for into the void that the departure
> of his 'Indifferentism' had created conscience rushed in, and
> the last state of the man was seven times seven worse than
> the former. He felt her kisses showering on his cheeks, as
> though a rose were shaking its blood-red petals on to his
> face—and yet, and yet she was a murderess that gave them,
> and it was by murder she had gained the right and the power
> to give them, and yet her kisses were so sweet, and fell so
> softly, like summer rain on parched ground, and he had been
> yearning for them so long. How could he throw away the
> power to possess them for ever? And after all— [3]

Rudimentary as this psychologizing now appears, it offers for
its time a tacit denial of Victorian complacencies and so
points forward to the elaborately realized dilemma of *The
Good Soldier*. In *The Shifting of the Fire* Ford appears too
uncertain or unwilling to raise directly the question whether
or not Hallebone and Edith have been motivated from the
first by sexual impulse, so that the point remains unsettled at
the end of the story. But if, as seems probable, Ford had not
himself tried to reach a conclusion, he may have found the
question of passion itself absorbing enough from a Wagnerian
standpoint, one with which he had every reason to be familiar
through his father's influence as a Wagner expert. In *The
Shifting of the Fire* the triangle involving the lovers and the
aged husband carries an overtone of *Tristan* which derives
partly from the hint at the love philtre in the vial of poison
given Edith by Hallebone and kept by her secretly until it is
discovered by Kasker-Ryves. About the significance of Wagner
to contemporary views of passion Ford became much more explicit in his later collaboration with Conrad on the story *The
Nature of a Crime*, conceived in Edwardian times and in
knowledge of Dostoevski. In this tale the narrator, writing

to the married woman whom he has loved secretly, divulges his own motives while analyzing *Tristan:*

> It has always a little puzzled me why we return to Tristan. There are passages in the thing as intolerable as anything in any of the German master's scores. But we are held—simply by the idea of the love-philtre: it's that alone that interests us. We do not care about the initial association of Tristan and the prima donna: we do not believe in Mark's psychologizing: but the moment when those two dismal marionettes have drained unconsideringly the impossible cup, they become suddenly alive, and we see two human beings under the grip of a passion—acting as irrationally as I did when I promised my cabman five shillings to get me to the theatre in time for the opening bars.
>
> It is, you see, the love-philtre that performs this miracle. It interests—it is real to us—because every human being knows what it is to act, irrationally, under the stress of some passion or other. We are drawn along irresistibly; we commit the predestined follies or the predestined heroisms; the other side of our being acts in contravention of all our rules of conduct or of intellect.[4]

Centering in passion, *The Shifting of the Fire* indicates, clearly, therefore, the future path of Ford as novelist, one leading towards James and the exploration of the "dark forest of the heart." Hallebone's query in one place: "Why do people occasionally stumble by accident, as it were, on a clue that would guide them to the center of a labyrinth of motive and then pass it by without thinking it of any value?"[5] discloses Ford's native attraction to the labyrinthine form and to characters sufficiently complex to match it, even though his first novel lacks the structural properties of the web-like *Affair*. Likewise predictive, though the matter is only tentatively advanced, is Ford's attention to the bearing of financial pressure upon individual and sexual relationships, as the theme connects with Hallebone's bankruptcy as an obstacle to his marriage with Edith. Although Ford plainly follows out the consequences of this initial conflict in the mental strain imposed upon the lovers and in Hallebone's increasing hypochondria and impulses to suicide, he shows an inability to come to terms with anything concrete in the agencies resisting the hopes of the leading characters. After mentioning, for example, the materialistic objections brought by Edith's cotton-dealing parents against her art and her marriage, Ford quickly drops the subject and so betrays his ignorance of the real life of this merchant class.

In *The Shifting of the Fire* Ford was, therefore, dealing merely with isolated experience in a basically conventional narrative sprinkled with authorial asides and intrusions; the novel gives little sign of Ford the forthcoming Impressionist and fictional historian, except that in its provincial setting and banal events the book suggests his attempt to side with the literary current flowing from *Madame Bovary*. From this standpoint his next novel, *The Inheritors*, published in 1901 as the first fruits of his collaboration with Conrad, is so surprisingly different as to be considered a fresh start altogether; for *The Inheritors*, with its compressed epitome of the Imperialistic regime of Balfour and Chamberlain and other public figures, is completely impressionistic according to Ford's definition. His emergence here as contemporary historian no doubt owed much to association with the author of *Heart of Darkness;* yet the novel's exposure of political and cultural deterioration in an atmosphere of Imperialism reflects pointedly his own awakening to the changes in national life at the turn of the century and with the occurrence of the Boer War. Although *The Inheritors* was chiefly the work of Ford, Conrad merely retouching it in a scene or two, the novel, like *Romance*, displays evidence of struggle between the collaborators not only in theoretical experiment but also in temperamental bias, Conrad's liking for trenchancy pulling against Ford's for the muted effect. Whether Ford's professed dislike of the book embodied a certain resentment to drudgery under

Conrad's tutelage, his aim to create effects of delicacy and "silverpoint" [6] seems to have been a cause for dissention: "And do you not see the writer, at twenty-six, hitching and fitching with 'a something—a something—a something—' to get an effect of delicacy and Conrad saying: 'Oh, hang it all, do let's get some definite particulars about the young woman'?" [7] Perhaps such controversy helps to explain the rather synthetic quality of *The Inheritors* where Ford's historical assumptions seem to spring into shape in a Conradian atmosphere of crisis.

In spite, however, of some implausibilities in motivation and plot, the novel, using a Jamesian scenic structure, contains brilliant single episodes and conforms to a bold governing intention—that of rendering in a short novel the whole uneasy and shifting mood of Imperialism in its later phase. In this respect Ford's description of the book as exemplifying ". . . the superseding of previous generations and codes by the merciless young who are always alien and without remorse" [8] is inadequate; for a central theme is that of self-betrayal influenced in part by disintegrating historical tradition. Involved here is the narrator, Granger of Etchingham, a young man of aristocratic descent, who abandons his solitary dedication to pure literature and, by way of journalism, enters public life as a result of his sudden fascination for a girl who calls herself a "Fourth Dimensionist" and who asserts that she and her kind are to inherit the earth by ruthlessly scrapping the ideals of pity and love professed by Granger's ancestors and now weakened by the luxurious habits of the time. Even though he finds her sinister and her scheme mad, Granger, who has been ill from "trouble of the nerves," cannot resist the "incredible stimulant" of the girl's person, even when he learns of her political intrigues and her connection with a fraudulent enterprise for the building of a "trans-Greenland railway." Forced at last to choose between attachment to the girl and loyalty to his friend, Churchill, the Balfour-like foreign minister who stands for the old order of honor and integrity in government, Granger allows the publication of an article on the Greenland swindle which leads to the fall of Churchill; the victory of his opponent, Gurnard, the Chancellor of the Exchequer who represents both Chamberlain and the modern creed of opportunism and personal ambition; and Granger's own lapse into nonentity.

A main fault in *The Inheritors* is not weakness in idea, rarely a shortcoming in Ford, but rather too great audacity in attempting to convey by extreme Impressionist condensation meaning enough for a political novel of the size of *All the King's Men.* In order to keep the ideas in play, Ford has to skimp consideration of motive and character and push his narrator too rapidly through the spheres of art, politics, and journalism, so that in calling the work an "allegorico-realist romance," he is actually describing what is sometimes allegory raised to a single impression of the decay of art and ethics in an age of intrigue and mass values. Ford's logic is, therefore, better than his practice when he makes Granger an amalgam of neurotic aristocrat and artist and the girl a shadowy embodiment of the false modern glamor to which a decadent tradition succumbs. To some extent the Fourth Dimensionist girl with her Nietzschean arrogance in asserting that the meek shall no longer inherit the earth may be a parody of Wellsian utopianism; yet the irony of the novel's title strikes deeper in its implication that a weakening tradition of rule diverted to Imperialism will be destroyed by the same methods that it has used to subjugate others. The girl is in some way foreign with a hint of the odalisque turned insolent as Granger sees her: "She must be of some race, perhaps Semitic, perhaps Sclav—of some incompatible race. I had never seen a Circassian, and there used to be a tradition that Circassian women were beautiful, unfair-skinned, and so on." [9] Hence her enslavement of Granger, who admits that ". . . Of me there was nothing left but the eyes," [10] bears some resemblance to Aïssa's conquest of Willems in Conrad's *An Outcast of the Islands,* perhaps for which reason Granger through most of the novel experiences states of extreme visual excitation like those of

Willems under Aïssa's spell. In a symbolic light the girl appears a projection of Granger's own self-division and her oriental nihilism the complement of his own romantic dependence on fate.

Complex, however, as Ford's Impressionist parable may be in detail, it seems evident that Granger is far more significant than Hallebone in *The Shifting of the Fire* in commencing Ford's long study of the decline of a ruling class standard in the face of modern corruption, though the problem is still far from the subtler context of *The Good Soldier* and the Tietjens tetralogy. Granger's lack of stamina in defending his caste and its members like Churchill appears due to over-refinement and the accompanying nervous sensitivity represented by his strained visual faculties. In this respect *The Inheritors*, like the late novels of Conrad, signalizes the outgoing aestheticism of the 1890's and the shift in emphasis from art to life; for Granger's fault of excessive susceptibility to beauty after the creed of Pater undermines his political conscience and leaves him solitary. When he confronts the girl for the last time following his act of betrayal and the loss of his illusions, he is conscious not only that she is a Nemesis but that they both resemble immobile artifacts:

> "You have come," she repeated. She had no expression in her voice, in her eyes. It was as if I were nothing to her; as if I were the picture of a man. Well, that was it; I was a picture, she a statue. "I did it," I said at last.
>
> "And you want?" she asked.
>
> ."You know," I answered, "I want my . . ." I could not think of the word. It was either a reward or just due. She looked at me, quite suddenly. It made an effect as if the Venus of Milo had turned its head toward me. She began to speak, as if a statue were speaking, as if the passing bell were speaking; recording a passing passionlessly.[11]

Although Granger has appreciated the subdued manner of Churchill reminding him of "some forgotten medieval city," [12] his bond with the past has become too attenuated to enable him to resist aesthetic sterility. As a background to Granger's dilemma Ford creates a tawdry and largely metropolitan setting through a style now distinctly impressionistic which, as in Conrad's mature practice in middle novels like *The Secret Agent,* carries the central significance of the book down into the smallest details of atmosphere. The soiled luxury, for example, of Fox, the newspaper editor, reflects at close range the cultural state of the time:

> It was a palatial apartment furnished in white and gold— Louis Quinze, or something of the sort—with very new decorations after Watteau covering the walls. The process of disfiguration, however, had already begun. A roll desk of the least possible Louis Quinze order stood in one of the tall windows; the carpet was marked by muddy footprints, and a matchboard screen had been run across one end of the room.[13]

Something of the same theme of incompatibility between past and present values as in *The Inheritors* appears in Ford's novel of 1905, *The Benefactor,* though in this Edwardian work the emphasis rests more simply on the failure of a Victorian ethic in a society of adventurers and climbers. Working apart from Conrad, Ford adopts a key lowered nearer to his level for the muted Affair and by subduing the note of allegory creates a more plausible situation on the side of character. Perhaps conscious of superficialities in his handling of political elements in *The Inheritors,* Ford restricted himself in *The Benefactor* to a more familiar intellectual-aesthetic milieu but in doing so risked a suggestion of exploiting private sources of information. The central figure, George Moffat, a man of middle age, has with his brother Gregory, an art dealer, inherited a fortune from his father, Sir Graham, "the late great portrait painter," a Victorian genius who had headed a brilliant young band of fellow artists perhaps reminiscent of the pre-Raphaelite circle. Rather than his father's creative gift, however, George possesses only a dilettante's sensitivity to fine things and personal charm in manner and appearance that conforms to a sentimentally classic ideal: "Tall, with hair that waved away from his forehead, and in his moments of inspiration appeared almost like the wings on a Hermes' cap." [14] In keeping with his title role, George has spent his life in the practice of benevolence, distributing his wealth among artists who are usually shams or impostors or meddling with providential recklessness in the lives of others. In his main exploit of the latter kind, he attempts to rehabilitate the family of a country clergyman, Brede, who is on the verge of insanity, and in this way arrives at his own undoing. When Brede does go hopelessly mad, George's feeling of guilt as well as his bankruptcy prevents him from giving his love to Brede's daughter, Clara, who is left for George to dispose of and who bitterly resents his renouncing her with a halting plea on their need for self-sacrifice. The novel ends, therefore, in a dilemma of conscience and passion not unlike that in *The Shifting of the Fire,* though in *The Benefactor* Ford aims more sharply at forcing self-recognition by George of the deceit involved in his subtle form of Victorian hypocrisy.

The fact that George Moffat is a character with more life than the intellectually contrived Granger makes *The Benefactor* better than *The Inheritors* in organic quality. In some measure, as the abstract title of the novel suggests, Ford's purpose was to treat his main character as a type figure standing for a Victorian principle of benefaction at odds with primal instincts; and in doing so to strike incidentally at the genius cult of his boyhood with its memories of Swinburne's silliness and Ruskin's venomous tirades. From the allusion to George's unsuccessful marriage to a young Scottish girl who first views him as a godhead and then leaves him after becoming primly religious, it is evident that Ford modeled his main figure upon Ruskin, perhaps rounding out the irony by placing George in company with the mad clergyman, Brede, and thus momentarily foretelling the advent of the maniacal

Duchemin in the Tietjens tetralogy. But in satirizing the in-effectuality of a Ruskinian ethic in modern circumstances, Ford was likewise observing, and even more pointedly than in *The Inheritors,* the faultiness of a whole tradition; for as with many of his subsequent novels, *The Benefactor* abounds in ghosts of Victorian fathers beginning with those that over-shadow the lives of George Moffat and Clara Brede and render these characters pathetic. More strongly than in *The Inheritors,* too, Ford dwells on the plight of religious values in late Victorian society, setting against the altruistic George his ex-ploiter Hailes, an opportunist reminiscent of the Maupassant climber but also, in his foreign look, a recasting of the Nietz-schean girl in *The Inheritors:*

> He gave the impression of knowing a great many things of all kinds, and of being aware that he could be very, and very quietly, useful to ladies.
> He was thirty-five. One noticed most that his very black eyes—he remotely suggested a Japanese—moved continually from one's own to one's waistcoat buttons, and back again. He wore a navy blue suit, a dark blue tie with small white spots, and a tall, very shiny collar, open at the throat. There was a striking glitter of white teeth under a black moustache when he spoke, which he did—it was his mis-fortune—with an air of leaning against something and prac-tising the confidence trick.[15]

With the predatory glitter of his teeth for contrast to the romantic glamor of George Moffat, Hailes is much more be-lievably a product of late Imperial ambitions than the exotic girl in *The Inheritors.* Except in structure, therefore, *The Benefactor* marks an advance towards the creation of the Affair; for in its limited frame the novel covers a social field of representative scope and draws its central character gradu-ally into a labyrinthine predicament. By making George Moffat an art patron, moreover, and thus placing in the foreground the issue of increasing luxury and dilettantism with a corresponding decline in creativity, Ford gives more cogent expression to the problem of art in society than in *The Inheritors* with its view of aestheticism as a form of nervous ailment.

With *The Benefactor*, then, Ford had found himself in the role that he would assume through the remainder of his earlier fiction, that of the historian and analyst of a prewar society disunified by the loss of continuity from past to present. This point of view returns in his novel of 1907, *An English Girl*, which deals with the frustrations of young descendants of the Victorian generation even though the theme is somewhat veiled by Ford's unexpected change of setting to embrace for the first time American scenes and people. No doubt inspired partly by his visit to New York in 1906, the novel shows his desire to experiment with material of international scope; and the attempt proved germinal for his later work despite the fact that the form of *An English Girl* in itself reflects the early century taste for books with a travel motif that would feature the novelist as interpreter of an enlarging world picture with its interplay of new social forces and racial alignments, a fashion beginning to be represented by some of the writing of Dreiser. By an interesting coincidence Ford's novel appeared in the same year as James's *The American Scene*, a book that Ford noted for its method of rendering the essential qualities of American life; and *An English Girl* has a little in common with the Jamesian work in its element of simple Impressionism, the device of bringing an unfamiliar eye to bear on externals in such a way as to make the ordinary vivid. In some measure Ford's procedure is that of Conrad in *Heart of Darkness* in that the focus moves from quiet English surroundings, over the dissonant contrasts of a transatlantic voyage, to the ultimate encounter with an alien American environment as registered in the English Elinor Greville's first sight of a New York customs shed:

The native soil was of tarred planks: the building was apparently miles and miles long, roofed with a waving span of corrugated iron, decorated with the queerest advertisements she had ever seen. It was filled with a crowd of women in Paris frocks being shouldered by men in shirt sleeves—a bewildering crowd in the half light that, little by little, resolved itself into men in blue uniforms with bits of chalk and labels. They wandered about unconcernedly with their hands behind their backs amidst the largest travelling trunks in the world from which there foamed over, as if from tankards of stout, loose undergarments that delighted her eyes.[16]

Such elementary visual Impressionism could not have been difficult to Ford, who had employed the method in his three books on English life ending with *The Spirit of the People* in 1907; and *An English Girl* shows some signs of hasty composition, in particular the tedious block of informational data on the young American, Don Kellegg, in Part I. Yet Ford does not let the novel lapse into travelogue but develops an issue through which to explore an international aspect of contemporary history. Overshadowing the action is the ghost of the recently dead American tycoon and trust founder, Collar Kellegg, who, born in an English workhouse, drives ruthlessly to the position of multi-millionaire. Supposedly the inheritor of Kellegg's fortune, his son, Don, now a young man in his early thirties and vacillating where his father had been brutal, has been left to drift as he pleases in Europe where he has obtained a Harrow and Oxford education and so achieved dubious status as a "transatlantic." Although urged by his mother, who left her husband when the latter formed a liaison with an Italian woman, to enter politics, Don goes to Paris to study art, only to be told by Whistler that he is a hopeless duffer whereupon Don returns to England to accept a second-rate career as magazine illustrator and a long engagement with Elinor Greville, daughter of a good family, who, like Don, has tried in vain to become a serious painter in Paris. Living quietly at Canterbury with her rich father, who shuns the crudities of modern life, Elinor represents for Don the perfection of her type and class and its ideals of leisure and taste, though he feels no passion for her pseudo-classical calm; and in return she takes him for granted, with some reservations on his ancestry, not regarding seriously his socialistic impulses which she believes him too weak to act on.

News of his father's death and the opportunity to exercise financial power does, however, activate in Don an ambition to redress the harm done by his father by finding a way to improve conditions for the people at large; and he asks Elinor to join him in this effort and to accompany him to America, her sceptical father also traveling with them. In mid-Atlantic, however, as he watches the crowd of foreign immigrants aboard the liner and compares their quarters with the luxury castle of the first-class passengers, Don becomes not only aware of the complex extremes of the modern world but also dubious about his chance of employing wealth to realize his dream of greatness divorced from materialism:

> What could he—who, after all, had immense power—do for these people? He might make one—he might make them all—rich! But what good would that do? The good that they needed was to be taught that good did not come from riches. Yet in all probability they were flying from the tangible ills of hunger, cold, oppression, rapine and even butchery. They sought, perhaps, some of them, Liberty. Yet most of them probably were attracted by deeds such as those of his father's who had been born in a workhouse to die with an infinite power—to do what? To drink wine? buy women? purchase votes? What, in the inscrutable depths of those poor minds, did immense wealth signify? [17]

To these questions Don finds no answer in New York. Rather, he becomes progressively confused by the disorder and moral indifference of the metropolis and can see none of the modern beauty of its buildings and atmospheric effects that Elinor is detached enough to perceive. To complete his disillusionment, he discovers that his father has foreseen Don's disposing of the money in altruistic ventures and has so arranged the will that Don may inherit the fortune but have no power to use it, thus rendering his son impotent, "a gilded coupon." Don thereupon returns to England to accept a secluded existence with Elinor; but unable to compromise, he parts from her and returns alone to America to try to learn how at least some abuses may be remedied.

Although Ford does in *An English Girl* write from a tourist's perspective, he manages to create something like a single impression of "modernity" through playing upon the startling contrasts of contemporary life—the new beauty of the skyscraper set against the corrupt practices of Don's father, the harsh vitality of New York against the classical order of the Greville manner of life—so that the reader may be encouraged to attain a synthesis beyond the reach of the characters in the novel. With his alert historical sense, too, Ford grasps the traditional American problem of wealth without a guiding cultural purpose, a theme to which he returns with greater competence in late novels like *When the Wicked Man* and *The Rash Act*. But a major preoccupation, that of inadequate tradition, continues from *The Inheritors* and *The Benefactor* and focuses upon the mutual incapacity for life in Don and Elinor, both of whom have been thwarted by parental cynicism of its own kind, she by the fastidious inaction of Greville, he through the perverse will of the robber baron. Both have George Moffat's deficiency in creative vitality and, beyond this, an insufficient store of passion, though of the two Don is the more pathetic in his groping to understand and rectify his past.

Some indication, however, of an effort by Ford to imagine a counterbalance to cultural decline lies in his brief drawing in on the voyage to New York of the young Italian, Count Carlo Canzano, the son of the Roman noblewoman who had left her husband to marry Don's father. Canzano is, therefore, Don's step-brother; but their difference in blood and type appears in Canzano's light mockery of Don's "moral nervous dys-

pepsia" and in his surety of aristocratic descent, one of his
ancestors having been decorated for services to the Papal
troops. Representing Latin temperament, he is ". . . so polished, so unconcerned, so gay, so resigned, so very definitely
clear and 'all there.'" [18] Although Elinor charges him with
pessimism for declaring that his single purpose is to kill time,
he remains undisturbed, commending to Don the merits of devotion to fast automobiles:

> "I'm still interested in killing time! An automobile is a
> clumsy, evilly-smelling, odious contrivance. But so are most
> human contrivances and nearly all the beasts that you sit on
> or guide—horses and women and Constituent Assemblies.
> They're all a bother at one time or another, and if they go
> wrong you have to think yourself a fool for not having man-
> aged them better. It's so with horses, it's so with women:
> it's so with the pictures you used to want to paint. It's par-
> ticularly so with votes and voters. Whereas an automo-
> bile . . ." [19]

Being so little on the immediate scene, Canzano might be
taken for merely another counter in the play of diverse modern attitudes. Yet under his surface indifferentism lie vestiges
of an older Catholic tradition of positive right and wrong
which give poise to his gaiety and enable him to maintain his
own form of balance in the conflicts of contemporary existence. Perhaps also from his mother who has risked herself in
her attachment to Don's father, he has an inherited capacity
for direct passionate expression, a little like that of Forster's
Italians, which shows in his last letter berating Elinor for
having injured Don by her fear of emotion and loss of dignity.
In a sense, the letter gives Canzano the final word in the
novel; and even though Ford does not develop him or appear
certain altogether of his function, he does suggest Ford's early
glimpse of a cultural ideal outside Anglo-American tradition.
    Ford's refusal to commit himself to the standpoint of Can-
zano as a possible alternative to modern confusion alters in

his novel of 1908, *Mr. Apollo,* to apparent acceptance of the opinions of the god, Phoebus Apollo, who, in a form of satirical fantasy, descends upon contemporary London to rebuke the superstition and materialism of the age. Although the story demonstrates Ford's virtuosity, *Mr. Apollo* seems foreign to the main trend in his work towards structural complexity; for the book, in spite of a measure of suavity in presentation, is more openly didactic than Ford normally cares to be. Whereas the initial idea of the return of a classical god under a new dispensation may have been suggested by Pater's *Denys l'Auxerrois,* the actual tone of *Mr. Apollo* is closer to that of Wells's scientific fantasies like *The Sea Lady,* which pleased both Ford and Conrad; but if Ford here meant to compete with Wells on the latter's own ground, he lacked Wells's geniality so that the book tends to fall apart, with a society dominated by false dogmas and journalistic slogans on the one side and a pompous god uttering the maxims of Ford himself on the other. As the ironical title hints, Ford's chief aim was to chide a nationalistic self-importance too blind to recognize the exceptional even in the form of a supernatural manifestation because given over to cults of muscular Christianity, spiritualism, and telepathy and to the hypnotic pronouncements of the cheap newspaper. Included in the indictment is a type of aesthetic Catholicism represented by Margery Snyde, the daughter of a Kensington Museum official, whose pre-Raphaelite taste for flowing hair, low-necked gowns, and an accompanying "tinkle of little coins bearing the images of the saints, the Madonna, and the Popes of Rome" [20] seems to bring her close to the pretentious aestheticism of Mrs. Duchemin in *Some Do Not.* Though crudely sketched, Miss Snyde is notable as the first of Ford's modern types of Catholic women; and her fear and dislike of the radiant Apollo makes her one with the demoralized society around her. Under the caustic eye of the god the modern world in its Imperial pride assumes a look of late Roman decadence which occasions Apollo to utter a warning of cyclical change:

Egathistotheopompus, it appears, had been a philosopher
much esteemed by such worshippers of the heathen deities
as remained in the outer parts of the Roman Empire during
the fifth century. His works, however, presumably had
perished during the burning of the library at Constantinople,
for of them no trace remained. He it was who especially had
promulgated the theory that mankind was not perfectible,
but moved in cycles, that there had been a Golden Day in
Egypt that declined, till in Athens the wheel of humanity
was again exalted, and so in Rome, and so doubtless on-
wards into the unknown future and back into the unchron-
icled past.[21]

The overt reference to cyclical theory is unusual in Ford,
though it here adds point to his familiar portrayal of modern
cultural decline. Most important, however, to a consideration
of *Mr. Apollo* with reference to his development is the evidence of still another attempt by him to project, this time in
the figure of Apollo, the image of an effective cultural standard. Although in its combination of religious and humanistic
elements, the Apollo symbol is complex, Ford intended the
god to stand in one light for the Gallic traits of frugality and
diligence needed to correct the luxurious bent of the age; for
in the end Apollo's only disciples are the impoverished but
provident schoolteachers, Alfred Milne and his wife, who even
while being religious non-conformists recognize the miraculous in him. In his more positively religious aspect, however,
Apollo is notable chiefly for his tolerance of a diversity of gods
provided only that these be worshipped devoutly and not for
purposes of self-gratification. The single character to excite
his wrath is Mr. Todd, a hypocritical puritan minister whose
real creed is that of power and whose prurient fear of the
physical perfection of the god figures in Apollo's decision to
turn him into a bay tree. Already here Ford has in view some
of the essential components of the myth of disciplined grace
and gaiety to be formulated in his last novels; but the fault

at present is in both the inadequacy of Apollo to draw authority from any vital mythical context and the Wellsian situation
which forced the symbol into an incongruous sociological
frame. As a consequence, Apollo fades steadily into a priggish
moralizer caught embarrassingly in the mundanities that he
should irradiate and transcend.

Always surprising as are Ford's early leaps from one kind of
novel to another, none is more so than his progression from
the abortive attempt at satirical fantasy in *Mr. Apollo* to his
almost successful conception in 1910 of an Affair on the lines
of *The Good Soldier* in his novel, *A Call,* with its oddly and
perhaps ironically Dickensian subtitle, "The Tale of Two Passions." Whether, as seems probable, his desire to produce a
work conformable to the objectives of the *English Review* in
respect to furthering stricter critical sense led to this concentrated effort to fix the basic design of the Affair proper, the
"Epistolary Epilogue" attached to the novel leaves no doubt
that he wanted his intentions clearly understood. His rather
lofty badinage in the epilogue at the expense of readers who
might accuse him of failing to tie up his conclusion in Thackeray's manner is really a disguised advertisement of his own
true purpose: "His sole ambition was to render a little episode
—a small "affair" affecting a little circle of people—exactly
as it would have happened." [22] Inadvertently, in its stress on
method, the statement discloses the principal fault of *A Call,*
its too strict subservience to literary blueprint; for the novel
is an air-tight display of nearly every Impressionist resource
—swift opening, gradual revelation of character, justification,
progression d'effet. Such over meticulous craftsmanship no
doubt provoked Arnold Bennett's objection to the book as
"slick work," yet the technical care does invest *A Call* with
the quick and clean narrative pace that is not one of Bennett's
particular virtues. The novel has, however, an air of smartness
that may be a concession to prewar high life fiction; for although it employs the restricted milieu and the scenic method
of the later James, the accelerated rhythm and episodes pared

below the minimum normal for James suggest at times the manner of the early Evelyn Waugh. Satirical fade-outs like the following from a London party scene have a little of the Waugh touch:

> . . . Senhora de Bogota was leaning, a splendid mass of dark and opulent flesh, across her diminutive neighbor's form to whisper with a strong Brazilian accent to Madame de Mauvesine:
>
> "Regardez donc cette Etta! Ces Anglaises, a-t-on jamais ou rien de pareilles!"
>
> And Madame de Mauvesine, blonde with coppery hair and a peaked, almost eel-like face, raised her eyes to heaven, or rather to the ceiling that was painted to resemble a limpid blue sky filled with chains of roses and gambolling cherubs.[23]

This combination of bright surface with sombre theme results in a tone almost grotesque, which, although deliberate, lacks the validity furnished by the presence and character of the narrator in *The Good Soldier*. Yet with its stage as contracted as that in *Othello* and its labyrinthine plot, *A Call* so well answered to Ford's settled purpose at the moment as to point forward to a novel like Greene's *The End of the Affair* and to give new direction to the example of James in *The Wings of the Dove* and *The Golden Bowl*.

In *A Call* the almost static condition of outward life contrasts sharply with the wildest proliferation of hidden desires and motives. The action centers within a circle of upper-class people, a milieu ". . . of deep idleness, of high feeling, and of want of occupation—in this world where, since no man had any need of anything to do, there were so many things to feel." [24] Living so completely on its nerves, such a world can be exploded by the accident of a telephone call, a fit catastrophe for an Affair in which momentous consequences may follow from a trivial cause. Probably writing, however, with a view to an audience cognizant of findings like those by William James and Morton Prince, Ford more explicitly than James in *The Wings of the Dove* acknowledges the medical status of sexual repression as ground for neurotic illness and so bases his action on a recognizable case of nervous breakdown ultimately cured by a woman psychiatrist trained in Philadelphia. Yet the emphasis in the book is not merely sociological, for the inbred relationship of the characters provides the filaments for the structural web of the Affair. Ford thus seeks to retain the objectivity of traditional realism while incorporating materials suited to a stream of consciousness method.

In such an Affair the design is necessarily centripetal rather than linear and unfolds not by way of an initial event but by the radiation across the web of movement from an internal stimulus, adequately represented in *A Call* by the force of concealed passion which, being irrational as well as ignored, can violate the precarious adjustments of a fixed world. From the outset of his career, in his inexperienced treatment of passion in *The Shifting of the Fire*, Ford, independently of Conrad, had grasped the significance of irrational motive; but it may have been *The Secret Agent*, where the action pivots on an irrational impulse, that stimulated Ford at last in *A Call* to see clearly a structural form appropriate to the novel of submerged passion. If, therefore, *A Call* begins impressionistically with a strong initial focus on a character to be progressively anatomized in the course of the tale, this process inward leads rightly to the already fixed heart of the Affair, the passionate motive which Robert Grimshaw does not as yet perceive in himself:

It was once said of Mr. Robert Grimshaw: "That chap is like a seal"—and the simile was a singularly just one. He was like a seal who is thrusting his head and shoulders out of the water, and, with deep, dark eyes and sensitive nostrils, is on the watch. All that could be known of him seemed to be known; all that could be known of the rest of the world he moved in he seemed to know. He carried about with him usually, in a crook of his arm, a polished, light brown dachshund that had very large feet, and eyes as large, as brown, and as luminous, as those of his master.[25]

Grimshaw's seal-like appearance may be an echo of the impression conveyed by the spy, Verloc, in *The Secret Agent*, though the dachshund places Grimshaw in the class of the leisured, dog-carrying man. But the sleekness also betrays his unfamiliarity with the hidden passages of his own nature.

Although half-Greek, Grimshaw, the son of an English banker, identifies himself closely with the welfare of the class to which he belongs; and on the ground that he is acting out of class interest, he impulsively promotes a marriage between Pauline Lucas, a girl in love with him, and Dudley Leicester, Grimshaw's friend but a stupid idler and hypochondriac, and asserts that Pauline will make a man of Leicester and start him on a political career. The arrangement is not, however, as altruistic as Grimshaw pretends; for it offers him an outlet from a private emotional involvement not only with Pauline but also with his Greek cousin, Katya Lascarides, whose family raised him on the death of his parents. Finding that he did not love Katya, he broke his engagement with her, whereupon she suffered a nervous breakdown from which she recovered to embark on the profession of curing obscure nervous diseases.

Although the ostensible cause of their separation was Katya's insistence that Grimshaw live with her unmarried, her parents having formed a union of mutual "trust," her reason is merely a trick of her passionate "southern nature" to compel Grimshaw to force her to relent; but having no intention to do so in his growing attraction to Pauline Lucas, Grimshaw devises the ingenious compromise by which he may continue to see Pauline through her marriage to his friend while maintaining the pretext of a family bond of honor with Katya who remains indefinitely waiting. Circumstance, however, spoils this almost Iago-like scheme. Leicester falls victim of the malice of Lady Etta Hudson, an Edwardian siren later to become a

Catholic convert, who entices him to her house after a party in order to spite Pauline. While with Etta in her darkened house, Leicester receives a telephone call from an unknown person; and the shock to his hypochondriacal condition sends him mad with tendencies to violence, so that he must be kept under restraint by Pauline and Grimshaw who manage, however, to keep his condition secret. When the situation seems hopeless, Pauline appeals to Grimshaw to sacrifice their love by asking Katya to treat Leicester. Katya effects the cure but not until she has obtained Grimshaw's confession of having been guilty of the call to Leicester in an uncontrollable fit of jealousy and his promise to live with her on her own terms.

In some essentials, therefore, *A Call*, especially in its concern with the duplicities of the heart, develops from Ford's earlier novels, Grimshaw's final understanding that his attempt at a providential function has been a mask for passionate motive being very much, for example, like George Moffat's disillusionment in *The Benefactor*. The significant change from the earlier work is above all formal, including matters of character and background. In *A Call* Ford achieves the banality typical of the Affair by moving definitely into a late Edwardian atmosphere where leisured society has become not so much exclusive as luxurious and in some respects effete, capable through late Imperial wealth of indulging decadent tastes like those of Etta Hudson who dabbles in occultism and disseminates an odor of oriental perfume while yet having stronger traits of masculinity than the men she dominates. More even than in *Mr. Apollo* Ford portrays a world broken into a muddle of creeds, ranging from Christian Science to astrology, and of nationalities, as in the Greek and English relationships of the principal characters, and traces the effects of this disintegration in neurotic illness and the incapacity of governing class members like Dudley Leicester to exercise political leadership. Ford's irony over the loss of a tradition of rule in a post-Victorian generation is subtler here than in *The Inheritors* or *An English Girl*, being expressed through incongruities like those in which the soldierly-appearing Leicester sits mentally helpless below a window decorated with the legend of Saint George or a part-foreigner like Grimshaw, sneered at for an oriental by Etta Hudson, becomes the only serious propounder of the virtues of public service. Yet Grimshaw is not exposed to ridicule; for if his mixed English and Greek inheritance justifies making him the center for the conflict between morality and passion, he is also an anti-hero whose divided conscience is sufficiently acute to register the fundamental division of his world.

As central character in the Affair, Grimshaw, after his first impulsive gesture of promoting the marriage between Leicester and Pauline, becomes no longer the active director of events but rather a figure who awaits his own entanglement in the coil that he has created and the working of passive self-revelation. His story is, therefore, not one of action leading to tragedy but instead the modern tale of guilt and expiation, for which reason his predicament recalls slightly that of Razumov in Conrad's *Under Western Eyes,* the book so admired by Ford, or behind that of characters in Dostoevski. Hence an important feature of *A Call* and a presage of *The Good Soldier* is its evidence of Ford's increasing grasp of a form distinct from that of heroic tragedy and adapted to the restraints of an unheroic world. Obviously the heroically named and proportioned Dudley Leicester is a virtual invalid; and Pauline Lucas, having in one place impetuously used the word tragedy, quickly qualifies her remark with an almost Prufrockian insight: "Tragedies! Yes, in our day and in our class we don't allow ourselves easy things like daggers and poison-bowls. It's all more difficult." [26] In keeping with her words, Grimshaw responds to his jealous impulse for revenge on Leicester by the intangible means of the night call, the telephone assuming the guise of a weapon which draws no blood:

> . . . suddenly his whole body stirred in bed. The whites of his eyes gleamed below the dark irises, his white teeth

showed, and as he clasped the instrument to him he appeared, as it were, a Shylock who clutched to his breast his knife and demanded of the universe his right to the peace of mind that knowledge at least was to give him.[27]

Logical, however, as the telephone device is in furnishing the muted climax demanded by the Affair, its too obviously calculated function is a flaw common to the whole novel, a mechanism every part of which clicks into place despite Ford's effort to hide the massive plot by a rapid sequence of light scenes.

The shift in perspective on the question of luxury, which Ford had confined to the leisure class world of *A Call* or to a similar milieu in earlier works, remains perhaps the chief point of interest in *The Simple Life Limited* of 1911; for with this novel begins the consideration of luxury as a social phenomenon in and for itself which will continue on through *Mr. Fleight*, Ford's most accomplished book before *The Good Soldier*. Although cast in the form of anti-utopian satire on the follies of a community of cranks aspiring, along Tolstoy-Morris lines, to absolute innocence and simplicity in their Frog's Cottages outside the country village of Luscombe Green, the novel tends to hide its superiority as satire to *Mr. Apollo* by an array of topical hits at Edwardian fads and personalities not likely to be appreciated today except by connoisseurs of the period. Frequently such barbs, like those at Yeats and the Celtic twilight, are more malicious than amusing; and when Ford mocks living individuals thinly disguised after Mallock's fashion in *The New Republic* the ridicule cuts deep enough at times to suggest a reason for his publishing the book under the pseudonym of "Daniel Chaucer." Perhaps deservedly Frank Harris appears in the figure of "George Everard," manager of the Talavera Theatre and looking for girls for the front row of his "ballet"; but only some harsher antagonism, possibly the upshot of troubles connected with the *English Review*, seems likely to explain the spiteful portraits of what must cer-

tainly be Edward Garnett in the guise of Mr. Parment, an
outmoded critic of the 1890's, and Conrad as Parment's Simple Life associate, Simeon Brandetski, who has changed his
name to Simon Bransdon after being discovered by Parment
as a writer. While Bransdon, who has written a novel in a
construction camp in Africa, is recovering from black-water
fever at a seaman's hospital, Parment comes to his bedside,
salutes him as a master, and assures him of certain fame:

> So, upon the advice of Mr. Parment, Brandetski changed
> his name to Bransdon, and later he turned Simeon into
> Simon, thus becoming equipped with a name becomingly
> British for the title page of a book. His novel was published
> upon the day when he left the Hospital for Seamen. Mr.
> Parment set the note for the criticisms when he said that
> "Clotted Vapours" disclosed the coming of a new life-force
> in British Literature.[28]

Apart, however, from this topical element and the general
relevance of the content of the novel to "simple life" theories
circulating at the time, the satire goes beyond superficialities
in its handling of the more permanent issue of the contrast
between desire for simplicity and the inevitable bent of the
social order towards complication. Ford's criticism here of the
simple life community is not a denial of his previous emphasis
on the need for individual discipline but rather a rejection of
the idea that simplicity may be established by fiat and against
the record of history as one of human perversity and involu-
tion. His judgments on the self-sufficient type of community, of
which the period would have furnished numerous examples,
are essentially shrewd, as when he notes the futility of handi-
craft schemes set apart from an institutionalized society or,
with Orwellian point, the drift of planned equality towards
power control. But the heart of the satire lies in its insistence,
to be important in his postwar conceptions of restored tradition, that simplicity will not consort with the sophisticated
substance of human nature, a fact demonstrated by the work

of Miss Egremont, the community artist, in her attempt to produce simple life allegory with pre-Raphaelite materials:

> They represented mostly outlines of ladies very developed about the hips and obviously with no stays, who leaned their heads back in strained attitudes and saluted doves, the emblems of peace; butterflies, the emblems of the soul; or roses and vines, which are the emblems of the beauty and bounteousness of nature. As a rule this figure wore round her head a spiky halo of rays in the midst of which there was generally inscribed the words: "Sancta Beata Simplicitas!" [29]

More successfully than in *Mr. Apollo* Ford in the present novel fixes credible poles of satire by opposing to the fall of the Simple Lifers into excessive complication the attainment of simplicity after a naturally complicated past by Gerald Luscombe, a seemingly ordinary county landlord. The figure of Luscombe—a combination of Tory, family man, classical scholar and athlete—is a significant addition to Ford's stock of character types, for he not only incorporates for the first time Ford's image of an active man within a native English and Tory tradition, perhaps after the model of Ford's friend, Arthur Marwood, but also anticipates Christopher Tietjens in his attachment to outmoded values and in his semi-military appearance: ". . . a blonde, rather heavy man of perhaps thirty-five or a little more, he was dressed in a shooting-jacket, had a heavy jaw, a thick moustache and sagacious, rather dog-like eyes." [30] Because of the disruptions of his youth caused by passion—conflict between an adulterous mother and a drunken father and persecution at the university from cousins who hate him—Luscombe perceives the flimsiness of the simple life ethic from the standpoint of his classical morality; yet he remains kindly to individuals and scrupulous in performing his duties as landlord and royal subject. His cluttered drawing-room table appears to symbolize the real complexity behind his outward calm as it may also indicate Ford's own preference for an art derived from the labyrinth of human passions, since,

revealingly, the simple life prophet, Bransdon, desires secretly
to possess the table himself:

> Made of one slab of pink marble with green veins, with legs
> of gilded brass showing cherubs' heads, griffins' feet and
> ornaments in the style of foliage, the table supported a
> sombre mass of heterogeneous objects. The center of the pile
> was formed of three great books in stamped and gilded
> cloth. These supported three vases made of imitation lapis-
> lazuli. In between the three vases reclined two brown emu
> eggs. There was a crystal globe upon a white marble base,
> a fragment of stone from the Temple at Jerusalem, two
> silver-gilt pen trays, two Dresden china figures of a shep-
> herdess in pink, and a gallant in green removing a purple
> hat and, under a glass shade a model of the Taj Mahal exe-
> cuted in pith—a whole museum of objects which possessed
> for Mr. Simon Bransdon an almost unholy attraction. He
> found himself wishing that he could possess them all, finger
> them all and live with them all for the rest of his life.[31]

In the final turn of the satire, after the simple life colony
has been burned down by a mad Russian passing for a revolutionary idealist, the son of one of the co-founders, Hamnet
Grubb, whom Luscombe likes, decides that his rotten time in
the community has taught him that ". . . we learn in suffering
what we teach in parables" and goes to live alone in a hut in
the woods in the conviction that doing anything at all is futile.
He intends to "just live and see where you come out"; and
since the rest of the Simple Lifers shrink in bewilderment
from this exhibition of pure simplicity, the concluding irony
seems to clinch the point that complication is inevitable so
long as society wills to continue and, by inference, that Luscombe's Toryism is the only way of making the best of the
bad job that modern life necessarily is.

Luscombe's position is, however, more or less that of an
exile in a society that has no use for his virtues of abstinence

and duty, so that he lives on like a Waugh character within the confines of his provincial orbit. In this respect Ford's derogatory view of late Imperial luxury and decadence has not changed but merely, though importantly, come to embrace a figure more adequate than Mr. Apollo to incorporate and silently proclaim values and attitudes that society excludes but cannot altogether eliminate since they are complementary to its public ethical conventions. In his novel of 1912, *The Panel* (entitled misleadingly in America *Ring for Nancy*) Ford again created a main character with a touch of Luscombe's separateness in Major Edward Brent Foster, a career army officer returned to England from service in India and Africa and knowing himself ". . . a poor Irish fool, and that will be always in the wars like the father before me, and his fathers for ever and ever!" Ford rightly called the book frivolous and in doing so betrayed what he could not do convincingly, for *The Panel* seems a venture into the now largely ignored genre of Edwardian comic fiction spiced with dashes of erotic playfulness. Trifling, however, as the form in itself might have been in other hands, Ford did not take it on its own terms but, converting it to a satirical aim, turned an ostensibly popular romance of high life love between Major Foster and Lady Mary Savylle into an intrigue story which mocks its own substratum of pulp fiction. In outward appearance merely another tale of the kind that the Elinor Glyns of the time fed to mass readers, *The Panel* becomes an attack on such writing beginning with the condemnation by Major Foster, who has come home with a taste for Henry James, of novels by Mrs. Kerr Howe that he sees displayed at station bookstalls:

> The name "Juliana Kerr Howe" met his eye at least twenty-seven times. There was *Pink Passion* by Juliana Kerr Howe, with a picture of a lady in a pink nightgown. There was *All for Love*, by Juliana Kerr Howe, with the gilt design of a pierced heart and a broken globe on the cover. There

was a lady's monthly periodical with the inscription in pur-
ple letters, "*The Lovely Girl.* Read about her inside. By
Juliana Kerr Howe." [32]

Instead, therefore, of being wholly detached from the central
line of Ford's work, *The Panel* concentrates on one facet of
his examination of cultural deficiency, that of the impoverish-
ing of literature, which like Orwell later, he viewed as an
index of the state of popular taste. Although nearly all of his
contemporary novels include reference to the condition of art
in society, *The Panel* has a close bearing on at least one of
the issues in his satire, *Mr. Fleight,* published in 1913, the
year of his start on *The Good Soldier.*

Cast as political satire, *Mr. Fleight* appears to have enjoyed
a fairly good general sale which may have been due in part
to its being the most ambitious of Ford's early novels in social
range. Not only does it attempt to touch on all sides of contemporary politics, art, morals, and religion but also, which is
rare in Ford, to include a variety of class levels. In this respect
it is a cardinal example of Ford's Impressionist aim to reduce
potential Zolaesque breadth to the restricted focus of an Affair,
an effort resulting in *Mr. Fleight* in evident technical difficulties, one of the principal being the failure to create the illusion of time flow or lapse between sections. Because of digressions from the central plot movement the novel tends to
look fragmentary; yet this is the outcome of Impressionist
method, subsequently refined in *The Good Soldier,* which allows for cross reference from part to part in a unified mosaic.
Rather than by discursive means, the novel strives to carry
its point by a succession of rendered episodes, each one of
which furthers the mood of the whole. Such an incident as
the following, for example, contributes to the unstated but
dominant "impression" of the book, one of sham magnificence
accompanied by human futility:

> Mr. Macpherson, in evening dress, and with the attitudes
> and action of a mad rabbit, was rushing from end to end

of a hall, so brilliantly lit, so immense, and so empty, that, beneath the high pink arches like those of St. Peter's at Rome, beneath the high dome reminiscent of the Mosque of St. Sofia at Constantinople, in front of the set of boxes in the style of the Empire Music Hall in London, he appeared to be a mere speck of agitated matter.[33]

Again, as in *A Call, Mr. Fleight* is interesting mainly for its gain in formal subtlety. The society depicted is once more luxury-ridden, though the novel may reflect something of Ford's animosity against the invasion of Rand millionaires which he had expressed directly in 1911 in his autobiographical volume, *Ancient Lights*.

Ford's control of the main satirical plot is more expert still than in *The Simple Life Limited*, since the action begins immediately when Mr. Fleight, a wealthy Jew, asks another member of his London club, "a heavy, grey man of ferocious aspect" named Blood, to help him to a public career. Blood, an enigmatic figure with a reputation for violence in having strangled a groom in Rhode Island, has utterly renounced any part in active affairs and remains an onlooker of eighteenth century Whig disposition; yet he accepts Fleight's proposal, partly because both men have had the same tutor at Oxford, "the great Plodge," partly for the ironical pleasure of steering Fleight to victory in a parliamentary election which Blood regards as a contest of bad against worse. His extensive knowledge of the facts of public life and his ability to pull strings, especially with a group of intellectuals behind a fashionable review, enable Blood to win for Fleight both the office and a handsome German wife. But Fleight, who has suffered injury and indignity during his campaign, has lost his taste for glory in his initiation into what Blood calls "the dirty comedy of life," even though he has no choice but to carry out to the final letter the terms of his almost Faustian bargain.

The satirical design here attains force beyond that in Ford's earlier novels not only because it is mordant but also because the issue of action or withdrawal, raised by Ford as far back as *The Inheritors,* stands in direct relation to the mainstream of national life. In the cynical compact between the landed gentleman, Blood, and the cosmopolitan Fleight Ford appears to symbolize a radical and ominous split in the existing order due, perhaps, to a basic failure in the Imperial ideal; for as products of the teachings of "the great Plodge," whose task was to turn out pro-Consuls for the Empire, Blood and Fleight have been trained in the school of Jowett, as Ford interpreted Jowett's mission, and Fleight's timid venture into politics is partly an attempt to make up for Blood's defection as Plodge's "pet tragedy." To some extent the relationship between the main characters foreshadows in blunter fashion that between Tietjens and Macmaster in *Some Do Not,* although there are signal differences, among them the heavier emphasis on Blood's surname as suggesting both traditional aristocracy and a repressed inclination to bloodshed. Yet the act of violence initially assigned to Blood, his outright strangling of the groom who has been bribed to drug a horse, cannot be detached from the whole satirical context which aims to castigate the modern habit of condoning evil by refusing to betray feelings of horror, since the root cause of Blood's contempt for society is his memory of having offered himself for punishment to authorities who moved only to conceal the crime. With the impulse of Culpepper in *The Fifth Queen* to retaliate directly when injured, Blood refuses to participate in the affairs of a society so corrupt as to compel him to go on strangling grooms, men that he likes too well to think of harming further.

Ford develops his satirical antithesis by contrasting the principle of "blood," in its various implications, with the "pinkness," of a false and luxurious society, using a method of color symbolism intimated in *The Panel* with the pink romances of Mrs. Kerr Howe and anticipating a similar device in *The Good Soldier.* The motif occurs, for example, in the scene where the Baroness di Sonnino, Fleight's mistress, devours a meal in the ornate surroundings of his Palatial Hall, Hampstead:

Beside the fountain there was set a small table with shining napery at which there sat a fair creature devouring a lobster. She held a cracked claw between two delicate fingers. Her features were very pink and white. Her figure was very long and clothed in a very tight dress of broderie Anglaise with a tight collar that went up behind her ears, and she continued to nibble the pink flesh that came from the scarlet shell. Upon the tablecloth in front of her there stood a green Venetian glass vase filled with sprays of pink godetias, a green bottle, a tall glass containing sparkling water and a lump of ice, a small bottle of Beaune, the dish which contained the remainder of the lobster and a plate with much of its scarlet shell.[34]

The image of aristocratic gluttony meets by color complement with another glimpse of disorder in the aesthetic portion of the social field, when in his exotic room the malicious poet, Cluny Macpherson, works in a scarlet kimono reminiscent of the lobster shells of the puppet-like Baroness:

The room resembled a battle-ground, where opposing forces marched the one upon the other; it was difficult to tell where the territory of the books began, or the chinoiseries ended. Indeed, upon an armchair there lay six large brown volumes and two pieces of Chinese embroidered silk, whilst someone had upset half a tin of yellow tobacco over the chairful.

In a vivid scarlet kimono Mr. Cluny Macpherson, with his slightly bald head, his closed eyes, and his high features, was sitting on a red lacquered umbrella-stand, which he tilted towards an immense sheet of blotting-paper in a cleared space on the large round table.[35]

The allusions to orientalism as an adjunct to luxury in the key spheres of manners and aesthetics may recall James's use of Chinese imagery in *The Golden Bowl*. But in Ford's own practice as early as *The Inheritors,* the tendency to associate late Imperialism with the exotic reveals itself, though in *Mr. Fleight* the effect borrows overtone from *The Satyricon*.

From the upper classes the pink tinge spreads to the lower and colors the illusions of Gilda Leroy who sells tobacco in a subway stall and, like the telegraph girl in James's *In the Cage*, reads penny novelettes in which governesses win belted earls, her escape from squalor into sentimental dreams touched by suicidal impulses. When Fleight, seeking relief from public ambition, slips incognito into the cozy atmosphere of Gilda's shopkeeping family, the girl identifies him with her fictional heroes; and Fleight in turn to salve his vanity nourishes Gilda's fantasy with champagne and drives in his automobile. Her idyll smashes, however, when a gang of slum youths give Fleight a savage beating and hurl him through the glass door of the Leroy shop. Where he manages to survive, however, Gilda perishes under this blow to her illusions by committing suicide, in fidelity to pink novelette logic, in the grounds of Fleight's Palatial Hall. Her death somewhat resembles that of Winnie Verloc in *The Secret Agent*, since, in conformance with the theory of the Affair, catastrophe occurs outside the realm of official activity and its particular concerns. With a notable resemblance to the enquiry into the death of the boy, John Andrew, in Waugh's *A Handful of Dust*, the coroner's inquest on Gilda is more than eager to prove no one to blame:

> . . . the coroner's inquest was very decorously conducted. Mr. Fleight gently gave evidence that there was no particular reason why Miss Leroy should have called upon him, though there was certainly no reason whatever why she shouldn't. It appeared, indeed, from the evidence of Mrs. Leroy that Gilda's only motive was to gaze upon Mr. Fleight's marble halls before she committed suicide. And she had determined to commit suicide as soon as, behind the sheet, she had heard that Mr. Fleight was unquestionably not for her. And Mrs. Leroy, who was really quite sorry for Mr. Fleight, did her very best to make him come off without the reputation of the betrayer of her daughter.[36]

Although Gilda's case proves to Fleight that intercourse between individuals from different levels of society must result in fatality in a system complicated by luxury, it also confirms Blood's contention that the modern world of intrigue murders in secret. Recalling her namesake in *Rigoletto,* Gilda has been strangled as effectually as the groom despatched by Blood but for no crime other than having worshipped illusions fostered by the same society that evokes the violence of the toughs who have assaulted Fleight. Her anti-tragic death thus becomes the banal center of an Affair which has moved decisively beyond the halting effort in *A Call* to distinguish the muted crises of contemporary circumstance from the high catharsis of tragedy in the past. It is Blood, consequently, whose killing of the groom links him to the world of *Macbeth,* who possesses the capacity for tragic passion that modern existence rejects and who is thus rendered inactive except in playing through Fleight the contemporary game in order to expose the game itself in his role of master of a Faustian puppet-show. Properly, therefore, he assumes the guise of Lear when he carries in his arms the body of Gilda fallen unconscious on learning that Fleight does not want her; [37] for, again, *Lear* represents tragedy at furthest remove from the modern temper that finds its reflection in *Hamlet* or *Othello.* The nontragic hero is, properly, Fleight who ends with power over "gentle imbeciles" like Cluny Macpherson rather than a "set of brutes" like Blood.

Ford completes the irony by arranging that Fleight's apotheosis shall take place in a factual realization of the pulp fantasies of Gilda, whose idea of heaven was to see Fleight, with a blue ribbon and on a marble staircase, receiving six thousand guests to the strains of the *Meistersinger.* Her dream turns true in the party celebrating Fleight's political triumph, "a silly fairy tale" fusing the color of sentimental romance and of sham statesmanship in a cloud of pink from salmon, Turkey carpets, and the scarlet costumes of Russian dancers:

Mr. Fleight remained perfectly still, gazing into vacancy in front of him. They were all crowding round Augusta, and suddenly the words that he had uttered to Gilda Leroy in

the little shop on the Saturday before he had begun his
election campaign came into his head. For the rest of his
life—there would be the palm plants, and the marble staircases, and the Christian wife he was only too sadly aware
he had purchased, standing at the top of the stairs in white
satin, whilst the invisible orchestra played the Preislied out
of the "Meistersingers." He was standing quite alone; all
the rest of them were crowding round Augusta. He shrugged
his shoulders right up to his ears and let them slowly fall.[38]

Although Fleight's wife, Augusta, experiences a premonitory
chill of disaster, his victory, like Gilda's death, represents the
normal operation of social forces which move automatically
without the uncomfortable intrusion of tragic terror. As the
poet, Cluny Macpherson, sums matters up in an observation
worthy of Aldous Huxley, the agnostic dismissal of Providence
has eliminated the bothersome emotions connected with tragedy:

'We are all friendly agnostics,' and that's what we are.
There's not a single thing that we can know. We haven't
any of us got any religion; and science, that everybody used
to be so frightened of, has given up the attempt to prove
anything. But we're a nice pleasant lot, and we don't burn
anybody and we don't even write letters abusing each other
in the *Times,* as Huxley or Mr. Gladstone or that sort of
person used to do. And I'm sure it's much better like that.
Isn't it fun to think that you might be a Manichean—whatever that may be—if you wanted to, without any St. Dominic
to come along with an inquisition? [39]

With *Mr. Fleight* Ford reached an advanced point of self-
assurance after his twenty-year period of experiment beginning with *The Shifting of the Fire,* and the production of this
remarkable novel indicates a steady maturing of his powers
towards a form capable of furnishing a single impression of
the Edwardian age as he viewed it. In the fiction of the period
few works reveal so comprehensive a grasp of the essential

nature of prewar society except for those of Conrad in the middle stage of his career; and a comparison of *Mr. Fleight* with *The Secret Agent*, its nearest parallel, shows at once the difference in talent between the two novelists who had struggled to combine forces in the overstrained writing of *The Inheritors*. In *The Secret Agent* Conrad's final impression is much like that of Ford in *Mr. Fleight*, in that both portray a world subject to irony in its loss of moral hold upon evil; yet Conrad employs the basically more popular form of the detective story, with its strong contrasts between officialdom and underworld, whereas Ford chooses the larger territory of broad social satire with the accompanying difficulty of excessive shortcutting to maintain compression. The method, however, is deliberate with Ford in his persistent desire to key down every strong situation, the result being that he compels more effort from the reader in making correct deductions, for example, from the story of Gilda Leroy than does Conrad from that of Winnie Verloc, despite the use of similar Impressionist procedures in both cases. In this respect the Affair, the formal properties of which Ford had clearly come to understand in his progress from *A Call* to *Mr. Fleight*, seems more distinctly Ford's possession than Conrad's, although Ford recognized and acknowledged its elements in *The Secret Agent* and *Under Western Eyes*. The muted tribulations of ordinary people in banal circumstances could not have greatly excited Conrad's interest.

Ford had, nevertheless, sufficient reasons for looking back with some indifference to his earlier work. Certain of its themes have obvious period limitations, and the rather smug attitudes of racial superiority in several of the novels disappear from his postwar work. The course of later developments in his thought lies plainly marked, however, in the writing of this phase. The changes to follow were to occur largely in the province of language and style.

Chapter VII

The Perfected Affair: *The Good Soldier*

As IF to compensate for his careless attitude towards his earlier novels, Ford took pains to represent *The Good Soldier* as his literary monument, a view perhaps justifiable but one that distorts considerably the true pattern of his creative growth which was to extend into areas beyond the range of this crowning effort of his prewar phase. Among the most familiar of these memorial statements are his remarks to Stella Ford in the dedicatory letter of 1927 where he describes the novel, as he did elsewhere, as the triumphant swan song of a career ordained to end at the age of forty and, further, leaves the impression that without the help of the lady addressed he would not have resumed writing after the war interval—a graceful compliment but one that implies a division too absolute between his prewar and postwar output regarded from the standpoint of literary continuity. Although he encourages assent to his claim that *The Good Soldier* had been "hatching" within him for a full decade,[1] he omits reference to the fact that in the novels preceding it he had actually experimented with themes and methods relative to the design of this consummate Affair and substitutes instead the more engaging anecdote of having sat down on his birthday, the 17th December, 1913 to produce the one novel that is enough for any man to write and of precisely fulfilling his objective. Yet it is difficult to believe that any but a fairly old literary hand could have completed the book in the approximately six months that Ford alleges,[2] and with works like *The Fifth Queen* and *Mr. Fleight* behind him he could hardly be called a novice at forty. With the slipperiness of the eel to which he compares himself Ford had reached the deep sea in

172

The Good Soldier; but he had left other young on the way, if none so rare.

Like the bulk of Ford's anecdotes, however, that concerning the origin of *The Good Soldier* carries validity as impression rather than statistic. The novel does entirely surpass its predecessors in a unity of form and substance so absolute as to obliterate its period associations and thus to evoke in the reader a response largely free of historical ties. Here, perhaps, once and for all, Ford achieved in his own way an end in the search for absolute form that he held to be Conrad's lasting ambition, since at its higher levels *The Good Soldier* becomes an almost pure exercise in language, a notable example of a literary tradition reaching full self-awareness and hence the capacity for reflecting upon itself. This may have been Ford's meaning when in his Dedicatory Letter he calls the book his "great auk's egg . . . of a race that will have no successors," a comment seeming to apply not simply to the myth of his own creative demise but indirectly to the whole Impressionist effort through James, Crane, and Conrad which, at least in its initial phase and before the assault of the ". . . Cubists, Vorticists, Imagistes, and the rest of the tapageur and riotous Jeunes," [3] may well have terminated in *The Good Soldier*.

Although Ford's method has been imitated repeatedly in works from Katherine Mansfield's story, "Je ne parle pas Français," down to recent novels like John Hersey's *The War Lover,* qualities in the essential spirit of his book do not easily transmit themselves to the products of a later modernism. The vital associations of *The Good Soldier* lie, instead, within the field already won by Conrad with *Heart of Darkness* and by the later James, whose influence Ford manifests in chance echoes such as those in which the lighthouse-like gaze of Leonora Ashburnham recalls the floodlight eyes of Ida Farange in *What Maisie Knew* (p. 33) and the notion that Florence Dowell's "little heart might cease to beat" (p. 16) carries back to the death of Miles in *The Turn of the Screw*. Despite, therefore, the novel's formal distinction, its thematic and structural tensions reflect a transitional state in the manners and literary habits of Victorianism and so give rise to the comic ironies so well illustrated in Mark Schorer's interpretation. In common with so much in the late work of Conrad and James, *The Good Soldier* expresses Victorianism in the final stage of self-consciousness with respect to the hypocrisies of its conventions in morals and verbal utterance; and its superiority in this respect to a novel like *Mr. Fleight* lies chiefly in its command of a language veined throughout with the ironies pertaining to the story's whole effect. Ford's subtitle, "A Tale of Passion," modifies significantly "the tale of two passions" of *A Call*—though the latter novel seems unquestionably to have been a working base for *The Good Soldier*—in its double allusion both to a Victorian sexual dogma and to a Victorian literary mode of the sort that Ford had ridiculed less cunningly in *The Panel.* Yet to some extent, too, the novel memorializes a whole manner of erotic feeling and behavior for a future in which the term "passion" would be antiquated.

To this greatest of his penetrations into the heart of the basic sexual-religious ethic of an entire society Ford brought the full equipment of his Impressionism as a method of historical rendering. Stitched into the fabric of the prose is a succession of minute period references to ensure verisimilitude, and the novel likewise seeks conviction in the plain element of "case" as represented by the Kilsyte Case in which Edward Ashburnham stands trial for having kissed a nursemaid in a railway carriage. For all of his circumlocution, moreover, the narrator, Dowell, pursues his memories with the urgency of a historian who has witnessed the passing of an era:

You may well ask why I write. And yet my reasons are quite many. For it is not unusual in human beings who have witnessed the sack of a city, or the falling to pieces of a people to desire to set down what they have witnessed for the benefit of unknown heirs or of generations infinitely remote; or, if you please, just to get the sight out of their heads.

Someone has said that the death of a mouse from cancer is the whole sack of Rome by the Goths, and I swear to you that the breaking up of our little four-square coterie was such another unthinkable event. (p. 5)

The comparison between the death of the mouse and the fall of Rome may reveal more than simply Dowell's pettiness; for like many other asides in the novel the metaphor offers a comment on method, in this instance the Impressionist practice of rendering the character of a period by means of a selective and compressed illustration. In the pose of Tiresias, furthermore, Dowell sets the key for the mood of historical apprehension, of a social class on the brink of catastrophe, that may express Ford's own forebodings of war, perhaps heightened by the predictions of his politician friend, Masterman, of the outbreak of war with Germany one year from the second of August, 1913. His use, in any event, of the fourth of August as a date of superstitious recurrence is one of the peculiar features of the book.

Just as Dowell's assumption of the historian's part serves to enlarge his capacity as narrator and observer without drawing him outside the orbit of the story itself, so also the running topical motif extends the range of suggestion without distracting from the purely formal appeal. The small foreground Affair epitomizes the historical landscape of the time, and the crash of Dowell's supposedly "safe castle" with the Ashburnhams echoes larger rumblings of disaster in the Imperial distance. Although the main characters, as Dowell points out in his brief survey of the Ashburnham-Dowell-Hurlbird genealogies, (p. 5) descend from the same Anglo-Saxon tradition, the scheme of the novel is "international" in something like the manner of *An English Girl*—the chief locale being, as in *The Waste Land*, central-European, the people of varying nationality. From the Ashburnham side, however, the stress falls distinctly on the British Empire threatened by dissolution, as in the hints at Anglo-Irish friction surrounding the hurried marriage of Edward to Leonora and of declining Imperial power connected with the moral laxities of Ashburnham's period of soldiering in India. As in Ford's earlier novels, moreover, the English characters seem to inherit weakness from the blunderings of a previous generation of Empire makers, a point touched in reference to the army parents of Edward and Leonora but urged forcibly in connection with Nancy Rufford's father, a bad officer and a cynical Imperialist who, like Conrad's Kurtz, can dismiss maltreatment of Congo natives with the words: "Oh, hang humanity!" (p. 128)

Probably, however, because of the character of the period as well as of the imminence of war in the year when Ford wrote the novel, the record of Imperial distress bears heaviest on the military lapse associated with Ashburnham's frustrated career. Separately considered, the details of military vice and intrigue make up a severe indictment capable of disturbing readers who, like Ford himself, retained memories of the Dreyfus affair. Besides specific items of individual futility—such as Major Basil's collecting of horses' bits (p. 165) or Ashburnham's oiling, in evening clothes, the breech action of a gun (p. 213)—the book contains a succession of passing hits at such evils in the military set as gambling, blackmail, adultery, and abuse of rank, a telling instance being the Ashburnhams' virtual buying of Maisie Maidan from her young officer husband. (pp. 180–181) As a model for this type of criticism Ford may have had in mind the amateurish but notorious novel by the German officer, Fritz von der Kyrburg ("Lieutenant Bilse"), A Little Garrison (Aus einer kleinen Garnison), which, published in 1904, sought to expose the luxurious living of officer circles in small garrison towns as well as in the more aristocratic of the Kaiser's regiments. The book, in any case, shocked Violet Hunt; [4] and it seems likely that Ford, with his interest in current German affairs, would have known so widely publicized a work. Whether or not by coincidence, the evils attacked in A Little Garrison are quite similar to those imputed to the British army in The Good Soldier; and by a remote parallel the Kyrburg novel happens to end with the suicide of an officer who has fallen victim to the habits of the army system. While no question of literary influence need be raised, the stir created in a time of military apprehension by the book of the pseudonymous German author, with its stress on the problem of luxury so often treated by Ford, casts light on the significance in *The Good Soldier* of allusions to falling army morale for an alert reader in 1913. But what finally separates altogether Ford's novel from Kyrburg's is the Impressionist method which compels mere social data to shape themselves into the "rendered" materials that intensify the single effect of *The Good Soldier*.

As in his earlier novels, including the historical, Ford implies that this contemporary disorder in both public and private spheres has resulted from the splitting of a once unified religious and cultural tradition; and he enhances the gravity of the crisis by elaborating proof of its consequences on an Imperial scale. Central to this dominant theme is the Ashburnham-Dowell excursion from Nauheim to the castle in Prussia, ground always unhallowed to Ford, since it is here, at the summit of the "winding corkscrew staircases" that lead to the historical rooms of the castle, (p. 43) that the party stops before the Luther protest and at the same time becomes conscious of the act of betrayal, Florence's adulterous signal to Ashburnham, that begins the active deterioration of their relationship. In its religious and historical associations the scene is tightly packed, and the portentous shock of evil bears with it an emanation from the Lutheran disruption of Catholic unity that Ford had dwelt upon in *The Fifth Queen:*

> I was aware of something treacherous, something frightful, something evil in the day. I can't define it and can't find a simile for it. It wasn't as if a snake had looked out of a hole. No, it was as if my heart had missed a beat. It was as if we were going to run and cry out; all four of us in separate directions, averting our heads. In Ashburnham's

face I knew that there was absolute panic. I was horribly
frightened and then I discovered that the pain in my left
wrist was caused by Leonora's clutching it. (pp. 44–45)

Here for the first time, in Florence's display of the Reformation
spirit of secularism and in Leonora's confession that she is an
Irish Catholic, the true nature of the sexual-religious predicament underlying the novel becomes plain. To complete the
figure, Dowell's circuitous move to conceal the situation accords
wholly with the manners of a society habituated to the suppression of primal terrors.

In support of this undertone of factual verity and urgency
given *The Good Soldier* by the careful laying in of the historical motifs, Ford adheres throughout to the Impressionist
rule of making a work seem true rather than the result of
literary fabrication. Hence Dowell as narrator insists that his
story is "real" and told in a real way (p. 183) and that it is a
"tale," the latter term implying an account based on remembered facts. As Conrad often does, Ford in places relies upon
the authority of immediate experience in modeling some of
his minor characters on actual persons, examples in point being the German count and polo player von Lelöffel, a man
known to Violet Hunt,[5] and the two Hurlbird aunts of Florence Dowell, maiden ladies from Connecticut whom Ford
mentions having known while a patient at a German health
resort.[6] In one instance this practice extends to a major character when Ford takes the surname of Edward Ashburnham
from that of a lesser known historical figure of the seventeenth
century and thus provides Ashburnham with ancestral "justification" going beyond his parental record in the story itself.
Although the text notes briefly the descent of the Ashburnhams
from ". . . the Ashburnham who accompanied Charles I to
the scaffold," (pp. 4–5) the allusion derives from a longer
anecdote in Ford's book *The Cinque Ports* of 1900, perhaps a
further trace of the novel's slow hatching period. Besides drawing attention in this topographical volume to the long and

honorable connection of the Ashburnham family with the Ports
and to the Ashburnham House and lands near Battle, Ford includes a detailed survey of the relationsip between the Stuart
Ashburnham and his king:

> Charles I, a prisoner in Carisbroke, had for a time a body-
> servant, Ashburnham, whom the Parliamentarians removed.
> Ashburnham, returning to his home near Hastings, received
> a letter from Carisbroke bidding him have in readiness a
> vessel to carry the king over-seas. Ashburnham got ready the
> ship, which lay off Hastings for some three weeks; but at
> the end of this time news came from the luckless king. Some
> of his jailors were not sufficiently complaisant, could not be
> bribed; Charles would not trust those that had been bribed
> —Charles, one must remember, would trust no one suffi-
> ciently: the matter fell through. Hastings did not witness the
> memorable event. Instead, at Ashburnham House, near Bat-
> tle, are preserved the blood-stained relics of a martyr, the
> clothes that Charles wore when the axe fell.[7]

For the purposes of the novel the abbreviated reference to
Ashburnham's accompanying Charles to death sufficiently emphasizes the tradition of service behind the character of Edward. Yet it is significant that Ford should have chosen to
identify a principal actor in the story with a legend of kingship
and martyrdom, particularly since Edward himself assumes
the guise of a flayed martyr in later sections of the novel. The
theme of betrayed and severed tradition permeates the atmosphere of *The Good Soldier* and so appears to anticipate Ford's
return to the topic in his novels of the 1930's, *The Rash Act* and
Henry for Hugh.

Other evidence, moreover, demonstrates that germs for *The
Good Soldier* originated in Ford's personal experience. For the
episode of Ashburnham's driving Nancy Rufford to the station
in the dog-cart, Ford drew upon an anecdote in his 1907 survey of national life, *The Spirit of the People,* a case wherein
a married couple of "good people" have to deal with the em-

barrassment of the growing affection of the husband, P——,
for his ward, Miss W——, a girl living in the household. The
couple quietly decide to send the ward on a trip round the
world, meanwhile giving no sign of anything out of the ordinary until, on the morning of the girl's departure, the husband
asks Ford to drive with them to the station in order to prevent
a scene:

> Neverthless, I think he need have feared nothing. We
> drove the seven miles in the clear weather, I sitting in the
> little, uncomfortable, hind seat of the dog-cart. They talked
> in ordinary voices—of the places she would see, of how long
> the post took, of where were the foreign banks at which she
> had credits. He flicked his whip with the finest show of un-
> concern—pointed at the church steeple on the horizon,
> said that it would be a long time before she would see that
> again—and then gulped hastily and said that "Fancy ought
> to have gone to be shod that day, only she always ran a
> little lame in new shoes, so he had kept her back because
> Miss W—— liked to ride behind Fancy." [8]

Ford then comments on his own reaction, especially to the
parting of the man and the girl at the station:

> I won't say that I felt very emotional myself, for what
> of the spectacle I could see from my back seat was too in-
> teresting. But the parting at the station was too surprising,
> too really superhuman not to give one, as the saying is,
> the jumps. For P—— never even shook her by the hand;
> touching the flap of his cloth cap sufficed for leave-taking.
> Probably he was choking too badly to say even "Good-bye"
> —and she did not seem to ask it. And, indeed, as the train
> drew out of the station P—— turned suddenly on his heels,
> went through the booking-office to pick up a parcel of fish
> that was needed for lunch, got into his trap and drove off.
> He had forgotten me—but he had kept his end up. [9]

While commending this behavior as a distinct achievement, Ford adds that the girl died on her tour at Brindisi and the husband spent his next three years undergoing nerve cures on the Continent:

> That I think proved that they "cared"—but what was most impressive in the otherwise commonplace affair was the silence of the parting. I am not concerned to discuss the essential ethics of such positions, but it seems to me that at the moment of separation a word or two might have saved the girl's life and the man's misery without infringing eternal verities. It may have been desirable, in the face of the "eternal verities"—the verities that bind and gather all nations and creeds—that the parting should have been complete and decently arranged. But a silence so utter: a so demonstrative lack of tenderness, seems to me to be a manifestation of a national characteristic that is almost appalling . . .[10]

So lasting an imprint did this incident leave on Ford's memory that in recasting it for *The Good Soldier* he retained even the specific place reference to Brindisi. Evidently the occurrence appealed vividly to the curiosity regarding settled traits of English temperament which he had shown as early as *The Shifting of the Fire;* and it had, furthermore, all of the marks of the condensed "impression," which better than any number of statistics could epitomize the manners of the class of good people that he saw as furnishing a standard of conduct for the nation at large, a standard fixed in emotional repression. Already in *An English Girl* in 1907 he had drawn close to the point of the episode in the letter of the Italian, Carlo Canzano, reproving Elinor Greville for her want of feeling; but in *The Good Soldier,* where good people occupy the center of attention, the tactics of emotional restraint enter, by way of their bearing on sexual relationships, directly into the structural pattern of the novel itself.

Evidence of this kind does much to validate Ford's claim

for the decade long period of germination undergone by *The Good Soldier.* Of greater significance, however, though more conjectural than the foregoing pieces of direct borrowing, is the possible influence upon the novel of material from the deeper ore of Ford's private experience of nervous illness which, on his own testimony, sent him to Germany for treatment between the years 1903 and 1906. Although he alludes to this interval of frustration from time to time in his earlier reminiscences, his most extended account of his breakdown in a published source occurs in *Return to Yesterday* in 1931, where, long after *The Good Soldier,* he reports on a wandering search for health that brought him back to England for recovery under Conrad's doctor. In his reference to physical disability as a cause for his rejection in youth by the Indian Army and the Civil Service, Ford specifies as part of his handicap the supposed possession of a defective heart,[11] though of the latter organ, which assumes major symbolic importance in *The Good Soldier,* he has much more to say in his subsequent remarks on his tribulations while nervously afflicted. In summarizing his trials as a patient under diagnosis by specialists in various Rhenish health resorts, he conveys quietly his feeling of depression as well as of resentment against the *kur* regimen of that day.[12] With particular bitterness he speaks of a certain "Kaltwasser-Heilanstalt" as a monstrous institution which had tortured him. A chief reason for this hatred appears to have been the resident doctor, a figure with beard and black glasses, who declared Ford's trouble to be of "an obscure sexual origin" and attempted to prove this, without evident result, by suddenly flashing indecent photographs before the patient's eyes.[13] The commoner diagnosis was, however, agoraphobia, usually attributed to sexual abnormality and treated on that assumption, though no one bothered, Ford asserts, to examine his heart.[14] The analysis after a time took a special turn when Ford confessed that he had been thinking of a golden cup, a gift that he intended to buy, an item which the doctor seized upon as "a symbol of something improper" though Ford believed the interpretation probably "a hit at the Holy Grail." [15] His response to the specialist's delighted announcement was distinctly cold:

> *"Kurz und gut,"* he said, "you are suffering from . . ." some sexual disorder or other. As a matter of fact I was suffering from a slight fluttering of the heart which, after periods of intense overwork and fatigue, caused—and indeed does still cause—me to feel slightly faint for a second or two. This will actually sometimes happen in the street. The result therefore a little resembles agoraphobia which is, in effect, a disease of the will-power and may be attributable to sexual disorders—but which equally well may not. Those were the early days of that mania that has since beset the entire habitable globe. [16]

To what extent Ford was here, in a fairly late work of reminiscence, exploiting supposedly autobiographical memoir with a polemical aim is a question for the biographer; but the remarks throw light on a deprecating attitude towards doctors and psychiatric findings which is much more evident in his fiction of the 1930's, like *The Rash Act*, than in such earlier novels as *A Call*. There seem to linger, however, in the passages cited remnants enough from an authentic and critical phase of Ford's intimate experience to stimulate enquiry into the difficult problem of their relevance to the conception of *The Good Soldier*. A few debts of this kind appear obvious: the familiarity shown in the novel with spa background and routine and the attention directed to types and symptoms of mental disorder which, more comprehensively than in Ford's earlier work, contributes in *The Good Soldier* to a prevailing atmosphere of spiritual malaise that raises the book to a symbolic level not far from that of *The Magic Mountain*. If, for example, a character like Dowell appears to exhibit in his feeling of nakedness in any great space or in the counting of his footsteps (pp. 21–22) traces of the agoraphobia known to Ford, the matter is not reduced to clinical proportions as in the case of Leicester's hypochondria in *A Call;* nor do doctors have anything like the emphasis given them in the earlier novels. As Ford may have implied in his remark to Violet Hunt that he was writing a book with "'heart' in it," [17] his true concern is with the "dark forest" of the heart,[18] the realm already penetrated by James in *The Turn of the Screw* and by Conrad in *Heart of Darkness.* What, then, came perhaps most importantly out of his health resort ordeal was a consciousness of human duplicity and guile far deeper than the objective rhythms of organic or mental illness and cure.

Beyond these means employed by Ford to obtain conviction by striking roots for his novel in the soil of actual life, he took every advantage, through his narrative method, of the Impressionist device of leading the reader to forget that he has to do with a book at all. Yielding at once to the illusion that Dowell is talking much more than writing, picking his way to fulfill his conviction that ". . . real stories are probably told best in the way a person telling a story would tell them," (p. 183) the reader, further carried on by the mounting *progression d'effet,* participates vicariously in the action throughout. Although Ford had for precedent, of course, the advances made by James and Conrad in first-person narration, he arrived through Dowell at the end posited by his own theory—the oral, vernacular, and generally un-bookish style that he had not achieved in his earlier novels; and Dowell's occasional comments on the matter of style in itself testify to Ford's satisfaction with his results.

One possible reason for the use of an American narrator was to benefit by the informality of American speech, a language to which Ford had been introduced young in his boyhood reading of Artemus Ward, Mark Twain, and "ever so many other American books." [19] But more than merely a modern form of spoken utterance, Ford acquired a style in the larger sense, one that completely infuses the novel after the fashion of the later James, in which respect Ford's reminder of the small amount of direct conversation in *The Good Soldier* is significant of his agreement with James that a novel should be a work of sustained prose rather than a compromise with drama in the free employment of dialogue. The style corresponds exactly, moreover, with Ford's maxim that an effective speech should create the image of a person discoursing spontaneously and in an intimate, low-voiced manner, since Dowell imagines himself reminiscing to a sympathetic soul by the fireplace of a country cottage, ". . . talking, in a low voice while the sea sounds in the distance and overhead the great black flood of wind polishes the high stars." (p. 12) The level of pitch thus established holds throughout the book and by its very banalities—"Nancy must have been a very emotional child . . ."—reveals the nature of a speaker not only unable to say just what he means but also reluctant to express fully the tensions held down by his muted words. For Dowell's narrative is a confession uttered under mental strain, a typical Ford situation; and the guarded tone heightens, as in *The Turn of the Screw*, the sense of apprehension imparted by the substance of the tale itself.

Likewise in Ford's preferred manner, Dowell's talk is largely anecdotal, compounded of seemingly digressive fragments like those on the Troubadour Peire Vidal or Uncle John Hurlbird with his oranges and folding chairs. As a further support to the anecdote in altering the pace and direction of the narrative, Ford employs from time to time a device reminiscent of Conrad, that of introducing passages of moral generalization which become part of the whole ironical exposure of Dowell's character through his own words:

> But the real fierceness of desire, the real heat of a passion long continued and withering up the soul of a man, is the craving for identity with the woman that he loves. He desires to see with the same eyes, to touch with the same sense of touch, to hear with the same ears, to lose his identity, to be enveloped, to be supported. For, whatever may be said of the relation of the sexes, there is no man who loves

a woman that does not desire to come to her for the renewal of his courage, for the cutting asunder of his difficulties. And that will be the mainspring of his desire for
her. We are all so afraid, we are all so alone, we all so need
from the outside the assurance of our worthiness to exist.
(pp. 114–115)

While such a passage, like Dowell's frequent "poor dears,"
falls within the general framework of Victorian parody, it
also exhibits Ford's mastery of cadence as an instrument of
stylistic variation.

By installing Dowell as narrator, Ford resolved the irksome
problem of his earlier novels, his inability to suggest time
lapse which is so obviously a shortcoming in a book like *Mr.
Fleight*. Rather than taking his former course of dismissing
the time question by merely ignoring it, he adopted in *The
Good Soldier* precisely the opposite method of pressing it
upon the reader's attention by a cunning system of exactly
numbering days and years and by attaching specific dates to
critical events, such as the death of Florence. These dates,
which are among Dowell's obsessions, act partly as a comment
on the design of the novel, which is not developmental like
Washington Square or *The Old Wives' Tale* since none of the
characters alters very much physically but remains, except
for Nancy Rufford and Maisie Maidan, in the condition of
"young middle-age." The book has, in fact, been removed
from the historical dimension of *Mr. Fleight* to the metaphys-
ical plane where the issues connect with the enduring and inward evil of the heart, so that time marks chiefly moments
of moral or psychological import. Ultimately the theatre of
action is the mind of Dowell and the time scheme his mental
tactics in ordering and reconstructing the content of memory.
This internalizing, which recognizes the association of mind
and event, not only justifies Ford's use of "time-shift" that dis-
poses happenings according to a psychological rationale but

also endows the time scheme with a flexibility hitherto lacking in his work.

What Dowell mainly provided, however, was a means of validating the labyrinthine design which Ford had already constructed for *A Call* but had been unable to reconcile with an omniscient and sequential narrative procedure. In almost every respect *A Call* and *The Good Soldier* are novels of the same type and of similar components: the closed circle of good people, the idleness contrasted with the hidden currents of emotion, the outbreaks of madness and passion. But whereas in these respects *A Call* is also in its own way "a tale of passion" in its subterranean ramifications leading back to Grimshaw's concealed threat by telephone, its flaw is the discrepancy between structure and theme. In an objective framework the intricate turns of the plot appear simply contrived and melodramatic. This fault *The Good Soldier* overcame completely by its use of a narrator who, devious and neurotic as his accustomed milieu, supplies by his own mental attitude the shape of the story and at the same time absolves Ford from any charge of sympathy with this conception of experience, Dowell's meandering path of the serpent: "I have, I am aware, told this story in a very rambling way so that it may be difficult for anyone to find his path through what may be a sort of maze."(p. 183) In recognizing that the pattern of external action in *A Call* could not accord with the labyrinthine intent, Ford introduced a change in *The Good Soldier* not unlike the shift by Joyce from *Stephen Hero* to *A Portrait of the Artist as a Young Man;* and in calling his novel a tale of passion Ford may have meant, among other things, to designate a story of passive suffering rather than active will, of people acted upon instead of determining their own fates. In this light the book, even more pointedly than *Mr. Fleight*, would stress the incompatibility between tragedy and modern circumstance as Dowell's leading remark seems to do: "I call this the Saddest Story rather than 'The Ashburnham Tragedy' just because it is so sad, just because there was no current to draw things along to a swift and inevitable end." (p. 164) The words are, to be sure, typical of Dowell in his want of tragic insight and recourse to banalities like "sadness"; yet the story is in the end his story, and his halting definition ironically fits with an account of human bungling monstrous to the point of imbecility.

Dowell also makes clear that his serpentine process of recollection is related inseparably to the Affair with which he deals: "And, when one discusses an affair—a long, sad affair—one goes back, one goes forward." (p. 183) Since the good people in the story, like those in *A Call*, are expert in the habit of polite duplicity belonging to the manners of their society and, in particular, ". . . the modern civilized habit—the modern English habit—of taking everyone for granted," (p. 36) Dowell's groping effort at reconstruction is a continued search through hidden corridors behind the screen of convention in the course of which he stumbles upon such discoveries in the angles of the maze as the dead Maisie Maidan clasped in the jaws of a trunk or Florence Dowell running to destroy herself. His hesitancies and shocks thus ensure the involvement of the reader in an experience which is always in process because constantly rendered and which results in the sense of behind-scene disclosure favored by Impressionist method, the surprise encounter with the unexpected in the apparently commonplace. The practice of taking for granted, upon which so much of the irony depends, creates the circumstances that Ford thought essential to the Affair, the muffling of disaster by the adherence to prescribed routine, a key example of which is the first meeting of the Dowell and Ashburnham couples in the "cold, expensive, elegance" of the dining-room of the Hotel Excelsior. Although the intrusion of Florence into the private life of the Ashburnhams has begun the downfall of the small coterie, the atmosphere is so discreet that even Florence's slight shiver as Dowell passes the basket of rolls hardly denotes alarm. (p. 34) At no time in the novel does anyone raise his voice.

The contrast of the pretended and the concealed thus results in the action moving simultaneously on two levels and in the presence of the often noted theme of appearance and reality. As a participant in the drama Dowell is conscious of the essential division in his world but not completely, since he does not understand the nature of the Ashburnham and European systems of moral compromise, and not willingly, since with his innate snobbery he wishes to be taken for granted and to restrict himself to the agreeable surfaces of life. If he is deceived, it is partly through his own compliance, a fact that subjects him to the condition of double vision so essential to his role as narrator. Being a rich cosmopolitan, he enjoys all of the small comforts of luxury, "the slow, smooth roll of the great big trains" (p. 41) and avoids such glimpses of suffering as the sight of a cow being gored into a stream: "I suppose I ought to have pitied the poor animal; but I just didn't. I was out for enjoyment." (p. 42) He lives, therefore, in a state of perpetual contradiction between what he wants to believe and what he is compelled to see, so that his confession must at once affirm and deny: "No, by God, it is false! It wasn't a minuet that we stepped; it was a prison—a prison full of screaming hysterics . . ." (p. 7) Nowhere does he more fully expose the inevitable confusion in his funambulistic posture than in the moment when he attempts to confront the fact of evil: "If for nine years I have possessed a goodly apple that is rotten at the core and discover its rottenness only in nine years and six months less four days, isn't it true to say that for nine years I possessed a goodly apple?" (p. 7)

This ambivalence in Dowell becomes the keynote of Ford's method in all aspects of the novel, character among the foremost. In accordance with the Impressionist precept of gradual revelation, Ashburnham, for example, is dissected bit by bit, like Grimshaw in *A Call* or Conrad's Lord Jim, from his first appearance of self-certainty down to his ultimate suicide; yet the process acquires the conviction and interest that it does not have in *A Call* by its reference to Dowell's uncertainties, his always frustrated hope in appearance, that cause him to regard Ashburnham in the double focus of hero and bungler:

> It is very difficult to give an all-round impression of any man. I wonder how far I have succeeded with Edward Ashburnham? I dare say I haven't succeeded at all. It is even very difficult to see how such things matter. Was it the important point about poor Edward that he was very well built, carried himself well, was moderate at the table, and led a regular life—that he had, in fact, all the virtues that are usually accounted English? Or have I in the least succeeded in conveying that he was all those things and had all those virtues? He certainly was them and had them up to the last months of his life. They were the things that one would set upon his tombstone. They will, indeed, be set upon his tombstone by his widow. (p. 151)

Although the words, again, reflect the temperament of Dowell, they are also in accord with the modern ambivalent view of character due not only to introspection but also to the awareness of non-rational factors in motivation. Ford had recognized the influence of the irrational, in the form of passion, as early as his first novel, *The Shifting of the Fire;* but his technical advance in *The Good Soldier* enabled him to represent all of the characters in the Dostoevskian or Nietzschean light of figures enacting roles under automatic compulsion from inner darkness. Such is notably the case with Ashburnham, outwardly the Victorian model of officer and gentleman but also in his twisted attraction to Nancy Rufford a sentimentalist on the order of George Moffat in *The Benefactor;* yet the cardinal instance of the revelation of the hidden self after the protracted strain of concealment is that of Dowell's insight into his own nature when, on his collapse following the death of his wife, he remarks to Leonora Ashburnham that he can now marry Nancy Rufford and discerns in this unaccountable statement the operation of "that mysterious and unconscious self that underlies most people." (p. 104)

In its labyrinthine form, therefore, the Affair takes shape under the governance of the passion that works secretly in the characters, for which reason *The Good Soldier* is eminently the novel of a society of extreme refinement wherein passion —as distinct from sexual license—exists only through the maintenance of a code of elaborate formality. As a consequence of the intricate skein of concealment and evasion which protects the social amenities, the characters cannot intervene forcibly to arrest the progress of their own destruction, key examples of which are the suicides of Florence Dowell and of Ashburnham, so that Dowell may well cry out in perplexity ". . . what should these people have done? What, in the name of God, should they have done?" (p. 233) In these circumstances the violence of natural death becomes an offense cloaked by formality, as when the dead Maisie Maidan is at once surrounded by candles and lilies, (p. 76) or by ambiguity, as in Florence's insisting to the end on the pretense that confuses heart disease with suicide. Suicide, in fact, seems best to represent the mortuary ideals of a society marked by the kind of orientalism suggested in the concubine status of Maisie Maidan, whose hair resembles that of a Japanese, (p. 76) or in the curious picture-bride arrangement by which Ashburnham is married off to Leonora. The Affair thus becomes a record of passivity which, as Dowell observes, has "none of the elevation that accompanies tragedy . . . no nemesis, no destiny" (p. 164) and ". . . not even any villain." (p. 165) As in *The Secret Agent* and in Waugh's *A Handful of Dust*, likewise anti-tragedies, the villainy lies entirely in the coil of misfortune issuing from the practices of society as a whole, a peril which, because unresisted, assumes for Dowell the character of a mysterious fate that he tries to assail in his complaints against "blind and inscrutable destiny" or the ". . . merciless proceedings on the part of a cruel Providence." (p. 77)

Since, therefore, *The Good Soldier* contains no contrasting measure of force like Blood, the restraint upon action is even more evident than in *Mr. Fleight;* and such violence as that

displayed by Major Rufford in his terrible blow to his daughter's forehead is merely proof of frustration, a cruder exhibit
of the passion that beats at the reserve of Leonora when she
imagines herself lashing at Nancy's face with a riding whip,
". . . drawing the handle at the same moment toward her, so
as to cut deep into the flesh and to leave a lasting wheal."
(p. 210) No such simple brutality, however, sends the girl
insane, just as no one in the book retaliates physically upon
another, since as Dowell says when he chooses to ignore
Leonora's implied threat to his wife and so lets the mischief
for himself and the Ashburnhams proceed, "Good people . . .
do not threaten each other." (p. 69) Only the vain flashes
of rage shown in Dowell's beating of his Negro servant or in
Leonora's boxing the ears of Maisie Maidan offer relief from
the ". . . long silent duel with invisible weapons" (p. 123)
that Florence fights with Dowell because of his ineptitude or
Leonora against her husband and Nancy Rufford. The results
are, nevertheless, as deadly as those from the older vendetta;
and the chief sufferer is Ashburnham, a potential hero in the
eyes of the young Nancy Rufford, and by report a man who
". . . they said . . . was a good soldier." (p. 26)

Although the only character in the novel with some vestiges
of tragic dignity, Ashburnham appears the victim of the confused and sentimental ethic of his class and time; and his
deterioration could easily have become overly dramatic had
not Ford taken evident care to keep the matter at proper distance by means of Dowell's interposed narrative. On Ashburnham's first entry in the glitter of the expensive hotel dining-
room, his almost too perfect manner as he whispers to the
subservient waiter betrays a slight effeminacy and the "curious" and "sinister" expression of his eyes conveys an Au-
denesque hint of inner defect. (p. 28) No longer a soldier on
active duty, he has acquired the habit of luxury revealed in
his elegant trousers and profusion of leather cases; and
whereas he exhibits skilled horsemanship in the Nauheim polo
match, he becomes progressively further removed from the

conventional military symbols of horse and sword. In a train of imagery connected with the horse in its epic associations, the decline in his capacity for action follows from his cat-like maneuvering of the polo pony at Nauheim to his inert brooding in the chair of his gunroom at Branshaw where, above his head on the mantelpiece, "a dark-brown picture of a white horse" seems an omen of disaster. (pp. 212, 249) Briefly in India he carries a sword, but it turns in his frustration to a Carlylean walking-stick used to slash at the flowers in a Burmese garden. At the end and in his final retreat from action the weapon to destroy himself comes from his waistcoat pocket, ". . . a little neat penknife—quite a small penknife." (p. 256)

Ashburnham seems, therefore, to represent Ford's most complex image of the pernicious effects of luxury, particularly since the theme in *The Good Soldier* includes signs of failure in a once unified religious tradition that are not observable, for example, in *The Inheritors*. In this respect the both cruel and pathetic warping of Ashburnham's relationship with Nancy Rufford attains singular importance in the novel; for what goes wrong is at first mutual regard between two persons with inherently fine standards and, perhaps more, something close to reverence by Ashburnham for a religious ideal in Nancy, since the image of the Virgin that she gives him immediately after she has left her convent is a prominently stressed detail. (p. 124) But in consequence of the web of misfortune the association ends in the perverse strait of Ashburnham's having to exhaust himself to let the girl alone and she herself to feel contamination in his mere presence. Although Dowell's picture of Ashburnham being flayed to rags between Leonora and Nancy is appalling, (p. 239) it is still a semi-religious portrait of a martyr torn asunder by carnal passion and so possibly one of the central images in the book in its play upon the distinctions in the term "passion" in its religious and secular bearings. That Ashburnham should end by muttering against his wife Swinburne's "Thou hast conquered, O pale Galilean"

is a trifle startling in the light of character but not in that of
Ford's customary antipathy to anything suggestive of pre-
Raphaelite ethics.

In the end, however, Ashburnham cannot be seen apart
from his involvement with Dowell; and by so closely interweaving the lives of the two men, Ford created the kind of
double strand that he had not been able to form with Leicester
and Grimshaw in *A Call* or with Blood and Fleight in *Mr.
Fleight*. His aim seems to have been for an effect that he had
discovered in Stendhal and Jane Austen: ". . . the juxtaposition of the composed renderings of two or more unexaggerated
actions" so as to obtain ". . . a sort of frictional current of
electric life"; [20] and this he accomplished by keeping Ashburnham and Dowell so constantly in touch that the one character
adds weight to the other, the advantage lying especially with
Dowell who gains body and vitality as a narrator by the
reference of his story to that of Ashburnham. In *A Call* the
Greek traits in Grimshaw are a hindrance to his immediate
plausibility for the reader; and in *Mr. Fleight* the element
of caricature in Blood and Fleight tends to relate them to
burlesque, whereas in *The Good Soldier* the pair of characters
are in certain respects so nearly complementary as to focus
and heighten the leading theme of division and betrayal.

Yet in the final count it is Dowell who matters most in imposing upon the whole novel the weird color of his personality
and outlook and thus fulfilling to the letter the Impressionist
objective of presenting a situation through the lens of a particular temperament. That Dowell is both dupe and cuckold
makes for great psychological complication; but it is his utter
negativism, the quality that Mr. Schorer defines as *Accidia*,
that first attracts notice and that remains the shadow which
he casts over the action. In a sense Dowell is a triumph in
absolute ineffectuality and hence, more completely than
Fleight, an image of modern rootless cosmopolitanism without
tradition or personal conviction. Unlike James's Americans in
Europe, Strether or Verver, Dowell has ceased to be an Ameri-

can or interested in his properties in Philadelphia except as
a source of income. He is "a wanderer on the face of public
resorts" (p. 21) and significantly the only character in the
novel with no record of parentage. The most concrete fact
about him is his wealth which will enable him to "cut up at
about a million" and which alone has counted in his marriage
to Florence. By means of this he has no call to want anything
strongly—he does not know why he has "wanted" Florence—
and after his nine-year residence at the German spa he has
nothing to show: "Not so much as a bone penholder, carved
to resemble a chessman and with a hole in the top through
which you could see four views of Nauheim." (p. 36) The
figure of the knickknack sharply illuminates his mentality and
tastes, for he is a personification of late Victorian idleness and
the intricate whims induced by the habit of luxury. In comic
perspective—and in conjunction with the flirtatious proclivi-
ties of his wife—Dowell is in the line of *Daisy Miller* and not
altogether remote from the current of American Gothic.

By his coupling of Ashburnham and Dowell, Ford secured
the double irony essential to his portrayal of Victorian ab-
surdity; for if, on the one hand, Ashburnham is the victim
in act of a faulty ethic, Dowell, on the other, is a Victorian
mentality introverted and reflecting upon its own disaster. The
result is a dramatic tension much more vital than the weaker
device in *The Inheritors* of attempting to suggest an inner conflict of aristocrat and aesthete within a single character like
Granger. While lacking artistic ambition, Dowell takes a dilettante's sensuous pleasure in the material benefits of luxury;
and from his first metaphor describing his acquaintance with
the Ashburnhams as ". . . as loose and easy and yet as close
as a good glove's with your hand," (p. 3) his preferences tend
to settle upon the colors and textures of personal possessions
—his favorite blue ties, Ashburnham's leather equipment,
women's dress—and other tokens of a world of appearance as
distinct from that of passion. His eye, slightly Ruskinian,
lingers upon the exotic surfaces of existence:

. . . the world is full of places to which I want to return—
towns with the blinding white sun upon them; stone pines
against the blue of the sky; corners of gables, all carved and
painted with stags and scarlet flowers and crowstepped
gables with the little saint at the top; and grey and pink
palazzi and walled towns a mile or so back from the sea, on
the Mediterranean, between Leghorn and Naples. Not one
of them did we see more than once, so that the whole world
for me is like spots of colour in an immense canvas. Perhaps
if it weren't so I should have something to catch hold of
now. (p. 14)

Among such appearances was, once, Florence—"like a gay
tremulous beam, reflected from water upon a ceiling"; (pp.
14–15) yet the discovery of her infidelity compels Dowell to
recognize under the beauty of appearances the disturbing element of passion. The memory of her obsesses him, despite his
effort to thrust it away together with the rest of the ugliness in
human relations.

To keep his equilibrium, Dowell must seek to draw an embroidered curtain over the unmentionable, so that he betrays
hypocrisy in sharing the awkward trait of the Victorian novelist of revealing an obsession in the attempt to circumvent it.
He cannot, then, vouch for the cleanness of his thought and
the absolute chastity of his life without thereby making plain
why he sees men as either eunuchs or raging stallions or why
he fixes intently upon every manifestation of hair—whether
it be olive leaves "like hair flying in the wind," the black hair
of Maisie Maidan and Nancy Rufford, or the "glorious hair"
of Leonora Ashburnham. With his peculiar Victorian blend
of chastity and sensuality goes an undercurrent of cruelty
which accounts for his remembering "poor little Maisie
Maidan" as something wrapped in lavender but at the same
time cherishing the recollection of the sentimental girl's
ludicrous death under a trunk lid. Similarly his affection for

"poor dear Edward" does not prevent his relishing the idea of Ashburnham being suitably paid off for misconduct:

> In Milan, say, or in Paris, Leonora would have had her marriage dissolved in six months for two hundred dollars paid in the right quarter. And Edward would have drifted about until he became a tramp of the kind I have suggested. Or he would have married a barmaid who would have made him such frightful scenes in public places and would so have torn out his moustache and left visible signs upon his face that he would have been faithful to her for the rest of his days. That was what he wanted to redeem him . . .
> (p. 61)

The ambiguities in Dowell's talk may be compared with those of the governess in *The Turn of the Screw* in taking their origin in a mind divided between respect for propriety and secret obsession with morbidity. The fancies cast up by this confusion are hideous; and even more distorted than the image of Ashburnham flayed alive is Dowell's nocturnal fantasy of eternal judgment which condemns his wife to solitude in the same hand of God that contains the embracing Ashburnhams. (p. 70) The picture is "too terrible"; yet terrible is a common word in his vocabulary and used with a complacence that shows no appreciation of *terribilita*.

Although his involvement in the Ashburnham disaster constantly forces Dowell to reckon with the issues of sex and religion, neither his Victorian temperament nor the language at his disposal provides him with means requisite to the endeavor. His generalizations on what he thinks ". . . a matter so elementary as the morals of sex" are, therefore, a shuffling of the abstractions of an evasive society:

> Of the question of the sex instinct I know very little and I do not think that it counts for very much in a really great passion. It can be aroused by such nothings—by an untied shoe-lace, by a glance of the eye in passing—that I think

it might be left out of the calculation. I don't mean to say
that any great passion can exist without a desire for consummation. That seems to me to be a commonplace and
to be therefore a matter needing no comment at all. It is a
thing, with all its accidents, that must be taken for granted,
as, in a novel, or a biography, you take it for granted that
the characters have their meals with some regularity. (pp.
114–115)

Typically, Dowell slips into the Victorian rhetoric of "desire,"
"passion," "the soul" as well as into the notion of identity later
raged against by D. H. Lawrence. The errors of his thought
find their parallel in Ashburnham's muddles in act, the recurrence of the dismal affairs in the sentimental quest for "the
ultimately satisfying woman" that begins with the nursemaid
in the Kilsyte case and ends with the entanglement over Nancy
Rufford, the nearly incestuous relationship between Ashburnham and a girl bound to him as a niece or daughter. Instinctively, he falls in with Dowell's habit of mind when, in attempting to explain his sudden ardor towards Nancy in the
Nauheim Casino park, he carefully assures Dowell that ". . .
there was no physical motive about his declaration." (p. 111)
    The two strands of Ashburnham drama and Dowell narra-
tive meet in the strident closing ironies of the novel when the
scene narrows upon the family feud occurring in the privacy
of Branshaw house, the violent sexual contest cloaked by perfect manners that ensnarls Ashburnham, Leonora, and Nancy
Rufford. In itself this exhibition of hysteria, drunkenness, and
threatened suicide, technically a vivid example of *progression
d'effet,* has patent elements of Victorian sensational fiction;
but the turgid rhetoric of Dowell as observer converts melodrama to satire for the omniscient reader, a satire more vigorous than that at the end of *Mr. Fleight.* As Dowell suspects
". . . there was a great deal of imbecility about the closing
scenes of the Ashburnham tragedy"; (p. 238) yet rendered in
his customary language the episodes turn irreparably into the

substance of the shilling shocker, as in such incidents as the letter informing Nancy that her mother is on the streets:

> Whether she was actually on the streets I do not know, but I rather think that she eked out a small allowance that she had from her husband by that means of livelihood. And I think that she stated as much in her letter to Nancy and upbraided the girl with living in luxury whilst her mother starved. And it must have been horrible in tone, for Mrs. Rufford was a cruel sort of woman at the best of times. It must have seemed to that poor girl, opening her letter, for distraction from another grief, up in her bedroom, like the laughter of a devil. (p. 211)

Dowell's finicky avoidance of epithets is annoying but not so disagreeable as his account of Nancy tipsily amorous which borrows its tone from the *Pink Passions* rhetoric of Mrs. Kerr Howe:

> Flame then really seemed to fill her body; her legs swelled; her face grew feverish. She dragged her tall height up to her room and lay in the dark. The bed reeled beneath her; she gave way to the thought that she was in Edward's arms; that he was kissing her on her face, that burned; on her shoulders, that burned, and on her neck, that was on fire. (p. 225)

Tragic catharsis cannot end such a situation; instead the predicament runs out in the banalities proper to an Affair: Leonora's second marriage, Ashburnham's suicide, Nancy's madness. The whole strained domestic drama collapses when Leonora, hitherto made desperate by frustration, takes the simple course of marrying a man by whom she will have a child—a step that irks Dowell by reminding him that society must perpetuate itself by breeding like rabbits but that is the logical fall into commonplace of an action rising not out of tragic necessity but out of the same kind of denial or ignorance of the full potentialities of human nature that Conrad had satirized in *Chance*. Ford protracts the irony by reducing Ashburnham's suicide to an afterthought by Dowell, who has perfectly lived up to the convention of taking for granted by refusing to violate good form through interference with Ashburnham's proposal to commit hara-kiri with a penknife. Although the episode is fantastic, it is in key with Dowell's apparently more fantastic assertion: ". . . I can't conceal from myself the fact that I loved Edward Ashburnham—and that I love him because he was just myself." (p. 253) Dowell's claim may seem the ultimate in self-deception; yet to the end both characters are the reverse sides of the moral coin of their age, and in his fashion Dowell has loved Ashburnham with a sentimental mingling of admiration and contempt: ". . . I wanted to say: 'God bless you,' for I also am a sentimentalist. But I thought that perhaps that would not be quite English good form. . . ." (p. 256)

Like the involute pattern of the Affair itself, the curious bond between Dowell and Ashburnham is inbred and ultimately nihilistic in its concluding acceptance of death as a gesture of oriental politeness. The effeminacy of an upper class connives at the extinction of its own active powers, as represented by Ashburnham; and Ford implies that the essential flaw accompanies the breakdown of the religious and cultural unity which shows plainly in the sexual-religious dissension between Ashburnham and his wife but which is complemented by the basic hedonism of Dowell and Florence. In this respect *The Good Soldier* offers the most concentrated statement of the religious problem in modern society that Ford makes after his earlier trials at the theme in the novels beginning with *Mr. Apollo;* and his attitude seems to remain one of discontent with the adequacy of contemporary types of faith. Especially notable in his presentation of a Catholic point of view in Leonora Ashburnham, a much better rounded character than his former merely sketched pretenders to Catholicism like Margery Snyde and Etta Hudson and also more seriously conceived in that Leonora's faith is sincere and her psychology, a little like that of the embittered Mary Tudor in *The Fifth Queen,* affected by a sense of isolation engendered in the minority status of her creed. Yet Leonora appears as much as the other characters harmed by the evils of contemporary existence; and Ford attaches particular significance to the fact that the emblem of the small golden key which she wears upon her wrist attracts attention, first, as belonging to a dispatch box (p. 32) and, second, as entangled in the hair of Maisie Maidan, (p. 53) whom Leonora has had in reality to buy in order to appease Edward. But in addition to these compromises with a materialistic society, Leonora stands throughout as devoid of the traces of gaiety originally exhibited by Nancy Rufford, a clear image of corrupted innocence and faith. To Dowell, who watches her closely, Leonora fails to "set much store by the joy of life"; (p. 158) and with even greater objectivity he equates her rigid English Catholic conscience with the New England conscience, (pp. 60–61) an attitude to be condemned increasingly by Ford in his later work. Already Ford seems to be moving towards the distinction between forms of Catholicism that he begins to make explicit in his postwar work, as, for example, in *Great Trade Route* of 1937 where with reference to Spanish art in Malaga Cathedral he writes:

And we had to examine that form of Papistry because it is the only form of the cult that is completely without gaiety. It is the cult that still finds its expression in the black gondolas of Venice and the pictures of flayings alive in the Flemish Galleries. It is, if you like, the expression—the only possible expression—of the Catholic Reaction after Luther. So Mr. Symonds says in his *Renaissance in Italy* and, though I do not agree with him I don't want to argue the matter . . . Catholicism of course differs widely and evolves national types in every nation. But, for Catholics at least, it is everywhere distinguished by one thing . . . by, precisely, a sort of gaiety.[21]

In *The Good Soldier* gaiety dies completely after its brief glimmer in the youth of Nancy Rufford; and although Dowell in his wanderings in France momentarily commends ". . . that Provence where even the saddest stories are gay," (p. 13) he abandons any hope of salvation from that quarter as he implicates himself totally in the Ashburnham predicament: "It is no longer in the olive hills that I shall find my heaven; because there is only hell. . . ." (p. 234) The direct, if passing, allusion to Provence is, nevertheless, significant; for if in *The Good Soldier* such an image of cultural harmony takes only negative shape, it returns for positive consideration in Ford's last novels.

In the whole scheme of Ford's development *The Good Soldier* is not, therefore, a point of final attainment but one of temporary fruition, chiefly with respect to form. The questions here left standing or regarded as insoluble within a social order culturally disunified become central again when Ford resumes creative work after his matured knowledge of the Great War and seeks to reinstate the values that a civilization now really shattered demanded more urgently than the merely threatened society portrayed in *The Good Soldier*. But the latter novel, aesthetically considered, does retain its own kind of eminence, just as *A Portrait of the Artist as a Young Man* and *Sons and Lovers* hold their reputation in the full scale of the literary achievement of Joyce and Lawrence; and it is with these works that *The Good Soldier* properly belongs as a main example of the transitional spirit of late Victorianism. Indebted as he was to the practice of James and Conrad, Ford moved beyond these novelists in his more open attack on the Victorian sexual and religious hypocrisies that were engaging the attention of Joyce and Lawrence; and in doing so he evolved a form of contemporary irony that Conrad was seeking more awkwardly in his late novels and that bears comparison in its own time with Jane Austen's purpose in *Northanger Abbey*. Thus even though the discarded remnants of Ford's earlier novels contain rough analogies to the book that superseded them, *The Good Soldier* marks a departure from the preceding modes of conventional satire and novel of ideas towards a modern form governed by the play of consciousness. The book contributes independently to the advance in formal experiment.

Chapter VIII

Muted Epic: Society and War

FORD'S CLAIM that he put into *The Good Soldier* everything that he knew about writing sums up those qualities of the novel which account for its special place in the whole body of his work. In the sense that it came closest to his ideal of technical perfection it remained for him his best book, the consummate realization of his Impressionist theories; and from the standpoint of craftsmanship alone he had after this comparatively little more to learn. The novels that followed in the 1920's and 1930's, in the light of the finished art of *The Good Soldier,* leaned almost necessarily towards formal impurity in their inclusion of argumentative and doctrinaire principles which Ford cultivated on his emergence from the trials of the Great War and which altered his position from that of detached historian of the attitudes of late Victorian society to that of analyst of the ills of Western civilization and proponent of remedies, a change of front that aligned him with a main trend in the literature of the time. Yet the loss on the side of aesthetic rigor was to some extent offset by a gain in humility and deeper understanding of the general human plight.

As Kenneth Young has remarked, *The Good Soldier,* despite its formal brilliance, may seem a little too tightly constructed, too rarefied in tone; [1] and although Ford continued to apply essentially the same method in his later novels written in a period becoming less responsive to this kind of literary refinement, he understood in his own way the anxieties and dissonances of a postwar age. Aware as he has been in his earlier fiction of omens of disaster in the Edwardian world, the actual shock of the barbarian invasion of civilized territory produced in him the radical change of heart demonstrated by his obsessive references to the moment when ". . . on the 4th of August, 1914, the Germans crossed the Belgian frontier 'near a place called Gemmenich.'" The event followed by his own participation in the war as an infantry officer brought to his outlook a strengthened capacity for astonishment and compassion which finds expression in his 1915 *vers libre* poem, "Antwerp," when he asks of the unknown defenders of the city "In the name of God, how could they do it?" [2] and acknowledges, not unlike Yeats, that modern war compelled acceptance of ". . . a strange new beauty." In the works that draw immediately upon his life as a soldier—and among them the remarkable and too often neglected *No Enemy* of 1929— Ford displays more than a knowledge of writing when he records, even in the impersonal mode of fiction, his intimate sense of connection with human suffering and endurance. For this reason his major novel of the war years, the *Parade's End* tetralogy, is at once a work of deep pathos and, as he himself noted, likelier than *The Good Soldier* to find itself dated, since the tetralogy as a whole cannot be detached from a Victorian spirit which Ford, temporarily identified with it as he had not been before, commemorated elegiacally as it passed to extinction.

Going to the war as an officer past forty, while it enabled Ford to enter the march of "les Jeunes" of his day and so to ally himself once again with an advance guard, also imparted to the writing affected by this experience a character different from that commonly associated with the examples of Continental war literature produced by men like Remarque, Barbusse, or Aldington. Inevitably his age imposed upon him an avuncular perspective which colors his fiction and besides endowing his representative soldier, Tietjens, with an air of gravity somewhat unusual for his comparative youth likewise resulted in Ford's drawing with particular success the figures of elderly men who have a past to recall before their army service at the front. But to Ford this circumstance was not altogether a limitation, since it freed him of some of the narrowness in outlook and feeling of personal grievance that could not help being part of the reaction of younger writers facing war without a previous opportunity to mature. That Ford became subject to the disillusionment and anger felt by other men as the war dragged on is evident; yet his resentment seldom derives from acquaintance with physical suffering, which he tends to avoid partly out of literary conviction, or from concern with imminent death, which had for him perhaps less of the threat of unfulfilled promise that it carried to those with careers abruptly broken off. Like other war writers, he sought in his own fashion to warn; but he does not linger upon horrors not only because he recognizes that such details serve to anaesthetize or morbidly fascinate the reader but also because he sees that these are matters of relatively ephemeral significance by comparison with the major issue of general war as a catastrophe for civilization at large. This latter emphasis sets his work in this phase clearly apart from the ordinary stream of war poetry and fiction and lends it merit deserving of wider recognition. Perhaps at this time Ford really came to full power in his role of fictional historian; in any case his earlier training in historical reflection helped him to the breadth of view upon war as a manifestation of cultural disorders which he displays forthrightly in the informational books that he published in 1915, *When Blood is Their Argument* and *Between St. Denis and St. George*, works that attempt to explore the cultural grounds for Prussian barbarism, as Ford regarded it, and the contrasts between German and French civilization.

This maturity which permitted Ford to comprehend the waste and pity of war from the standpoint of the individual— his own exposure to gas and shell shock helping to make the lesson personal—and yet to look beyond to the struggle as involved with the fate of civilized traditions extends also to his fictional writing and makes it distinctive. To some extent the novels of this stage carry forward into the climate of war the judgments of society expressed in the more limited field of *Mr. Fleight* and *The Good Soldier,* so that despite Ford's somewhat creatively barren years between 1913 and 1923 the breach in continuity from earlier to later work is not absolute. Among the standing convictions that Ford took with him into the Army was a content with militarism of a particular kind, not an aggressive mood but a certain belief in the inherent worth of a military profession which may have been an inheritance partly from the age in which he had grown up, partly from his own youthful attraction to an officer's career; and this acceptance of necessity accompained his adherence to what he regarded as a cause essential to defending France, a matter also relevant to the views of Christopher Tietjens. Ford's portrayal of soldiers engaged in duty is notably free of a disposition to render his characters pitiful or brutal, so often the bent in modern war writing; and besides the touches of blunt humor and courage in the trench scenes of *Parade's End,* episodes reminiscent of *Henry V, No Enemy* contains memorable tributes to individuals of the rank and file without public distinction but admirable to Ford for traits that he continued to hold in respect, those of mute and humble fidelity without thought of reward.

In his novels, therefore, certain epic virtues survive; and whereas he may indict aspects of military stupidity or intrigue, his censure does not fall, as it tended to do in *The Good Soldier,* upon the Army itself, once the latter is in the field and standing in defense of what remains of a civilized world. Instead he turns the blame upon civilian treachery or callousness and treats the modern soldier as afflicted far more from the mental strain of worry over troubles at home than from the occasional risks of battle, as rendered unheroic not by the degrading conditions so often connected with present-day warfare but by the unrelaxing pressure of home front interference and cruelty. Like other war writers Ford recognized that the day of the professional soldier had passed and that armies retained civilian habits, but he also insisted more emphatically than others upon the fact of total war and upon the obliteration of any clear line separating the areas of home and front. War is simply another expression of the character of society as a whole, the vices existing among civilians reappear in the Army; and for this reason none of Ford's novels are war books in the conventional sense. All of his work holds a balance between the two fronts behind and in the fighting line, so that the war itself seems not only an extension of social motives and compulsions but also in some degree in the nature of a gigantic Affair. When, therefore, in 1922 Ford set down at St. Jean Cap Ferrat ". . . the first words of an immense novel," [3] he was not beginning the Tietjens tetralogy on lines altogether foreign to his earlier practice. But he was more definitely estranged than he had been from the old ways of civilian life, much more now one with the fraternity of veteran soldiers.

Ford's renewed ambition in the 1920's to turn to fictional history on an immense scale was not altogether in accord with his earlier Impressionist preference for the single compact novel, and his impulse to greater scope cannot have been due merely to regard for breadth in subject. On his own testimony he felt that the death of Proust had left a vacancy in the office of novelist-historian that required filling; and although he denies any intention of bidding for the post, he does admit that the news of Proust's death in 1922 affected his resolve to write again seriously and with something immense in mind.[4] Just how to proceed towards this latter aim without abandoning Impressionist method, which Ford clearly did not intend, must, however, have raised an immediate structural problem; and it seems likely that suggestions for the basic plan of *Parade's End* with its compressed units and shifting points of view came from *The Fifth Queen* trilogy, hitherto the only model within Ford's own practice of a fictional work in several parts. But the difficulty of presenting the complex issues of a decade centering in the Great War by means of an Impressionist scheme of selective and foreshortened incident demanded that Ford exercise all of his technical skill, and this should be weighed in any evaluation of the tetralogy. That he had perhaps tried the experiment of dealing with a subject approaching the range of *Parade's End* in a single book but had found this unsatisfactory is suggested by his novel, *The Marsden Case*, published in 1923 while the tetralogy was in progress. Although Ford defended in *The Marsden Case* his treatment of a subject admittedly weak, the book is topheavy and too intricate in its mechanism of plot and character to achieve balance and depth.

To judge by its theme and method, *The Marsden Case* may represent an attempt by Ford to regain a foothold with a post-war reading public. The title of the novel carries an overtone of the detective story, whose popular appeal Ford had long recognized; and the plot complications introduce an element of suspense and discovery which helps to sustain the narrative even though a reader might overlook less obvious intentions. The nature of the story itself, moreover, would have been likely to catch the attention of an after-war generation ready to blame its Victorian predecessors for moral and political blindness and confusion. In essence, the situation, which Ford appears to have built upon an actual case, concerns the predicament of an upright young man, calling himself George Heimann, who while serving in the war as a Guards' officer finds himself driven almost to the point of suicide by worry and grief caused by the long legal action taken by his sister to win family rights of inheritance and by the resulting publicity which makes George a scapegoat for mass hysteria and abuse arising out of the hatreds of the European crisis. George and his sister are the children of Earl Marsden, in Victorian times a Whig aristocrat and cabinet officer but driven into disgrace and exile on the Continent for a small misdemeanor during Gladstone's administration. As a result of ostracism Marsden has adopted the name of Hijmann from that of his French wife; and completely absorbed in his personal grievances and ambitions to obtain reinstatement in public life, he does nothing either to provide for his children, born abroad and raised in Germany, or to explain to them the reasons for their unsettled status, a consequence being that George, deeply attached to his father, becomes sensitive and obsessed with a fear of illegitimacy.

When, however, Marsden commits suicide on the outbreak of the Great War which destroys his hope of returning to public esteem, his son and daughter have the opportunity to lay claim to the family title and possessions by entering upon a complicated process of litigation, a course which the daughter insists upon following against the wish of George to avoid bringing old scandal to light or to distract attention from the national peril by forcing a demand for private justice. In achieving her end, the sister rouses antagonisms and passions most of which strike at George and afflict his mind with "the threefold or fourfold strains" of anxiety that bring him close to self-destruction like that of his father; and although Ford seems to overload the novel with a heavy mass of "justification" bearing upon the twisted facts of Marsden ancestry involving in particular the burden passed from father to son, the device serves the functional purpose of emphasizing Victorian duplicity and egotism and its consequences in the mental strain and sensitivity of the succeeding generation as represented by George. In one aspect the Marsden case deals with the problem of individual justice opposed to national right and need, thus resembling somewhat the issue raised by the Archer-Shee affair subsequently dramatized by Rattigan in *The Winslow Boy* or earlier the dilemma of the Dreyfus trial that continued to haunt Ford's memory. But in his novel Ford lays stress chiefly on the injury done to men enlisted in the defense of a nation that has victimized them not only through the mistakes of the past but also through the moral irresponsibility of the present. The indignation expressed by the narrator, Jessup, a novelist and officer friend of George Heimann, in referring to the strife occasioned by the Marsden suit underlines sharply a principal aim in the novel: "You would have thought those people would have shown some decency with the shadow of death falling right across the land." [5]

In its own way, therefore, *The Marsden Case* develops

themes similar to those employed in the Tietjens tetralogy; and the faults of the earlier book often cast light upon the reasons for the alterations in method adopted by Ford in the longer work. Although the two productions have in common a tendency to focus upon the social background of the war and to remove the division between civilian and military spheres of life, *The Marsden Case* appears oddly one-sided in its almost total omission of any war-front scenes except as such happenings can be reached by implication. The result is that the novel comes to seem limited to the handling of a specific instance of legal controversy and to this extent loses in Impressionist power of evocation, just as George Heimann, because too strongly implicated in details of private history, lacks the symbolic force of Christopher Tietjens as the embodiment of an established tradition and outlook which the war rendered obsolete. In spite, therefore, of its broad range in character and incident *The Marsden Case* seems thin and contrived, so that Ford must have recognized the impossibility of confining such abundance of material to a single book and have turned instead to the clearer and more flexible outlines of the tetralogy. About *The Marsden Case* there is something of the cumbersome mechanism of *Lord Jim,* an analogy heightened by Ford's attempt to use the single narrator, Jessup, who copies the serpentine manner of Dowell in *The Good Soldier:* "For of course when a man tells his story, and the story is very complicated, to be plain, he must emphasize points in advance, go back to others, advance, go back again, and so on." [6] In a book where Ford had every reason to wish to avoid didactic intrusion his employment of the narrator had everything to recommend it; yet unlike Dowell, Jessup, though "a recovered nerve patient," is neither ingrown nor self-deceived so that his wavering method of narration, while in keeping with the substance of his tale, is not really adapted to a character capable of firm and straightforward expression:

Wars are very terrible things. It is not merely that people die and suffer: people must die and people must suffer, if not here, then there. But what is dreadful is that the world goes on and people go on being stupidly cruel—in the old ways and all the time. I used to think that, once out there, we should be surrounded by a magic and invisible tent that would keep from us all temporal cares. But we are not so surrounded, and it is not like that. The one nail does not knock out the other. There is the never ceasing waiting about; and the cold; and the long depressions. Now and then there is a terrible noise—wearing, lasting for days. And some pain. All that is bearable. But what is desolating, what is beyond everything hateful, is that, round your transparent tent, the old evils, the old heart breaks and the old cruelties are unceasingly at work. And that is what you have to go back to. I think that if our splendid *Intelligentsia* knew how mournful, how terrible, and how long a strain on the mind war really was, they would not seek with light hearts to drive poor fellows again into such pain in the mind. There are other fields in which they may gain glory.[7]

What Jessup here says plainly reveals in Ford a reaction to the war so fierce that he does not for the moment care that the speech does nothing to illuminate Jessup's character and that it violates the Impressionist principle of rendering. In fact, the direct lesson seems in a way to dissolve poetry in pity and so to clinch bluntly the point of a novel hovering between didacticism and story. Yet in the Tietjens tetralogy Ford regained control of his materials; and if the simple end of the long work is to press home once again Jessup's warning, the richer effect of the tetralogy entirely justifies Ford's stricter adherence to Impressionist method.

On the evidence of scattered references to stages in the evolution of the ground plan for the tetralogy, it appears that Ford took a course familiar to himself and Conrad when shaping the raw material for a novel: that is, finding inspiration in immediate experience and adding to this the support of a number of concrete or observed facts in order to attach the work to the common verities of human life. The initial imaginative impulse might, however, spring into being from a chance or passing hint of one kind or another quite distinct from purposely collected data, for which reason the tetralogy, though a mine of exact social and military detail, has no air of naturalistic literalness. Whatever the point at which Ford discerned the general scheme of his immense novel, his own comment regarding an early intimation of the coming project suggests a possible origin in momentary personal fancy when, on service in France in 1916, he happened to wonder how the war would have looked to his dead friend, Arthur Marwood, the extinct English Tory.[8] That Marwood, a man of strong character who had influenced both Conrad and Ford, offered a model from life for Christopher Tietjens, Ford's central character, seems verified not only by Ford's direct testimony but also by physical and temperamental resemblances, especially in traits that Ford had come to associate with the eighteenth century, between Marwood and the modern Plutarchian hero of the tetralogy. Yet if Ford began with an "impression" of Marwood, the Tietjens of the novel certainly took form by a complex process of free invention, since besides incorporating qualities of Ford himself and the latter's war observations and memories, Tietjens also stands in some measure for the unrewarded virtues of personal discipline and endurance in soldiers of lower rank that the war and its perpetual expenditure of human valor had taught Ford to respect. As he had done in *The Good Soldier*, moreover, Ford likewise gathered first impressions of other characters in the tetralogy from living persons. Father Consett, Ford's best and almost unique depiction of a Catholic priest, derives partly from life [9] as do also some of the principal women characters. Valentine Wannop, the young suffragette in love with Tietjens, Ford admits to having based upon the actress, Dorothy Minto; [10] and Christopher's wife, Sylvia, he claims to have drawn in appearance from his glimpse in Amiens station of a woman in a golden dress and with light hair in bandeaux,[11] though it

may be possible that he likewise endowed Sylvia as a type
of prewar fashionable beauty with the height and sinuousness
that the period had admired in the actress, Mrs. Patrick Camp-
bell.

In accordance with his Impressionist theory Ford also extended the elements of verity in the work by obtaining one of
its important germs from a case reported to him before the
war by Marwood. The substance of the anecdote, with its
obvious parallels to the predicament of Tietjens and Sylvia,
concerned the misfortunes of an Englishman of good family
and with a promising career in the Foreign Office who had
made a disastrous marriage with a woman after a chance sexual relationship in a French train. In spite of her unfaithful-
ness and of doubt that he is the father of her child, the man
refuses to divorce his wife, a Roman Catholic and thorough-
bred member of the ruling class, because he thinks this would
not be decent; but when he falls in love with another woman,
his wife returns to him and he deteriorates into alcoholism and
eventual suicide. For his purposes in the novel Ford's chief
modification in the bare data of the tale was, of course, to
spare Tietjens from deteriorating like the man known to Marwood or like Ashburnham in *The Good Soldier*, the aim being
to allow Tietjens to bear up under his tribulations not only
because Ford thought afflicted characters the only ones worth
writing about but also because Tietjens could in this way
exemplify in his central position the intolerable strain upon
the mind that Ford associated with the conditions of modern
war.

The point is far more convincingly established through
Tietjens than it had been with George Heimann in *The Marsden Case*, since the roots of Tietjens' worries lie deeper than
public hatred and reach to the fundamental antagonisms of
sex and religion. Unlike George Heimann, moreover, Tietjens
is not merely a special instance of wartime injustice but, in
this respect somewhat closer to Blood in *Mr. Fleight*, an image
of the fatal rift in a society so corrupt as to expel and castigate

a representative of its traditional sources of strength. Solid as his character becomes, Tietjens also serves as a necessary index of the historical shift in outlook brought about by the war as he moves in the end to alienation from the attitudes of organized society; and the symbolic heightening of his figure indicates the greater imaginative flexibility with which Ford transformed the crude anecdote supplied by Marwood as compared with the more cramped treatment of the profuse data furnished by the Marsden case. Out of the Marwood tale Ford drew suggestions for a social and historical picture nearly Proustian in scope, the allusions to the Dreyfus affair in the first novel of the sequence perhaps being intended to stress the breadth in aim.

From the standpoint of theme the tetralogy might be considered more decisively than *The Good Soldier* the end of the earlier phase in Ford's career, since to some extent the long novel merely confirms in more elaborate detail and in terms of historical record the breakdown of the late Victorian world foreshadowed in *The Good Soldier*. But the principal change is one of mood; for whereas the tone of *The Good Soldier* is ironic, that of the tetralogy becomes increasingly elegiac and completely so in its concluding unit, *The Last Post*. Although with the war behind him Ford could view with even firmer hostility the evils of the luxurious society responsible for the catastrophe, the actuality of prolonged suffering widened his vision of tragedy and its admixture of pity, for which reason, perhaps, the chief characters in the tetralogy possess a kind of terrible beauty and awareness of doom that makes those in *The Good Soldier* seem a little flat by comparison. In itself the tortured emotional relationship between Tietjens and his wife, today almost incomprehensible in its Victorian aspects, is cruel; yet Sylvia Tietjens, the most superbly conceived character in the novel, is superior to Leonora Ashburnham as a tragic figure and Christopher almost by reason of his repressions and eccentricities seems intended by Ford to suggest a capacity for accepting and withstanding pain without which the burden of Allied defense could not have been sustained. As in *The Good Soldier* Ford indicates that the cleft in Imperial England resulted from cultural disunity in the past, and the consequences appear not only in the anguish of the Catholic and Protestant marriage of Sylvia and Christopher but also in the fatality that pursues the whole Tietjens family as it represents a Tory ruling class. In the war Christopher renounces all luxury as well as national bonds; yet Ford, while permitting the dying Mark Tietjens to muse upon the sordid patches in the family history, also leaves the Tietjens brothers with the force of character which tragic complexity has produced:

> The grandfather of Father scalped by Indians in Canada in the war of 1810; the father dying in a place where he should not have been—taking what he got for it and causing quite a scandal for the Court of Victoria; the elder brother of Father killed drunk whilst fox-hunting; Father suicided; Christopher a pauper by his own act with a by-blow in his shoes. If then there were to be any more Tietjens's by both name and blood. . . . Poor little devils! They would be their own cousins. Something like that. . . .[12]

Although Mark's survey is not correct in all details, the disorder and violence of the past in a people of Nordic origin, as Ford regarded the matter, constitute fate for the chief actors in the tetralogy; and while the members of the Tietjens family suffer through the intrigues and hatreds of the society around them, their line contains its private flaw which underlies the barrier of misunderstanding between the father and his sons. To the extent, however, that the characters bear their own fate and persist against its bitterness, as those in *The Good Soldier* do not, they attain the tragic distinction lacking in a society absorbed in conspiring for money or place. With those sharing this tragic inheritance Sylvia also belongs; for whereas she is a Tietjens only by marriage, she is bound to the family and in a sense struggles for acceptance by a group to which she acts as Nemesis. In a measure she resembles Leonora Ashburnham, since despite her fashionable status and patrician vices her Catholicism isolates her and makes her uncertain of the support provided by true kinship.

From Sylvia's first appearance in the foreign setting of the remote German spa at Lobscheid in the solitary company of her eccentric mother and the Irish priest, Consett, Ford continues to emphasize her lack of personal bonds; and, significantly, she can look to no father except the priest, whom she derides while he is living but whose execution during the war haunts her memory and leaves her imagining him as vested with the authority of a saint. Her "trepanning" of Tietjens into marriage through sexual enticement when she fears that she may have a child by her lover, Drake, is doubtless in one light an act of Victorian duplicity; yet it has also a quality of desperation, a craving for safeguards, which with his rational insight Tietjens appears to recognize even while he must undergo the misery that she inflicts upon him for his knowledge of her guilt. The episode of their sexual misadventure in the train becomes, therefore, crucial to the fatality theme in the novel, since it turns Sylvia into the agent of retribution that attacks the Tietjens family as a result of the cultural and religious disunity in their past and thus gives her a historical dimension larger than that assigned to Leonora Ashburnham. That Christopher recognizes this root cause of the family decline and makes some attempt at restitution seems evident in his desire that Sylvia be given the house at Groby and allowed to bring up her son, the heir to the estate, as a Roman Catholic, whether or not he really believes the prophecy in *Spelden on Sacrilege* that ill-luck must follow those who have despoiled Catholic owners of their property.

The tormented assaults by Sylvia upon her husband Ford treats, in a view similar to that in *The Good Soldier,* as expressing the perverse condition of a luxurious society which Tietjens repudiates at first by his growing attraction during the war to austere and contemplative habits and in the end by

his starting on a life of simple country living with Valentine
Wannop, the girl whose plain and direct manner makes her
not only the antithesis to Sylvia but also a type of the young
generation after the war. The course of the triangular relationship between Tietjens and the two women thus marks the
historical change in moral attitude through the decade of
European conflict. To broaden his portrayal of social dis-
equilibrium on the eve of the war, Ford added to his central
characters Mrs. Duchemin who although complementing
Sylvia as another kind of Edwardian siren differs in her Victorian sexual hypocrisy and in her attachment to the cult of
pre-Raphaelite aestheticism which Ford had earlier attacked
as pernicious in its influence upon moral standards. Like Lawrence's Hermione Roddice in *Women in Love* Mrs. Duchemin
combines an external appearance of beauty and refined taste
with an inner vulgarity which Ford tended to attribute to
the aesthetic disposition; and her sudden outburst of sexual
fury and profanity against her lover, Macmaster, which she
directs at Valentine Wannop, who has believed herself Mrs.
Duchemin's friend, both disillusions the girl and accounts for
much of the antagonism to Victorian manners which followed
the war. Although hardier than Nancy Rufford in *The Good
Soldier,* Valentine is likewise betrayed by her exposure to the
collapse of a pretended ideal into sordid emotionalism; and
knowing that ". . . you cannot suffer a great sexual shock
and ever be the same," she inevitably follows Tietjens' path
out of the late Victorian world:

> And she had never heard what had become of Mrs.
> Duchemin's baby. Next day Mrs. Duchemin had been as
> suave, as circumspect, and as collected as ever. Never a
> word more had passed between them on the subject. This
> left in Valentine Wannop's mind a dark patch—as it were
> of murder—at which she must never look. And across the
> darkened world of her sexual tumult there flitted continually
> the quick suspicion that Tietjens might have been the lover

of her friend. It was a matter of the simplest analogy. Mrs. Duchemin had appeared a bright being: so had Tietjens. But Mrs. Duchemin was a foul whore. . . . How much more then must Tietjens, with the larger sexual necessities of the male . . . Her mind always refused to complete the thought.[13]

For his depiction of the various conflicting passions in the prewar milieu, Ford may have drawn something from a work at that time considered notorious, Otto Weininger's *Sex and Character*. Although he speaks contemptuously of Weininger,[14] Ford undoubtedly shared the latter's interest in the problem of sexual attraction that provoked curiosity in the earlier years of the century; and from Weininger's theories of "characterology" based upon the notion of the dependence of sexual feeling on ratios of masculine and feminine components in men and women Ford may have taken a hint not only for the mingling of desire and hate in Sylvia's attitude to Tietjens but also for the stress on physical type differences between main characters like Sylvia, Tietjens, and Valentine. As a period note, in any case, the passing reference by Tietjens in the third volume of the tetralogy, *A Man Could Stand Up—*, to the Weininger hypothesis compels attention.[15] What is plain, at least, is that Ford intended to connect the sexual and religious discontent of a luxurious society with the increasing propensity to violence which broke out finally in the Great War. Through the opening portion of the tetralogy the signs of loss in civilized order are present in such divergent occurrences as the personal assaults upon suffragette demonstrators and Sylvia's longing to experience again the "dreadful feeling" of violation given her by her seducer, Drake. But even more conclusive is the line drawn from Valentine Wannop's disbelief in the purpose of the "tall candles in silver sticks" belonging to Mrs. Duchemin,[16] after the latter has exhibited the violence of her sexual rage, to the killing in France of the soldier, 09 Morgan, by the shrapnel "candlestick" which falls in the night.[17] The war is not only a particular aspect of the nature of society as a whole but also a reflection in the make of its weapons of the social custom of concealing its destructive methods.

This combining of the elements of domestic or social conflict with the traditional theme of military action lends to the tetralogy a special character in tone and design which places the work apart from the usual descriptive war front novel and suggests at times a certain analogy with Joyce's *Ulysses* in the crossing of commonplace and epic strains. With Ford, however, the historical aim remains primary; and his reference to the work as dealing with ". . . the world as it culminated in the war" and ". . . the public events of a decade" [18] indicates that his probable immediate model was Flaubert's *L'Education sentimentale,* so often praised by Ford as the greatest novel ever written. The tetralogy contains reminiscences of Flaubert's book, as in the opening motif of the journey and the friendship between the two young men, Tietjens and Macmaster, which recalls that between Frederick Moreau and Deslauriers and, more importantly, in the use of a central character as observer and reflector of the movement and incidents of a period. Yet despite Ford's agreement with Flaubert in avoiding a panoramic view of history, the final effect of the tetralogy is not that of *L'Education sentimentale* where time flows without purpose save to mark the course of human frustration; and although Ford did report the waste caused by war, he also acknowledged the truth that the battle had been carried to a finish by the resistance of men however unheroic and embittered. This admission, together with Ford's consciousness of the meaning of death in great numbers, accounts in some measure for the presence of the tragic and epic qualities in the novel. In Homeric perspective the work concerns itself with the epic theme of love and war as reflected in the long feud between Tietjens and Sylvia, a recognizable counterpart of the original Helen; and while Ford was recording the downfall of a once ruling class, the aristocratic status of

the bulk of his leading characters is in line with epic precept
—the nearest to the conventionally heroic being Tietjens with
his invariable courtesy and skill with horses.

These epic features differentiate the form of the tetralogy in
a marked fashion from that of a novel like *The Good Soldier*
and establish Ford's work as worthy of comparison in the development of a modern epic genre with that of Joyce, whose
interior monologue frequently resembles the rhythms of
speech employed by Ford, as, for example, in the talk of
Sergeant-Major Cowley:

> Epsom salts they say is the cure for it. . . . For seeing your
> dead. . . . And of course you should keep off women for
> a fortnight. . . . I know I did. Kept seeing Herring's face
> with the hoof-mark. And . . . there was a piece: a decent
> bit of goods in what we called the Government Compound.
> . . .[19]

The general quality of the prose, in fact, brings Ford closer
to Joyce than to Galsworthy and largely invalidates older attempts to compare the tetralogy with *The Forsyte Saga* and its
essentially different chronicle pattern. To some extent like
Joyce, moreover, Ford perceives that whatever remains of epic
formula is necessarily subject to the conditions of modern experience, the nature of war in particular being a principal
modifying factor. In this regard the tetralogy, especially in its
war front sections, heeded the precept of Crane in *The Red
Badge of Courage,* which Ford reports having read again
with renewed appreciation while on active service, with respect to the modern avoidance of heroics, Ford's direct acquaintance with war convincing him of the truth of Crane's
view that, "The idea of falling like heroes on ceremonial battlefields was gone for ever" and of the fact that the behavior
of Crane's protagonist under fire ". . . was exactly how we all
did take it twenty years later." [20] For the handling of the social
complication so as to provide a muting of the epic note, Ford
appears, however, to have turned from Crane to James, since

one of the most illuminating of Ford's casual remarks on the design of the tetralogy is his statement that while thinking vaguely of writing about the war he wondered how James would have treated this "intractible subject"; "I imagined the tortuous mind getting to work, the New England scrupulousness, the terrified involutions . . . and for the rest of the day and for several days more I lost myself in working out an imaginary war-novel on the lines of 'What Maisie Knew.'"[21]

This admission helps considerably to explain the modernized epic tone peculiar to the tetralogy which Ford achieved, much as he had done earlier in *The Fifth Queen*, by borrowing from the sombre atmosphere of domestic conflict in his favorite Jamesian novel. Looked at from a slight distance, the plight of Tietjens within a corrupt society is not unlike that of the child in *What Maisie Knew*, on which account Val Wannop reasonably calls him an Innocent; but in addition the centering of the narrative in a comparatively small number of foreground characters follows Jamesian practice. Although these people have the privileged status found in epic literature, they are so closely related through blood or standing acquaintance as to constitute almost a family drawn within the boundaries of an Affair, the war affecting them in some measure like prolonged illness or debt as a cause for personal alliances or antagonisms. Composed in this way, the tetralogy remains alone within the loose category of war writing in its time, though it anticipates in certain respects some experimental tendencies in writing of the 1930's; and its adoption of the Impressionist method of reflecting events in the minds of various observers divests it of the crudities of the literature of outright protest or denunciation to which Ford had moved temporarily in *The Marsden Case*. The work, moreover, maintains its subdued tone by adhering to the scenic pattern which led to its division into parts, each with its own individual rhythmic movement and unity; and despite the separation into four books Ford clearly intended the whole to be accepted as a single novel with interwoven motifs and overlapping episodes

—in short, as a complex total impression of a distinct but vanished stage in the life of a people.

By comparison with the three more compact units succeeding it, the first novel, *Some Do Not,* appears somewhat diffuse because of its partly expositional function, Ford having the task of presenting an impression of society before and during the earlier years of the war through a group of representative characters, at least eight of which—Christopher and Mark Tietjens, Sylvia, General Campion, Valentine Wannop, Mrs. Wannop, Macmaster, and Mrs. Duchemin—required substantial "justification." Ground clearing of this kind obliged Ford to resort to shifting point of view and to a measure of disguised authorial comment; and to avoid the danger of retarded movement, he injects currents of narrative tension, among these the most obvious being the contrasting fortunes of Tietjens and Macmaster and the sexual conflict beginning in the marital strife between Tietjens and Sylvia and leading to the affinity between the former and Val Wannop. But the principal means for ensuring tautness in structure is radical foreshortening of the time scheme by which a span of some ten years is compressed into about four selected days, though the memory flashbacks of individual characters cover much longer intervals. The first, or prewar, section of *Some Do Not* contains no more than three days; and the second, longer part occurs during the single last day of Tietjens' leave in England before his return to the front in 1917. These main sections, furthermore, reduce themselves to a few carefully elaborated scenes like those of the Duchemin breakfast party or the discussion between Tietjens and Sylvia in their Gray's Inn rooms on the afternoon preceding his departure. In this book Ford pressed his technical skill to the limit, even managing effects of simultaneous action, in order to make certain of a rapid overlap from the prewar to the war years at the center of the tetralogy and a sense of the close interlocking of incidents. The succession of peak moments provides, however, an Impressionist script rich in implication; and causal sequence yields to a pattern of charged psychological units, external event to mental and emotional undercurrent.

At the outset, therefore, the procedure common to the tetralogy as a whole becomes familiar; yet the arrangement of abruptly juxtaposed scenes also contributes to the impression which *Some Do Not* attempts to create, that of a complex and neurotic society veering towards barbarism and disaster. The omens of the dissolution of surface refinement into violence are everywhere apparent, though they are particularly stressed in a cultural setting as when Sylvia and her mother hardly notice the pictures of animals slaughtered or bleeding to death on the walls of their room in Germany until the outraged priest denounces them or when Duchemin, the clergyman, personally handsome and in the midst of the aesthetic appointments of his house, breaks out in a fit of Ruskinian madness before his guests and has to be restrained by force to stop the scatological ravings that presage his ultimate lapse into homicidal lunacy. Throughout the novel, moreover, Ford underscores the theme of social agitation and decline by a running motif of gradually arrested movement. At the opening, in a passage of evocative prose with images denoting the *nouvel art* taste of a complex and outwardly confident Imperial society, the train carrying Tietjens and Macmaster to Rye runs with the swift precision of advanced science and mechanization:

> The leather straps to the windows were of virgin newness; the mirrors beneath the new luggage racks immaculate as if they had reflected very little; the bulging upholstery in its luxuriant, regulated curves was scarlet and yellow in an intricate, minute dragon pattern, the design of a geometrician in Cologne. The compartment smelt faintly, hygienically of admirable varnish—the train ran as smoothly— Tietjens remembered thinking—as British gilt-edged securities.[22]

The sinuous design of the upholstery, emblematic of luxury but also slightly sinister in its brief allusion to the sexual en-

counter of Sylvia and Tietjens in the French train compartment which causes fatality, reflects a social order excessively
involute and so ripe for the descent into savagery. With the
advance of war, mobility gives way to images of primitive and
hampered locomotion—the lumbering knacker's cart, a war
symbol, which appears at the end of the first main section of
the novel, and the transport lorry which picks Tietjens up in
the final sentence of the book. To complete the impression of
a society betrayed from within, Ford relates the theme of
breakdown to at least three main failures in character relationship: the marital breach between Sylvia and Tietjens, the disillusionment of Val Wannop with the aesthetic and Ruskinian
moral ideals of Mrs. Duchemin, and the sullied friendship between Tietjens and the weak but ambitious Macmaster who
observes the rules of society by exploiting Tietjens for the sake
of a knighthood. As one of Ford's most subtly drawn characters, the venal but unfortunate Macmaster comes in the
course of the novel, and particularly in the fine and muted
scene of his farewell to Tietjens shortly before the latter's return to France, to represent the hero by intrigue that society
elevates in preference to the simpler virtues and strength of
Tietjens who becomes the scapegoat of its catastrophe on the
Western Front. In his last important appearance before fading out of the tetralogy, Macmaster pathetically seeks to evade
the knowledge of his private damnation:

> With his black, short beard quivering and his wretched eyes
> turned down, he had said:
>   "I wanted to explain. . . . This miserable knighthood. . . ."
>   Tietjens patted him on the shoulder, Macmaster being on
> the stairs above him.
>   "It's all right, old man," he had said—and with real affec-
> tion: "We've powlered up and down enough for a little thing
> like that not to . . . I'm very glad. . . ."
>   Macmaster had whispered:
>   "And Valentine. . . . She's not here to-night. . . ."

He had exclaimed:

"By God! . . . If I thought . . ." Tietjens had said: "It's all right. It's all right. She's at another party . . . I'm going on . . ."

Macmaster had looked at him doubtingly and with misery, leaning over and clutching the clammy banisters.[23]

The hesitant and unfinished speeches in the foregoing passage, a rendering of conversation as it actually occurs in cases of emotional stress, exemplifies an Impressionist method of handling dialogue with which Ford had experimented as early as *The Inheritors;* but in *Some Do Not* he employs it with full assurance and so obtains the effect of intense personal suppression of feeling and unspoken thought that distinguishes the long scene between Tietjens and Sylvia, a memorable impression of the ironical nature of the modern soldier's departure for battle, that opens Part Two of the novel. Through the whole of *Some Do Not,* moreover, the procedure of limiting mere physical happenings while allowing the private reflections of the characters to ramify at will results in an emphasis upon almost painful restraint and inner tension. Ford's purpose in this respect seems to have been partly to suggest a principal trait of the English temperament memorialized in the tetralogy, and a digressive remark on this point in *Some Do Not* indicates that Ford was here applying in full force the theory that he had evolved from the dog-cart incident germinal to *The Good Soldier.* But the further aim in *Some Do Not* is to make individual constraint of passion a key to the rift in Victorian character between surface amenity and the concealed violence of primal instincts which can explode, on the one hand, in the mania of Duchemin or the sexual tirades of his wife, or, on the other, in the final conflagration of the war. Because of this unbalance the late Victorian generation reaches the point of madness that Tietjens approaches at the opening of the novel when tortured by Sylvia's cold proposal to return to him after her affair with Perowne:

He wanted to stop scandal if he could; he wanted them to live within his income, he wanted to subtract that child from the influence of its mother. These were all definite but difficult things. . . . Then one-half of his mind lost itself in the rearrangement of schedules, and on his brilliant table his hands set queens on kings and checked their recurrences.

In that way the sudden entrance of Macmaster gave him a really terrible shock. He nearly vomited: his brain reeled and the room fell about. He drank a great quantity of whisky in front of Macmaster's goggling eyes; but even at that he couldn't talk, and he dropped into his bed faintly aware of his friend's efforts to loosen his clothes. He had, he knew, carried the suppression of thought in his conscious mind so far that his unconscious self had taken command and had, for the time, paralysed both his body and mind.[24]

By thus describing the psychological torments of a complex civilization, Ford can proceed much more convincingly than in *The Marsden Case* to identify the modern war of civilized peoples with the infliction primarily of mental suffering and shock. Victorian in habit at the beginning and through a good part of the tetralogy, Tietjens survives, nevertheless, by his wartime conversion to the ordered and contemplative state of mind that he attributes to the English seventeenth century Anglican tradition and by his love for Val Wannop, the daughter of a woman novelist with a trace of descent from Jane Austen. At the start, however, his friendly relationship with Val is so warped into self-consciousness by the salacious fancies of a sexually morbid society that they reject the opportunity for consummation; in this respect the title and leit-motif of the novel, *Some Do Not*, refers both to existing Victorian codes and to the rise of antithetical attitudes during the war.

Ford's emphasis on internal experience in *Some Do Not* also enabled him to introduce a system of organic rather than chronological progression between the units of the tetralogy,

a pattern of symbolic associations well illustrated in the episode of Val's night ride with Tietjens in the dog-cart at the
close of Part One. Drawn by the horse that belongs to the declining aristocratic world of Tietjens, the lovers wander in an
eerie, low-lying mist which both forebodes the later fog-
covered battlefields of the war, as Tietjens psychically appre-
hends them in his momentary reflection on smoke-screens,[25]
and recalls the cloud of scandal surrounding the two characters. Rounding out these signs of imminent war is the accident in which the car blindly driven by General Campion,
society's warrior in full uniform, rakes and injures the horse
driven by Tietjens—an incident made vivid by Impressionist
rendering:

> Not ten yards ahead Tietjens saw a tea-tray, the under-
> neath of a black-lacquered tea-tray, gliding towards them;
> mathematically straight, just rising from the mist. He
> shouted: mad: the blood in his head. His shout was drowned
> by the scream of the horse: he had swung it to the left. The
> cart turned up: the horse emerged from the mist: head and
> shoulders: pawing. A stone seahorse from the fountains of
> Versailles! Exactly that! Hanging in air for an eternity: the
> girl looking at it, leaning slightly forward.[26]

The collision anticipates the forthcoming destruction of an
obsolescent chivalry, in the heraldic semblance of the horse,
by late Victorian mechanized war with its tea-tray or candlestick missiles. The crash, "like twenty tea-trays: a prolonged
sound," [27] prepares the reader without further exposition for
the opening of the second novel, *No More Parades*, with the
shell thundering down like "an immense tea-tray."

The screaming of the wounded horse in *Some Do Not* por-
tends catastrophe, but means of a kind still exist to staunch the
blood. In the war zone of *No More Parades*, however, the tea-
trays of civilization have become weapons which kill without
apparent cause and produce death which cannot be atoned for.
Hence the killing by shrapnel of the Welsh private, 09 Morgan,

in the base camp under Tietjens' command impels Tietjens, who must for an endless moment hold the man's body in his arms, to think at once of his own past in a social order responsible for the casualty:

> In the bright light it was as if a whole pail of scarlet paint had been dashed across the man's face on the left and his chest. It glistened in the firelight—just like fresh paint, moving! The runner from the Rhondda, pinned down by the body across his knees, sat with his jaw fallen, resembling one girl that should be combing the hair of another recumbent before her. The red viscousness welled across the floor; you sometimes so see fresh water bubbling up in sand. It astonished Tietjens to see that a human body could be so lavish of blood. . . . He felt as he did when you patch up a horse that has been badly hurt. He remembered a horse from a cart on whose chest the blood had streamed down over the off foreleg like a stocking. A girl had lent him her petticoat to bandage it.[28]

This great scene in which Tietjens must wash the man's blood from his hands is central to the entire novel and, though held to lowered key, gains sharp outline by reason of the Impressionist device of registering shock directly upon the senses. For Tietjens it is, in a sense, a blood ritual which, while permanently obsessing his mind with Morgan's phantom, marks the beginning of his severance from the Victorian world and his former class allegiance and his growing attachment to those without place or power. Through his personal reaction, moreover, the incident stands linked with the governing theme of the novel: the obliteration by modern war of everything traditionally connected with military procedure or ceremony as represented by professional soldiers like General Campion. Death of the kind that strikes Morgan abolishes "parade"; and the action as well as the title of the novel affirm the truth of the anecdote related by Tietjens from a memory of War Office talk:

Well, the end of the show was to be: the adjutant would
stand the battalion at ease: the band would play *Land of
Hope and Glory*, and then the adjutant would say: *There
will be no more parades.* . . . Don't you see how symbolical
it was: the band playing *Land of Hope and Glory*, and then
the adjutant saying *There will be no more parades?* . . .
For there won't, there won't, there damn well won't. . . .
No more Hope, no more Glory, no more parades for you and
me any more. Nor for the country . . . Nor for the world,
I dare say . . . None . . . Gone . . . Na poo, finny! No
. . . more . . . parades! [29]

The word parade—connected not simply with army custom
but with nearly all that the past has venerated in morals, sex,
and religion—furnishes, therefore, a leading motif in the novel
but with ironical stress upon the canceling of the term by the
upheaval of older life routines. This meaning emerges by
steady reiteration of the irrationality of wartime affairs, as in
the madness of Captain McKechnie, the relationship of Colonel
Levin to an agent of the sultan of Turkey, the discussions at
mess of schisms in Christianity, the dependence of the fate of
an army upon the efficiency of an orderly-room clerk, and a
series of other absurdities crowned by Sylvia's arrival at the
camp in the General's Rolls-Royce. Customary time adjustments are, moreover, dislocated or blurred; for although the
action of the book, reduced to little more than forty hours,
occurs during a night, the following day, a second night, and
a brief portion of the succeeding morning, the night episodes
—like the delayed readying of the draft for the front or the
meeting of Tietjens and Sylvia at the hotel—seem intermin-
able, the daytime intervals short and hurried. As if to mark
firmly the dissociation between human events and the normal
course and significance of day and night, the concluding scene
in which Campion virtually passes a death sentence in ordering Tietjens back to combat duty takes place in a radiance of

morning sunlight. But vaguer than the uncertain line separating night from day is time progression by clock measure; and Tietjens' occasional inability to recall exactly when something happened further emphasizes the disturbance of ordinary perception by reason of constant strain upon the mind.

In spite, however, of the apparent illogicality in temporal order and event *No More Parades* is the most compactly designed unit in the tetralogy, partly because of its brief time span, partly because of the restriction in point of view, which is mainly that of Tietjens with short interludes focusing on the thoughts of Sylvia and Campion. Also the structural plan itself, unlike that in *Some Do Not* which is to some extent a prologue, is inherently dramatic, the material falling into the three major divisions of the night-long scene wherein Tietjens struggles with the problems of dispatching the draft of Canadians to the front, the episode of the second night involving the relationship between Sylvia and Tietjens at the hotel and the ensuing fracas in her room, and the final protracted discussion between Tietjens and Campion a few hours later which concludes with the General's face-saving act of relieving Tietjens of his command at the base and sending him to a fighting regiment. Apparently in order to prevent slackness in this tripartite movement, Ford omits direct treatment of Sylvia's journey to the army camp and of the actual conflict between Tietjens and the other officers in her room, these happenings being accounted for only by flashback. The closely linked design never becomes rigid, however, since the underlying advance of related themes—in particular that concerned with the forwarding of the draft—provides lines of digression which are ultimately caught in with the central issues at the end of the book. In these respects *No More Parades*, by strict Impressionist standards, is the most perfectly shaped volume in the tetralogy and justly the one likely to appeal most immediately to a reader.

The suggestion in the book of a somewhat formalized dra-

matic pattern in three phases set over against a background
of seeming confusion and illogicality is, moreover, an acces-
sory to meaning, since the causal progression of the main seg-
ments of the story carries an overtone of fate which applies
both to the extinction of parade and to the removal of Tietjens
from the Victorian social order. From the critical moment
when he participates in the death of 09 Morgan by a drenching
in the man's blood and a consequent assumption of guilt,
Tietjens is subconsciously in resistance to the forces responsible for the war; and only the arrival of Sylvia as an agent of
civilian interference and malice is necessary to complete his
alienation both from her and from the society that she moves
in. During his dinner with her at the hotel Tietjens puzzles
and annoys Sylvia by fraternizing with the elderly and lower-
class Sergeant-Major Cowley, with whom Tietjens now shares
the soldier's fellowship of remembered deaths; but even before thus inciting Sylvia's capacity for reprisal, Tietjens has
made several gestures of opposition to the prevailing military
system, among them his permitting the young Canadian soldier on draft order to visit his mother in the town off limits.
Such violations of formality draw Tietjens into the net of fate
which delivers him first at the hotel to the trap rigged by Sylvia
and immediately afterwards to the judgment of Campion,
duped by Sylvia but also her defender under a class code.
As a commanding general Campion is the godhead of an Imperial regime and thus descends fully clothed in emblems of
power upon Tietjens, the offender waiting sentence:

> A shadow—the shadow of the General Officer Command-
> ing in Chief—falling across the bar of light that the sunlight
> threw in at his open door seemed providentially to awaken
> Christopher Tietjens, who would have thought it extremely
> disagreeable to be found asleep by that officer. Very thin,
> graceful and gay with his scarlet gilt oak-leaves, and rib-
> bons, of which he had many, the general was stepping at-
> tentively over the sill of the door, talking backwards over

his shoulder, to someone outside. So, in the old days, Gods had descended.[30]

As "the apotheosis of the Regular Soldier" and with his clipped Sandhurst manner and Boer War reminiscences, Campion wields authority in the last great Victorian war. But eminent late Victorian though he is, the General, while still "radiating glory," reminds Tietjens of "an old apple inside a damascened helmet"; and making, like Sylvia, his final main appearance in *No More Parades*, he embodies a passing world and all of its spirit of parade. His last scene with Tietjens is, in its Impressionist power of multiple suggestion, one of the high points of the tetralogy; for here the Victorian father and god must not only condemn to seeming death the son whose predicament he cannot understand but also in doing so confront the already irreparable split in the order that they are both defending. In his bewilderment and feeling of remorse in casting off a member of the Groby family with whom he has had a lifelong friendship, Campion is in one light pathetic; yet Ford also endows him with the traits of subterfuge and cunning so often attributed in the novels to the Victorian generation, and it is not wholly clear in how far Campion's motives in disposing of Tietjens have for influence a private desire to be rid of an embarrassing hindrance to the General's social and political reputation and hopes. Campion, in any case, is perhaps the most ambiguous personage in the tetralogy with a veiled personal history touched on only through occasional hints, as may be considered fitting to a spurious godhead. Although evidently not married, he has a son, mentioned only once,[31] and, in *The Last Post*, a mistress bearing the name, whether by chance or intent, of the Colonel commanding Tietjens' battalion in the front line. Conceivably, in so closely knit an upper-class group, the father of Perowne, Sylvia's former lover, Campion, while actually godfather to Tietjens, has been reputed in some quarters the latter's actual father; and Ford's innuendo through much of the tetralogy en-

courages the supposition that the two men are in some way
blood kin, a device that further implicates Tietjens in the Victorian moral duplicity which he rejects even in submitting to
Campion's baffled notions of justice:

> Military operations sweep on. But my problem will remain
> the same whether I'm here or not. For it's insoluble. It's
> the whole problem of the relations of the sexes.
> The general said:
> "Good God! . . ."
> Tietjens said:
> "No, sir, I've not gone off my chump. That's my problem!
> . . . But I'm a fool to talk so much. . . . It's because I
> don't know what to say."
> The general sat staring at the tablecloth: his face was
> suffused with blood. He had the appearance of a man in
> monstrous ill-humor. He said:
> "You had better say what you want to say. What the devil
> do you mean? . . . What's this all about? . . ."
> Tietjens said:
> "I'm enormously sorry, sir. It's difficult to make myself
> plain." [32]

From his failure to comprehend in Tietjens' plight the nature
of the forces undermining the world he defends—a situation
not unlike that between Lingard and Willems in Conrad's
An Outcast of the Islands—Campion turns away with a certain relief to his formal inspection of the camp cook-houses,
a customary routine that he can understand. Among regular
soldiers and in professional surroundings "like a cathedral's
nave," he is once again the god, fully assured in confronting
petty deceptions that are part of an old army ritual. Yet the
inspection, taking up the main theme of the novel, is parade
become obsolescent and ending ". . . like the sudden burst-
ing out of the regimental quick-step, as after a funeral with
military honours the band and drums march away, back to
barracks." [33] The real war progresses, without ceremony but

to the credit of Tietjens and the lower ranks, in the final clear-
ance of the replacement draft to the forward line.

In typically Impressionist manner each novel in the tetralogy
bears a structural form proper to the single effect that the
particular unit seeks to impart; and from this standpoint *No
More Parades*, intricately designed in order to project an
image of the conflicting forces present in modern war at full
tide, differs from the apparently simpler design of the third
volume, *A Man Could Stand Up—*. In the latter, intentionally
less dramatic in rhythm and consequently looser in arrangement, the shift from the opening scene on Armistice Day,
which centers in Val Wannop's reactions at the girl's school
in London, back to a day on the Western Front several months
earlier and the point of view of Tietjens awaiting a German attack and, finally, back once again to the Armistice setting and
the joining of Val and Tietjens establishes an interrupted forward movement which is appropriate to the atmosphere of
historical irony. By delaying until the middle of the novel
any further reference to war action in itself, Ford once again
notes the merely contributory function of military events in
the whole record of critical social change over a decade as well
as the increasing remoteness of conventionally heroic exploits
from the concerns of modern life. In *A Man Could Stand Up*
—the last battle of an exhausted army is far distant from the
hysterical effort of a civilian world to return to its customary
habits, even though the collapse of Victorian authority stands
plainly marked at the outset of the novel in Val's rebellious
escape not only from the moral warnings of her headmistress
but also from the Gothic surroundings of the school itself. The
war ends devoid of glory, and the novel concludes on no scene
of military triumph. Even the solemn moment of the Armistice
with its ceremonial guns and whistles occurs while Val is
hurrying to answer a telephone call from Mrs. Duchemin who
is still scheming against Tietjens.

The recurrence of frantic telephoning throughout the book
—in particular the long message from Mrs. Wannop in which

she attempts to deter Val and Tietjens from living together "maritally" [34]—indicates not only the excited atmosphere of the Armistice declaration but also the futile effort of the Victorian generation to retain the prestige held by them still confidently in *Some Do Not*. Characteristically, persons like Mrs. Duchemin and even the more scrupulous Mrs. Wannop resort with Victorian guile to the telephone that enables them to screen themselves and to compel attention; but the distance that protects them also muffles their voices which recede in the din of a new era uncertain of the future but no longer responsive to the past. To some extent, therefore, the plainer lines of the novel contrast with the crowded stage of *Some Do Not;* and the points of view are rightly those of Val and Tietjens, the characters most active in the war and hence most representative of a reasoned denial of Victorian standards in the spirit of individual freedom and integrity as intimated in the title, *A Man Could Stand Up—*. In opposition, however, to the anarchic turbulence of the Armistice crowds, the lovers choose a personal discipline as austere as the meagre furnishings that Tietjens has installed in his former Gray's Inn rooms and as little governed by secrecy as the open hospitality of Tietjens to his former comrades in the informal gathering at the end of the novel. As against the sinuous filaments of intrigue that encircled Val and Tietjens in *Some Do Not*, the background of their new relationship in *A Man Could Stand Up—* has an air of classical simplicity and restraint which Ford expertly suggests in moving Val, who feels identified with Alcestis, away from the Victorian school and the street mobs and into the quiet eighteenth-century square to which Tietjens has returned:

Coming into the Square was like being suddenly dead, it was so silent and so still to one so lately jostled by the innumerable crowd and deafened by unceasing shouts. The shouting had continued for so long that it had assumed the appearance of being a solid and unvarying thing: like life.

So the silence appeared like Death; and now she had death
in her heart. She was going to confront a madman in a
stripped house. And the empty house stood in an empty
square all of whose houses were so eighteenth century and
silver-grey and rigid and suave that they ought all to be
empty too and contain dead, mad men.[35]

What Val finds on meeting Tietjens is, however, neither the
madness and death that belong to Victorianism and the war
but the contemplative virtues which Tietjens has adopted to
counteract his experience of death at the front. For the purpose, therefore, of justifying this development in his outlook
without having to mar the intensity of the closing scenes with
explanatory material, Ford takes advantage of the long middle
section of the book and its trench setting in order to render
the growth of Tietjens' convictions in the midst of circumstances most conducive to such thinking. Simply in itself this
part of the novel is a superb example of purely Impressionist
writing; for within the confines of an ordinary day during
the British retreat of 1918 Ford manages to include reference
to nearly every aspect of the battle conditions of the Great
War—the flattened landscape, the varied types and sounds of
weapons, the construction of trenches, the tactics and equipment of infantry, the treatment of prisoners, the spread of in-
fluenza through the armies. Yet although the section is in
some measure condensed history made convincing by the
presence of an eyewitness, it has the selectivity and suppleness
of fiction as demonstrated in the minimal use of technical
jargon and the reflection of events in the particular mental
field of the observer, Tietjens, which makes possible the
copious employment of anecdote and digression. Faithful to
his conception of the true nature of modern war, Ford puts
little emphasis on the isolated instances of direct physical injury but concentrates instead upon the barbarities of mechanized weapons, the dreariness of fatigue and apprehension,
and the ceaseless mental strain induced by petty annoyance.

Especially telling in the last respect is the incident, so veritably rendered, in which Tietjens listens to the embittered protest of his colonel, an excellent combat officer broken by the worries of line service, muddle, debt, and disease:

> He looked at Tietjens with infuriated eyes. "Look here you!" he said. "You're an educated man. . . . What's the worst thing about this war? What's the *worst* thing? Tell me that!" His chest began to heave. "It's that they won't let us alone. Never! Not one of us! If they'd let us alone we could fight. But never. . . . No one! It's not only the beastly papers of the battalion, though I'm no good with papers. Never was and never shall be. . . . But it's the people at home. One's own people. God help us, you'd think that when a poor devil was in the trenches they'd let him alone. . . . Damn it: I've had solicitors' letters about family quarrels when I was in hospital. Imagine that! . . . Imagine it! I don't mean tradesmen's dunnings. But one's own people." [36]

Episodes like this are active factors in fixing Tietjens' resolve to quit his own class, to join the company of those whom the war has not profited, and to owe allegiance only to the English land itself and to a past tradition rooted in the seventeenth century. In this novel his sympathy with men who are courageous regardless of rank or nationality, like the private soldier, Eisenstein, or the young Portuguese lieutenant, Aranjuez, seems much more pronounced than in *No More Parades;* and his turn at the close of the war front section from the rebuke given him by Campion to solicitude for the wounded Aranjuez is clearly significant. His gain in strength of character comes through association with the queerly assorted but undaunted Cockneys of his line company, who in their cheerful impudence carry something of the old spirit of Agincourt into the desperate last hours of a Victorian war. Not only here but also in the brilliantly conceived party scene in Tietjens' rooms which ends the novel Ford grants to a declining order its moments of individual heroism.

Writing so inspired as that forming the conclusion of *A Man Could Stand Up*— provides strong evidence for Douglas Goldring's claim that Ford would have preferred to end the novel sequence at this point with its implied reversal of all the Victorian habits in force in *Some Do Not*. Adding *The Last Post* to complete the tetralogy may have been to Ford rather an onerous task, as the occasional irritability in his dedicatory letter suggests, even though as an individual work the novel displays his usual intelligence and scrupulous craftsmanship. Despite the sense of freshened vision imparted by assigning the chief point of view to Mark Tietjens, Christopher's brother, *The Last Post* does not substantially deepen the reader's understanding of familiar characters like Campion, Sylvia, Val, or Mrs. Duchemin; and although among the people introduced here for the first time, Marie Léonie, Mark's French wife and former mistress, is a strong and partially comic figure, some of the other newcomers—in particular Sylvia's son, Michael, and the burlesqued American, Mrs. de Bray Pape—are uninteresting, to some extent, no doubt, because of their absence from the earlier sections of the tetralogy. Ford's predicament here seems to have been one that, as he implies in his dedicatory letter, an Impressionist could only face with repugnance —the need to supply his work with an ending; and whereas Ford expertly disguises the matter, mainly by locating his full close in the death of Mark while permitting the more important Christopher to live on in a continuing Affair, he is clearly for once compelled to humble himself to Thackeray and to dispose of loose ends left on his hands by his choice of the tetralogical form, among these principally the removal of ordinary doubts like those connected with the circumstances of the death of Mr. Tietjens or the situation of the child born to Christopher and Sylvia in *Some Do Not*. This process of house cleaning undoubtedly deprives *The Last Post* of some of the vitality of the earlier volumes, and the ensuing flatness does much to validate the Impressionist defense of the single-book novel.

In spite, however, of these defects *The Last Post* is, in its own right, a work proper to the general scheme of the tetralogy and in many places profoundly moving, especially in the scene of Mark's reflections at the moment of death. The meditative quality of the novel in its relation to a character who is both head of the Tietjens family and sufficiently detached from smaller conflicts to review the whole course of the past helps to reaffirm the historical scope of the tetralogy; and even though Mark's recollections frequently drift into mere factual unraveling, Ford takes care to offset any danger of slackened tempo by furnishing a time plan restricted to a few hours of Mark's last day of life and with the steadily mounting *progression d'effet* which culminates in both the final confrontation of Sylvia and Val and the death of Mark. But the main achievement of *The Last Post* is that which distinguishes the other units of the entire work in its adherence to Impressionist method: the creation of a unified sense of the period to which the book refers. As the title indicates, *The Last Post* is an impression of the aftermath of war, so that its prevailing mood is in some measure one of weariness and its tone elegiac. After the stir and tension of the preceding volumes the range narrows to the level of the only occasionally interrupted musings of a single character, immobilized like Mr. Eliot's Gerontion and withdrawn completely from the affairs of a world which has been repudiated in contempt. As often in his work, moreover, Ford enhances the period impression by investing the atmosphere of the novel with reflections of cultural taste in the 1920's. Thus Marie Léonie's amusing resentment against Tietjens and Val for their failure to appreciate the romantic classicism of her favorite sculptor, Casimir-Bar, whose productions like *Thetis informing Neptune of the death of a son-in-law* she regards as the finest display of pathos and passion, offers an aesthetic counterbalance to the almost Egyptian immobility of Mark with its hint of the mystery of life in death so frequently celebrated in postwar art.

In the death of Mark, who has been stricken into an obstinately willed paralysis by what he considers England's betrayal of her own cause and of her war dead, Ford brings to an ironic but dignified conclusion his leading theme of the passing of an older national spirit with roots deeper than Victorianism. That Mark at the end should hold the center of the stage is understandable, since, eccentric in a different manner from his brother, he has typically English habits of life and thought that cause Marie Léonie to picture him as the Continental image of ". . . the English Milor with *le spleen.*" [37] With Mark, too, the original Tietjens line, severed by the mutual rejection by the brothers of the Groby inheritance, reaches its close; and Ford gives weight to the event by endowing Mark with a shadow of kingship alluded to in Marie Léonie's instinctive view of him as the Jove or Jupiter of the family group.[38] From this standpoint it follows that the immediate agent in his death should be Sylvia, who plays to the end her role of Nemesis to the family even while haunted herself by the memory of Father Consett and the faith which, though never congenial to the Tietjens clan, prevents her at the last from harming Val's unborn child. Although she is again in character in effecting the uprooting of the Groby Great Tree, a symbol of family and Empire, her act does not greatly disturb Mark who with the clairvoyance of imminent death recognizes the cedar as malign and not really indigenous to English soil. In his own way Mark in dying appears to dismiss all of history and its violence which Christopher brings home sharply in reporting the destruction of Groby:

> Christopher was at the foot of his bed. Holding a bicycle and a lump of wood. Aromatic wood: a chunk sawn from a tree. His face was white: his eyes stuck out. Blue pebbles. He gazed at his brother and said:
> "Half Groby wall is down. Your bedroom's wrecked. I found your case of sea-birds thrown on a rubble-heap."
> It was as well that one's services were unforgettable! [39]

The muted closing scene with its pathos of hard affection and the restrained emotion of the English temperament raises *The*

Last Post to equality with the finest effects in the tetralogy as a whole. Although Mark's death logically concludes Ford's theme of the dissolution of the Tory class, the novel really ends not only with the Impressionist note of life continuing in its ordinary way but also with a further implication of continuance in a more symbolic key. The sudden personal appearance of Christopher for the first time at Mark's deathbed is like a portent emphasized shortly afterwards by Mark's clasping of the hand of Val. Through Christopher and the altered way of life that he desires for his coming child, Mark's quality of kingship promises renewal in some fashion; and in this respect *The Last Post* contains intimations of the trend in Ford's work in its later and final phase.

Bringing Mark Tietjens to the foreground in *The Last Post* made necessary Ford's relegating Christopher to an off-stage role until his direct entry in the closing scene; and whereas his absence does effectively provide a kind of dramatic counterpoint to Mark's brooding upon their relationship, it is also possible that Ford left Christopher in abeyance partly because the latter's postwar occupation as country old furniture dealer did not altogether represent a sufficiently positive image of his change in personal belief. In his dedication to *No More Parades* Ford had promised to show Christopher ". . . in process of being re-constructed"; and although this had been done in the war front section of *A Man Could Stand Up—*, Ford in the meantime may have reached other or fuller private conclusions regarding the exact nature of reconstruction. Significantly, in any event, he attached to *No Enemy*, which appeared the year after *The Last Post* in 1929, the subtitle, "A Tale of Reconstruction," and turned in this book, perhaps with some feeling of relief, from the logic of fictional narrative to a work freer in form and nearer belles-lettres in its mingling of stylistic virtuosity and submerged argument. Holding a place of its own in the body of Ford's work, and one of his most perfectly written productions, *No Enemy* also remains among those books—like Hemingway's *Death in the After-*

noon or Orwell's *Down and Out in Paris and London*—which resist formal classification but even in that respect belong to a characteristic trend in the literature of the present century.

In nearest affiliation, however, *No Enemy* relates to such independent essays in the Impressionist mode as James's *The American Scene,* which Ford had recognized for its possession of extra-dimensional qualities, and, still more pertinently, to Conrad's *The Mirror of the Sea,* which in a similar way combines credo with a concern for distinction in style. Although *No Enemy* develops the warnings in the tetralogy against luxurious habits and again recommends frugal and contemplative virtues as a means of avoiding war, it does so not only with an air of new found assurance perhaps deriving from Ford's own postwar experiment in rural small farming but also with one of more determined insistence that a model of individual hand production to ensure food economy—hereafter one of Ford's dominant ideas—might save the world. In one respect, therefore, *No Enemy* is a "long lay sermon"; [40] yet the didactic element keeps indirect, for one thing, by Ford's use of an invented main figure—Gringoire, the Gallophile veteran and expert cook as well as poet whose heart has been changed by the war—and for another, by the adoption of a narrative method seemingly as impromptu as Gringoire's recipe for curry:

> Oh, you take any old thing—tinned lobster, bully beef, cold mutton. . . . And of course you fry. . . But curry powder is good for any dish. . . . Because of the garlic in it. . . . And which curry are you talking about? There are hundreds. The only thing that unites them is that the curry must be cooked. Don't you understand? The curry— the powder—itself must be cooked. For hours and hours. Do you see? No, you don't see. How can I remember what I put into the curry for your friend? Any old thing. . . .[41]

From what begins as seemingly no more than a casual discourse on the art of cookery between Gringoire in his rural cottage and his visiting friend "the compiler," both veterans of the war and both serving as dramatic versions of Ford's experience and belief, Ford as master literary cook creates a work intricate in its interweaving of themes yet so flexible in structure by reason of the constant play of time shift, anecdote, and digression that, rather than being exhorted, the reader moves through a series of rendered episodes that win his assent by emotional persuasion and a feeling of direct involvement. In this light *No Enemy* is one of the ripest examples of Impressionist strategy and of a language devised to eliminate abstraction, one of Ford's aims being to leave a record of the war which might defy time in that the account would consist not in material description of specific data but in the impressions of a sensitive observer, the hope being that ". . . the record of his emotions might well interest people who have such memories still vivid within them." [42] Memory, varied war reminiscence, is, consequently, the method of the book, but memory comprised largely of moments of vivid sensory awareness taking shape in advance of the word labeling and so hardening them into sterile concepts:

> Then, indeed as the eye was to look into the pellucid sky, there became visible a number—some one counted fourteen—of tiny, shining globes. They appeared to be globes, because there was a fresh wind blowing straight from them and they turned end on. So, but slowly and incessantly heaving, did the immense one close at hand; a spider's network of cordage went with its movements. Tiny and incredibly pretty, like films of gold dust floating in blue water and like peach blossom leaves—yes, incredibly pretty in the sunlight—airplanes were there. Because the—just as pretty —little mushrooms that existed suddenly in the sky, beside the sunlit dragonflies and peach blossoms, were purely white, one officer said:
> "Hun planes!" [43]

As always in Impressionist writing at its best, the foregoing passage carries the significance of the book in its sensory details; for by tabbing the aerial wonder with an artificial term of hatred and thus canceling the moment of pure vision, the watching officer betrays what to Ford is the sorriest injury of war—the mental strain and bitterness, largely a product of mechanized hostilities, which deprive men of the opportunity for contemplative vision that in normal conditions supplies a basis for peace both within the individual and in common human relationships. In this sense the title of the book, *No Enemy*, offers a dual meaning, not simply the obvious post-war assertion of anti-national spirit but also the implied protest, as in the Tietjens tetralogy, against the concealed adversary of scientific weapons which strike from afar and thus cause universal sickness of mind by contrast with their relatively limited power of sheer physical destruction. In keeping with this theme, *No Enemy* is to a great extent a rendering of memory under the weight of emotional pressure, the time-shift method of *The Good Soldier* being employed again to emphasize the dislocation of visual focus and stability experienced by Gringoire: "During the four years that the consciousness of the war lasted, he had noticed only four landscapes and birds only once—to know that he was noticing them—for themselves." [44] By this confession Ford provides at least one clue to the ensuing decline in prewar and Ruskin-inspired taste for visual observation as a cultural aim.

Complementing the theme of mental unrest is the motif growing firmer as *No Enemy* advances—the need for attainment of serenity through the gaining of a form of sanctuary which engages Gringoire's thought during the great battles of the war and which he attains through his self-sufficient manner of country living upon the land that he has learned to value in proportion to the destruction visited upon it. Fixing his confidence in serenity are his wartime encounters with persons so thoroughly endowed with this trait that no external

afflictions can deprive them of it, people as diverse as the
sculptor, Henri Gaudier; [45] the old Tommy of the Lincolns; [46]
the Canadian, Lieutenant Morgan; [47] and the stoical Belgian
woman, Rosalie Prudent.[48] In this remarkable collection of
informal sketches of men and women possessing simple dignity without official honors Ford not only gave concrete support to his guiding theme but also reiterated the sympathy
demonstrated in the Tietjens novels for people seeking nothing for themselves but exhibiting qualities of calm endurance
of hardship.

These lessons Gringoire brings to his postwar existence, a
lived discipline rather than a theory, which by its devotion
to subsistence farming, fine craftsmanship, the cultivation of
friendship, and—as a unifying virtue—the art of cookery as
a pursuit furthest removed from the barbarities of war and
industrialism supplies a plan according to which persons with
small incomes may learn ". . . how to lead graceful, poetic
and pleasant lives and so to save the world." [49] Properly, therefore, No Enemy is essentially a contemplative book, pastoral
in setting, which ends on the peaceful note, crowned by a
Spenserian echo, of Gringoire and his friends gathering for
an evening meal interspersed with poetry, a scene that gathers
in the book's central themes of frugality and human concord in
a single concrete impression. In no other work does Ford
achieve quite the same graceful integration of materials apparently so incongruous as curry recipes and memories of
soldiering. On this account No Enemy should stand with a
book like The Mirror of the Sea as, in final effect, an almost
pure demonstration of Impressionist prose and one that, in
its rhythms of memory, outlasts its temporal bearings and
continues to appeal to a taste for this art of overtone. The argumentative purpose is everywhere kept in leash to aesthetic
considerations, perhaps too subdued a balance today for
those who demand outright and unmixed protest.

With No Enemy, nevertheless, Ford quietly set down his
repudiation of the barbarism arising from the moment when

the German hordes crossed the Belgian frontier and attempted to prescribe a remedy for the mind harassed by the strains of the ensuing conflict; and in this respect the book is not only his final word upon the war itself but also a fitting sequel to the prolonged analysis and depiction of the collapse of a society which he had undertaken in the Tietjens tetralogy. In breadth of aim and scope the latter work must be regarded as the greatest of Ford's achievements, the fullest expression of his talents as a fictional historian, despite the fact of its temporal restrictions and late Victorian elements. In its avoidance of the note of passive suffering condemned by Yeats, the tetralogy possesses the mature outlook absent from so much war writing contemporary with it; and no other novel of that time or later explores more profoundly the social and psychological roots of cultural disorder which are of deeper concern than extended accounts of the slaughter of inexperienced youth. With these novels Ford came to an understanding of the claims of common human nature which surpasses the sometimes peevish satire of his earlier work and which finds utterance in the withdrawal of Tietjens from a world of power and intrigue and over to the company of men without class or country.

Evidently, however, Ford did not care to rest with the somewhat uncertain view of individual reconstruction that he ascribed to Tietjens at the close of the tetralogy, so that he allowed himself the more complete and positive affirmation of personal belief put forward in *No Enemy*, which perhaps for that reason seems a book less evasive than *The Last Post*. From *No Enemy* with its increasing appreciation of the Gallic virtues upheld by Gringoire and its tentative hints at a new basis for communal relationship within even a restricted orbit, Ford had, in any case, reached a turning point anticipating the novels of his last phase in the 1930's.

Chapter IX

Mythical Landscape: The Late Novels

THE PHYSICAL TRIBULATIONS of gas and shell-shock notwithstanding, Ford survived the Great War hardened, like Christopher Tietjens, in character and purpose; and much can be said to favor the opinion of Douglas Goldring that Ford's real literary strength came with the war and found best expression in the continued productivity of his later years with its varied output of fiction, memoirs, and critical and discursive writing in such works as *Great Trade Route* (1937), *Provence* (1938), and *The March of Literature* (1939). Whether or not due to active soldiering or the rout of the late Victorian world against which he had chafed in his youth, Ford gained maturity in release from the fidgeting over the dilemma of art and action which had earlier distracted him; and for all of its eccentricities, his writing during the 1930's and up to his death in 1939—an event which occurred with his work on a novel still in progress—has the assurance of a man exploring conviction and settled in the acceptance of his literary calling. No doubt the fact that he had proved himself capable of major performance in the Tietjens tetralogy gave Ford renewed confidence; but he had thriven, too, and as always in the atmosphere of avant-garde bustle, in the Montparnasse circles of the 1920's and on the prestige and excitement of the *transatlantic review* venture, acquaintance with innovators like Joyce, and grooming of the young writers from America. Besides helping to direct "L'Epoque Ford Madox Ford," he benefited himself from study of the postwar currents in taste and experiment, as the occasional echoes of Joyce and Eliot in the tetralogy indicate; and that he had assimilated the waste land outlook well before he made his familiarity with it

248

obvious in 1934 in the fictional autobiography, *It Was the Nightingale,* may be taken for granted.

By thus enlisting with the postwar literary forces, and through his own immersion in the process of Victorian breakdown, Ford moved inevitably from his earlier stand of detached historian to that of proponent of remedies for the illness of contemporary civilization, an impulse that became overmastering as he neared the age of sixty and lived in apprehension of general cultural collapse,[1] though its rise towards fuller statement may be seen clearly enough in *No Enemy.* This enterprise led to no abandonment of the historian's function which was still essential to social and cultural diagnosis. Nor did it mean discarding Impressionist method, since Ford held faithful to his adopted theories despite sociological trends in literature of the 1930's, though he did relinquish much of the Jamesian urbanity that he had cultivated in his Edwardian phase and introduced notes of the violent and sinister that recall Dostoevski or the Conrad of *Under Western Eyes* and that better accord with the darkening era of world depression and fascism reflected in the novels of such near adherents to his literary creed as Graham Greene and Faulkner. But Ford's preoccupation with the shaping of personal belief into something more tangible than the hints contained in early books like *Mr. Apollo* and *Ladies Whose Bright Eyes,* or even the temporary expedient suggested by the pastoralism of *No Enemy,* and with the formulating of schemes for the repair of Western civilization grows steadily into its central place in such semididactic works of his later years as *Provence* and *Great Trade Route.* In a purely fictional context this concern takes creative form in the related novels, *The Rash Act* (1933) and *Henry for Hugh* (1934), and the curious and elusive partly detective story, *Vive Le Roy* (1937), books in which the historian yields largely to the maker of a myth with features unique in the body of contemporary literature. By the 1930's, therefore, Ford had joined in the quest of that notable band of desert travelers, dismayed by the toppling of Christian culture and seeking roothold, that included Yeats, Eliot, Lawrence, Huxley, and had taken his own path among divergent roads.

While, then, essentially Impressionistic in manner, Ford's late novels display his customary adaptability to change in literary circumstance and fashion, most particularly in their employment of mythical elements as well as in their effort to incorporate the substance and tone of contemporary language and speech. But they are also notable for their broadened focus upon American scene and character, a more tolerant attitude of understanding towards such materials than Ford had shown in early novels like *An English Girl* or *The Good Soldier* and a fairer presentation of American types than he had offered in his war period books with such disagreeable caricatures as Senator Pappenheim in *The Marsden Case* and Mrs. de Bray Pape in *The Last Post*. His extensive use of American setting and foreground characters in all of his late fiction from *When the Wicked Man* through *Vive Le Roy* may be explained in part, no doubt, as a bid for an American audience, since he had lost touch with the English public but had enjoyed a good sale of *The Last Post* immediately upon its publication in the United States.[2] Yet that his intentions could not have been entirely mercenary seems evident from the late novels where he is no more disposed than ever to flatter the ways and institutions of a society now far advanced, by his measure, in the vices of industrialism and canned food, a society, moreover, that he had not hesitated to warn (in his 1927 volume of personal commentary, *New York is not America*) against leanings to Prussianism in bullying over the European debt. From the beginning of his career, and through his desire to extend the international mode in fiction, he had been steadily if intermittently attentive to American characteristics and developments; and his close association in the Paris of the 1920's with young American artists and his enthusiastic view of their promise in all likelihood not only refreshed his critical interest in the United States but also stimulated his reflection on its cultural possibilities. In his novels of the 1930's, in any event, the mythical landscape tends to embrace the polarities of France and America, even as his personal life came to establish itself between those two regions.

Except for the fact that Ford had been cognizant of the increasing power of America in the international scheme during the early years of the century and had questioned its potential role in *An English Girl* in 1907, he approaches the subject in a different way in his late novels. Although still manifesting a European disdain for the provincialism and crudities of American life, his postwar attitude takes for self-evident the now dominant position of America in what survives of Western civilization and thus becomes less patronizing, more disposed to arrive at understanding of the real nature of the past, so that he dispenses with the hesitance to explore beyond external impressions that he had shown in *An English Girl*. Quite clearly, in fact, he undertakes in the 1930's to turn from his previous commitment as analyst and critic of the English people to a similar task with respect to America; and in doing so he reveals in an illuminating way both the limitations and resources of his Impressionism as a tool for the novelist-historian.

In accordance with the assumptions of this doctrine, Ford is often at fault in matters of specific detail, in which department he betrays the restricted knowledge of the outsider or of the writer dependent for general information on books of social summary like Dorothy Dudley's *Dreiser and the Land of the Free*. His attempt, for example, to portray American adolescents in *When the Wicked Man* is plainly weak, even though he had never at any time been much attracted to child characters. Yet with respect to what he regarded as the principal aim of the Impressionist novel, not documentation but the shaping of a single and imaginative vision of a selected milieu, Ford often wins assent for his impression of America sheerly by the strength of his literary intelligence and intuition, his customary sensitiveness to atmosphere and to the signs of historical disturbance or crisis, an ability by which he was able to hold his ground against many of those better provided with a store of facts. In the end, furthermore, his concern is not with local events but with the placement of America within the large scale cultural map that to the end of his life he was striving to design, for which reason in the late novels American scene and character tend increasingly to occupy an orbit which includes that part of the continent of Europe which Ford thought worth salvaging from the waste land. The rescue of an "ersatz-civilization"[3] from further ruin makes necessary the creation of a bond between America, as the new leader of Anglo-Saxondom, and the remaining vestiges of a Provençal-Mediterranean tradition.

Although incentives to this plan for a reconstructed and unified culture certainly at times were present in Ford early in his career and now and again affected the themes of his novels, they did not become urgent until he had seen and grasped the consequences of the war; and the clearest proof of his personal understanding of the modern sexual-religious dilemma lies in the Tietjens tetralogy with its persistent emphasis upon the tortured relationship between Sylvia and Christopher. The problem that he confronted was that of the great moderns generally, but that the solution which he looked for came nearer to beliefs like those of Yeats and Lawrence than to the convictions of Eliot may be assumed from his statement as late as 1938 in *Provence:* "Faith, in short, died after the war—every sort of Faith and it is time to get back to life."[4] At the close of the tetralogy the faith adopted by Tietjens has no relevance to existing society, and the pastoralism of *No Enemy* supposes an independent communal association apart from any church, so that Ford appears to have been as firmly persuaded as Shaw or Wilfred Owen of the failure of institutional religion:

And so the whole Western world once the war was finished plunged into a sort of Albigensism. . . . What else could it do, the parallel being so very exact? . . . For the appalled soldiery saw all the churches of the world plunge into that hellish struggle with the enthusiasm of school boys at a rat hunt. Not a pulpit thundered that if you slay your fellow man your forehead will bear the brand of Cain. Great lights of the churches plunged into the whirlpool it-self—and not armed only with maces, either. . . .[5]

The Albigensian reference, though it had sometimes oc-curred in statements by Ford when young and had perhaps been made familiar to him through his father's study of the troubadours, develops in his last years into a fixed analogy be-tween the modern world depressed by war and the old culture of Provence disrupted by the massacre which had rooted out the gentle heretics. By the same measure he comes to assert the need for a recovery of original Provençal virtues, these be-ing associated in his mind with qualities of art and a spirit of graceful conduct somewhat like Gringoire's individual stand-ard in *No Enemy*, this opinion having evolved seemingly from his prewar idea of a basic antagonism in civilization due to the incompatibility of barbaric "Nordic" habits and the amenities of the Mediterranean South. Although this antith-esis hovers in the background of *The Good Soldier*, it acquires solid dimensions with Ford after the war, which he regarded as a culminating riot of Nordic savagery, motivated by a Prussian temper that he by no means charged to the Germans alone or as a people and leaving for its aftermath a world doomed to the Nordic tyranny of business power and scientific weapons. Common to its time as this attitude may be, it assumes in Ford an independent aspect through ex-pression in the terms peculiar to his imaginative outlook. For him the war had been another devastation of Provence and the ensuing world torpor a recurrence of Albigensian despair:

As it is we are in a world of Albigenses. I do not think it is exaggerating to say that the proper man to-day—the man

of some culture and reflection believes that there are two
first principles, forgets the Divine Birth of the Saviour, regards the rest of the Christian creeds, if with affection, yet
as legends having no relation with the life of the day. He
believes in the necessity for personal and mental purity,
like the Cathartes; in the necessity for the reduction of the
population; in the absolute sinfulness of wars and in the
right to suicide. . . . His religion in fact, like that of the
gentle people who were destroyed at the battle of Mount
Muret is rather one of negation than of any positiveness at
all. It is a product of doubt coming after immense public
catastrophe in which, as he sees it, all his leaders have been
found wanting—of a doubt and languour that distinguish at
once the populations of London as of New York.[6]

If Ford here merely presents his own description of the
waste land state, his chart for reclamation of the dismembered
territory follows original lines and is typically cultural rather
than political. As set forth in *Great Trade Route,* published
in the same year as Ford's last novel, the proposal is to restore a lost circuit of civilized commerce over a road steering
away from the Nordic area of swamps and marshes and in
this way to outlaw the tradition of the sword by reviving the
free movement of peaceful traders or merchants carrying along
the latitude of Washington, Constantinople, Samarkand, and
Peking wares beneficial to culture, the products of graceful leisure and the arts.[7] Such a retracing of the buried
thoroughfares of a world civilization might conduce to the
unburdening of the mind that stands for one of the features of
Provence:

> For it is certain that I think that the only things that can
> save the world are a certain Mediterranean brand of slack-
> ing off in every department of life—a slacking off in every-
> thing from conscious rectitude and its heathen sense of
> acquisitiveness to the sense of efficiency and the hours of
> labour worked. So that it would be dreadful if at the end of
> great labours and my wanderings I should find myself lik-

ing the New England Conscience or States which at present
seem to me to be the most detestable things in the world
and the source of all our present evils.[8]

In itself a figure of considerable charm, the Great Road likewise belongs to the time when literary visions of a return to
cultural unity could produce symbolic forms as different as
the Byzantium of Yeats and the dark god community of Lawrence. To Yeats, perhaps, Ford stands closer than to Lawrence,
since Ford's desire is for an urbane and harmonious culture
grounded in civilized tradition and allowing for commerce
between West and East. Nothing in his outlook suggests a
yearning after pre-mental sources of vitality, although he
shares with both Yeats and Lawrence the hope for a change
and freshening of the rhythm of existence, a revival of the
dance as image of joy:

> Thus arose and spread throughout the world the great
> road and the great civilisations of that Road. So that today
> we still await the second coming of Arthur and his knights
> who were their vassals . . . or of Christ who, like their own
> Confucius, gathered together their traditions that still re-
> mained on a ruined Road, and made them into a perdurable
> book. They had carried with them ivory, apes, peacocks, per-
> fumes; and perhaps more than anything they evangelised
> with the dance. For it was not their younger sons, dipso-
> maniacs, criminals and the degenerate that they sent to
> those people to stay with them but their gravest and most
> erudite dancers, who were their priests. This cult was one
> of joy—and rhythm.[9]

Ford's Trader, therefore, as purveyor of the means of enjoyment and art, displaces the soldier and the priest—participants in the Nordic massacre of the War—in assuming the
leadership of a cult of pleasure connected with the forgotten
basis of civilized life. Such a role, possibly, Tietjens approaches, since at the end of the tetralogy he is in his own way
a trader free of national ties and prejudice. In its recognition

of the merchant and of the place of Christianity within the tradition Ford's myth, too, has something in common with Eliot's in *The Waste Land,* both writers employing an inclusive symbol recalling sources of order prior to the Christian synthesis and Ford designating the Trader as precursor on the great route to Christ as well as Arthur. Through the myth Ford may well have resolved at last the religious perplexities that enter into early novels like *Mr. Apollo* and *Ladies Whose Bright Eyes,* where already he seeks to embody in some way the image of joy that he proclaims frankly in his work of the 1930's. That germinal properties for the ultimate Road symbol had thus been latent well before the myth began to appear in his late novels seems to indicate that the conception did not spring into being with the 1930's mood of resistance to national frontiers, even though Ford could not have been unsympathetic to the latter position. Being something of a selective internationalist, he concentrates upon the special hope of seeing English and American differences reconciled within an imagined Mediterranean environment. But his private tastes strongly color the ideal and render it in its own fashion exotic and somewhat exclusive, as though capable of realization only outside existing society and by those fortunate enough to obtain passage to the south of France.

Through the final phase of his work, consequently, Ford has in view a double purpose: from the historical side a demonstration of the Albigensian ills of contemporary life including the suicidal impulse so prominent in the late novels; from the remedial a piloting of the way towards the Great Road— these aims coalescing in his main accomplishment of the 1930's, the related books of *The Rash Act* and *Henry for Hugh.* The resulting effects are often bizarre, one of the more eccentric devices employed in all of the novels being that of double or mistaken identity frequently associated with a *doppelgänger* motif. Although Ford had experimented with the theme of mutation of personality in early books like *Ladies Whose Bright Eyes* and had made the confusion of identity between Ney and

Fréjus a central feature of *A Little Less Than Gods* in 1928, the pattern becomes so insistent in the fiction of the 1930's as to surround the latter with an aura of fantasy. The theme is, nevertheless, germane to the context of the novels and its two aspects complementary—the doubling or *doppelgänger* incidents expressing dramatically, and after the manner of Dostoevski or Conrad, the ailment of modern self-division; the exchange or fusion of identities representing a conception of the self transformed or unified through awareness of tradition, the latter state probably being connected with the myth of the cycle of kingship and so affording an answer to the problem of disrupted inheritance involved in works like *The Good Soldier* and the Tietjens sequence. Whereas this emphasis upon doubling seems a natural outgrowth of Ford's handling of self-recognition in such early novels as *A Call*, it is notable in the later work not only for its elaborated reference but also for the presentation of the issue not in terms of current psychology but instead in those of the legendary or occult. If the choice doubtless exhibits Ford's preference for the magical, as approximating the religious, rather than the scientific, of which, according to Goldring, Ford refused to believe a word,[10] it also conduced to technical advantage in the way of narrative interest and suspense.

Although *When the Wicked Man,* finished in 1930, is the first of the late novels to display a blend of the modern and the legendary, it alludes to the Provençal ideal, if at all, only by inference, the action being directly concerned with big business as a version of the Inferno. In comparison with Ford's depiction of anxiety and guilt a work like *Babbitt* appears comparatively genial; for if *When the Wicked Man* deals ostensibly with a world of Manhattan company directors, the latter reveal traits originating in the Nordic swamps and forests to the north of the Great Trade Route. Thus a salient fact behind the English descent and American career of the principal character, the middle-aged Joe Notterdam, acting head of the publishing house of Post, Gellatly, and Jeaffreson, is

his recognition of himself as "Nordic" in type ". . . heavyish
in build, light-haired, blue-grey-eyed and tall and high col-
oured." [11] Whether or not supplemented by an acquaintance
with Spengler, Ford's assignment of Nordic features to Notterdam's private history of violence and alcoholism appears
a development from the contrasting racial types in the early
novels towards the evolving Provençal theory, a progression
having something in common with the ideas of D. H. Lawrence in that the bearings are less racial than psychic and
cultural in their reliance upon points of coloring and physique.
Though tamed in some degree by the conventions of middle-
class affluence, Notterdam remains a barbarian—individual-
istic, irreligious, and superstitious like the society to which he
belongs—on which account his personal legend becomes associated with the blacker medievalism of such fabulous ante-
cedents as Nostradamus and Faust, (pp. 178, 309) from whom
he imagines himself as deriving in name and temperament,
and his fate entangled in a visitation of *doppelgängers* and
vampires. By this overtone of fantasy Ford perhaps intended
to attach to his New York setting incidental qualities of American romanticism suggestive of Hawthorne, Poe, and even
James. Yet in specific relation to Ford's Provençal outlook
Notterdam also descends from a general tradition of Nordic
romanticism, the banditry periling the Great Route.

At first sight the fact that Notterdam is by birth English
rather than American may encourage a supposition that Ford
wishes to avoid betraying weakness in the drawing of native
American character and milieu, and it is evident that he succeeds better when revealing Notterdam by a Jamesian method
of indirect narrative than when attempting to employ dialogue
for any of the characters. In the latter procedure Ford commits
errors in recording details of manners and speech from which
home-bred novelists like Hemingway or Fitzgerald would have
refrained by instinct. The book, moreover, often seems curiously insulated against the heavier cross-winds of real native
experience, an effect that results largely from the confinement

of the story to the sphere of book publication and professional authorship and that cannot be ascribed wholly to Impressionist liking for a restricted locale. Here Ford shows traces of the outsider's dependence upon inside knowledge at his command, though considerable allowance must be given to the point that in focusing upon the publishing business Ford was likewise advancing again his familiar enquiry regarding the status of art, and specifically literature, in a culture governed by commercialism. Measured, however, against the novel as a whole, which fails neither in technical competence nor in imaginative perception, such faults are minor; and beyond question *When the Wicked Man* is superior in depth and insight to *An English Girl*, Ford's early and hesitant venture in the rendering of American metropolitan life. From the melting-pot assumption which underlies *An English Girl* and attaches the book to the period of its writing to the unprovincial background of *When the Wicked Man* Ford accomplishes a stride in his own work comparable to the shift in American fiction from *Sister Carrie* to *The Great Gatsby*.

With local color, in fact, Ford has no further concern. Although he presents characters of contrasting national origin—Notterdam, americanized after a Dorset boyhood; Kratch, Notterdam's partner, who lives among imported Dutch relatives; Porter, the English novelist exiled by necessity in New York and parading his foreign mannerisms against the threat of failure—Ford is not merely commenting on the growing international flux within the metropolis but, more importantly, affirming the basic theme of all of his later writing: the loss of Western tradition generally and its accompaniment, the dissolution of personal identity which haunts Notterdam throughout the novel and aggravates his sense of homelessness. With an American setting Ford could stress the acuity of the problem, but that the question was ultimately postwar rather than simply American he indicated by employing characters not from established families but persons half-European and strongly reliant upon money for survival. In the novel, consequently, the familiar American subject of wealth enters in a significant way; but the central focus rests upon the muddle of cultural disunity and so brings Ford's environment closer to that of Gatsby than to the habitat of the Buchanans in Fitzgerald's work. His situation wholly different from that of Don Kelley in *An English Girl,* Notterdam, for instance, who has passed in the course of a lifetime through the stages of crude acquisitiveness to comparative luxury which Fitzgerald divided between the separate personalities of Cody and Gatsby, recognizes that his security depends not only upon what he can acquire and hold by a constant application of energy and cunning but even, in the last resort, upon aid from his multimillionaire partner, Kratch, who is, significantly, the real father of Notterdam's adopted children. Although less gaudy than Gatsby's Trimalchian palace, Notterdam's Long Island house is likewise a cultural farrago, including Assyrian bathrooms, and a medley of styles not unlike that which Ford had noted in expensive New York hotels in *An English Girl:*

> The house being an imitation of a Mexican adobe patio, the dining room had to be Spanish seventeenth century in character. The great reception room was eighteenth century, French; Elspeth's bedroom painfully *Nouvel Art,* with glass tops to all flat surfaces, blue squares, scarlet angles, turquoise and emerald spatterings. Even the chief bathroom was a hothouse arrangement of alabaster and porphyry. Having seen it once, he had never entered it again. (p. 110)

The "ersatz-civilization" here illustrated, and not money alone, is the primary cause of Notterdam's afflictions—his frigid relationship with his Scottish wife, Elspeth; his increasing alcoholism; his sense of loss of control and impending disaster. Since none of his supports, neither his business nor the family establishment that he has tried to create with the wife whom he counts as one of the spoils of his youthful marauding in San Francisco, affords permanence, Notterdam himself lacks certainty of selfhood, the whole novel being largely a continuing revelation to him of his divided nature: his private record as cuckold, cheat, lecher, and virtual murderer by contrast with his public image of prosperous efficiency. Underlying his discontent, in a novel with wandering for a governing motif, is his search for home that leads him in a circle, temporally and geographically, which at the end joins age and youth, New York and England, but never, seemingly, brings him within the circuit of the Great Route. In one of his strong but muted scenes, Ford illuminates Notterdam's homelessness by noting the latter's incapacity for sexual consummation with his young Southern mistress, Henrietta Felise, herself rootless in the city, until his car arrives in sight of the new house that he is building:

> Looking out past her he saw beyond a long pool a single light reflecting itself from the dark mass of a high-pitched house. There were elms. He could see that she had her hands over her eyes. He said:
> "Look! For God's sake look. . . . The gardener has a light. . . . You can see it on the swimming pool." He dropped the car window and fresh air came in and a very little more light.
> She was looking at him. Then she leaned erectly and deliberately forward, turning her head towards the house. (pp. 248–249)

Like that of Gatsby, moreover, Notterdam's milieu, lacking cultural pivot, merges readily with the underworld to which Notterdam must recognize himself as committed by reason of his youthful submission to the moral violence of the new continent over which he and his companion, Kratch, have wandered seeking plunder after their desertion from a British sailing ship. As his memory drifts back to this period from his present consciousness of the strain and futility of commercial ambition, Notterdam identifies himself with an American past of traditionless individualism of the kind that Fitzgerald had associated with Gatsby's benefactor, Dan Cody. Although in these scenes Ford's conception is slightly bookish, Notterdam and Kratch lacking the plausibility of the Duke and the Dauphin in *Huckleberry Finn,* his historical sense is as active as that of Fitzgerald:

> In the old days he had been accustomed to flatter himself that he could at any time take any Death Valley Liz, sentimentality and all, out of Kratch's very jaws. Then there would be blows, an estrangement for a month or more during which each, apart, would forlornly roam forlorn townships of the forlorner West. Then they would meet, ostensibly by accident, in a saloon, and, having wetted it, would, as often as not, go and buy the local paper. The one with the purchasing money became the editor and the other the local news reporter, each taking it in turns with the composing and machining. (p. 17)

A residual frontier myth thus lingers on in the mind of Notterdam long after he has adapted to the existence of a company executive and revives in his crisis of middle-age to provoke the question of what he has gained by his choice of the publisher's office. Ford here recognizes the romantic impulse at odds with American incomplete sophistication, the suppressed desire for physical action that impels the sick Kratch to carry with him to a company conference a trowel symbolic of his still unbroken attachment to the youth in which he had excelled as a bricklayer. (p. 6) The lifelong association of Notterdam and Kratch, even though based on antagonism, includes a certain romantic and emotional bond between men leagued for survival in conditions of relative lawlessness as well as a vestige of Nordic savagery in the predatory instincts of the Hollander and the Anglo-Saxon. The bond is, nevertheless, one between outlaws and becomes weaker in the more monotonous but equally traditionless system of metropolitan rivalry that has enabled Kratch to betray Notterdam secretly in the sexual field. Whereas both men appear to grope unconsciously for roots in a legendary Southern past by attaching to themselves Mediterranean types—Notterdam's Italian chauffeur and one-time South-American mistress, Kratch's confidential Maltese servant—the fact of their immediate displacement is sufficiently clear. Content neither with past nor present, Notterdam explores his life back to earliest youth only to recover a nightmare and to release a *doppelgänger* who stalks him malevolently.

> He remembered to have read as a boy a story by a German author with a name like Lippschuetz. . . . Of a man who had been haunted by a double of himself called a "doppelgaenger." The appearance of the double had always presaged disaster of a hideous nature. Finally he had fired a pistol through the double's heart—to see that he had fractured a mirror and to fall dead. . . . The story had been called, he thought, the *Student of Prague*—or it might have been Vienna. At any rate it had immensely impressed him as a boy, so that traces of the *doppelgaenger* legend had fixed themselves on his memory whenever he had come across them. There was a picture by an Italian painter called "How They Met Themselves!" . . . It represented a pair of guilty lovers—though there was nothing to shew their guilt —walking in a thin wood. . . A spinney like Goldencroft Shaw where he had gone wrong with Lottie. . . . The doubles of these two had appeared to them. The man was represented as grasping at the hilt of his sword under his cloak, the woman sinking back with arms outstretched. (p. 179)

Whether or not Ford knew an actual tale named *The Student of Prague* or, possibly, recalled the German film with that title and employing the *doppelgänger* motif which had been revived in 1926 after its original production by Paul Wegener in 1913,[12] he certainly remembered distinctly in the above passage Rossetti's picture "How they met themselves," which in his 1902 study of the painter he had mentioned as

one of Rossetti's best designs and as an example of the artist's
liking for subjects connected with the supernatural. In Rossetti's superficially romantic topic Ford may well have detected
a latent psychological content applicable to the predicament
of Notterdam, whose guilt-ridden fancy takes the spectre for
some kind of supernatural visitation. Hence whereas a *doppelgänger* suitably preys upon Notterdam as a type of Nordic
with Faustian traits, it also acquires psychological validity as
a hallucination engendered by his state of near breakdown,
induced by drink and mental strain, and representative of a
complex form of sexual and religious anxiety. By causing the
doppelgänger to confront Notterdam with increasing frequency as the latter feels himself deteriorating, Ford could
handle the issue in an objective and dramatic manner and so
proceed by rendering rather than internal analysis. Appearing
first in the semblance of Notterdam as a boy in Dorset, (pp.
40–41) the double moves by stages towards the man's present middle-age and in this pursuit grows progressively "more
detestable and older" (p. 178) like Dorian Gray's portrait.
More to the point, however, is a probably intended allusion
to James's "The Jolly Corner," a story written at Ford's request
for the first number of the *English Review*,[13] inasmuch as the
coarsening of Notterdam's double recalls the figure of the
phantom self of James's protagonist, the man Brydon might
have been had he remained in America, and thus intensifies
Ford's theme of the harrowing results of American experience.
Notterdam, however, reverses the situation of the anglicized
Brydon in having to cope with the menace of a rejected English past, a phantom that he succeeds in exorcising only when
he returns to his Dorset birthplace in the closing scenes of the
novel. The further he retreats from his native European origins
towards complete surrender to American habits, the more
hideous does his double become.

    Ford logically amplified his central theme of weakened
tradition and unstable identity by involving Notterdam with
the English novelist, Porter, and the latter's white Creole

wife, Lola. Coming from the same Dorset village as Notterdam, Porter has had nothing of the commercial success of his fellow countryman but exists on the fringe of the underworld through his want of foothold in the New York "writing machine"— his case being another illustration of Ford's view of the state of letters in an ersatz-civilization. Although Porter, slightly military and athletic in appearance, is as much the physical opposite of Notterdam as was Ashburnham of Dowell, the two men have an unrecognized tie of common nationality, decidedly English and different from the frontier-bred affinity of emotion between Notterdam and Kratch. This relationship, in some ways reminiscent of Conrad's use of opposites as in *Under Western Eyes,* pertains indirectly to the *doppelgänger* motif in that his contact with Porter, which serves as a reminder of English derivation, contributes to raising before Notterdam the ghost of his European past. Even though Porter dupes him over a publishing contract, Notterdam seems a not altogether unwilling victim; for despite the sordid circumstances of Porter and his wife, their "queer mixture of a household" is nearer than his own Long Island establishment to the home that Notterdam has lost. Porter's misery is an outward complement to Notterdam's inner distress, the novelist's wasted hopes a reflection of the other man's soiling of his once "shining and golden youth"; (p. 64) and when Notterdam later repudiates the contract and Porter dies, either by suicide or accident, Notterdam accepts the suicide hypothesis and accuses himself of betrayal, of having murdered "one's excompatriot alone in a strange land." (p. 203) The twinges of desire that he has felt for Porter's wife, "black as night— and very likely hot as hell and sweet as sin in certain circumstances," (p. 78) add a sexual element to Notterdam's guilt, the result being a sudden and sinister metamorphosis in the character of his *doppelgänger.* In Porter's apartment shortly after the novelist's death Notterdam finds himself in the presence of a gangster from the underworld circle frequented by Porter and his wife:

He saw suddenly, as if in a vision, the sordid apartment occupied by the late Edward Porter. . . . Mrs. Porter, her face pallid with drink and fear, had been stretched along a table with a green cloth: there had been folding doors between the sordid, nasty-smelling room in which he found himself and a sordid, nasty-smelling bedroom with the bed-clothes indescribably tumbled. . . . The doors had been apart and from behind them there had stepped a terribly evil-looking tough who held a gun that he proceeded to in-sert into his hip-pocket. He was in a tuxedo of extremely rakish cut, his hair greased into a divided fringe on his low forehead. Mrs. Porter had been in a black, extremely low-cut dress. She was extraordinarily thin, her backbone shin-ing all down her very white back in the V of her dress. (p. 165)

The gangster, McKeown, a hanger-on of Lola Porter from her racketeering past and on occasion her lover, Notterdam identifies, at least in his shock at seeing Porter dead, with the final transformation of his *doppelgänger*. Equating his be-trayal of Porter with the corrupt American ethic which tol-erates the underworld that had engulfed the novelist, Not-terdam himself begins carrying a gun in his hip pocket as a defense against his presumed shadower McKeown. By this turn of events he virtually assumes the identity of Porter and takes a redemptive step in protecting Lola, although the situ-ation entangles him ironically with a woman vampire of the jazz-age and her revengeful demon lover from the criminal underground. On his voyage to England to arrange for a memorial edition of Porter's works, Notterdam despairs of ridding himself of this pair of evil spirits, especially after his taking for portentous the sight of the shadows of Lola and himself reflected upon the sea fog like the doubles of the guilty lovers in "How they met themselves"; (pp. 307–308) and growing cynical, he decides to make the most of his damnation by raping Lola in the Dorset house of his childhood, an act interrupted by the final visitation of his *doppelgänger:*

> He was looking at himself in the dim light and grasped at his hip. He was enraged and determined. . . . His other self was a detestable monster: flushed, red-eyed, lecherous, obese, his clothes disordered. You should put a monster like that out of the world he soils.
>
> His gun was out. He said:
>
> "By God, I'm going to kill you. . . ." You can't of course kill a supernatural being—but he was going to. Lola screamed, desperately and piercingly. She had been lying on the couch before the fire where he had thrown her down so that the monster was hidden from her by the back of the couch. She must think he meant to kill her. She sprang up and ran into a corner of the room where she crouched invisible in the shadow. She screamed and screamed.
>
> Her screaming disturbed him. They began screaming in the kitchen. He felt nevertheless as if he were in a cathedral. Immense pillars went up into shadow. He was Nostradamus who had called up a devil. This was a black mass. This was villainy. (p. 342)

The fact that the shot kills McKeown, pursuing Lola, and not, according to legend, Notterdam himself through the attempt to destroy the image of the double seems to confirm not only the subjective nature of Notterdam's hallucination but also to signify his false and helpless role in a society without roots. By returning to England and so trying to atone for Porter's death, he recovers some measure of identity in ridding himself of the destructive potential embodied in McKeown; yet he ends a mock hero not unlike Ford's earlier Mr. Fleight. He lands in New York to the cheers of a crowd inspired by publicity to welcome him for eliminating a pest and saving a beautiful woman but blind to the truth that the supposed benefactor has merely slipped out of humiliating circumstances

made inevitable by the corruption sanctioned by society itself. Thus, a hero by accident and no conqueror of the evil
that has enmeshed him and Porter in the duplicity and mutual
betrayal of contemporary existence, Notterdam finds no escape from the circle in which he has moved before, though
he obtains some degree of personal knowledge.

In great part, therefore, the novel offers a satire on the plight
of Notterdam as a Faustian man with Henrietta Felise for his
Gretchen and Lola Porter for his sensual Helen, a creature of
romantic guilt and uncertain origins who can describe himself in affirming that ". . . Nostradamus and Notre Dame and
Notterdam were all the same." (p. 326) Devoid of religious
clarity but superstitious, he displays the irresolution and painful conscience of the sinner by default who achieves neither
heroism nor villainy because embroiled in the confusion of
Christian and pagan motives that lies behind his psychic illness. Although different in kind from Dowell's Victorian
hypocrisy in *The Good Soldier,* much of Notterdam's thinking is a process of evasion or forced compromise which Ford
skilfully illuminates by a language made up of tentative or
disguised assertions: "If one were maudlin one might well
say that one had slain one's brother." (p. 203) In a similar
light the *doppelgänger,* likewise the product of romantic tradition and so again characteristic of Notterdam, remains ironically ambiguous like the ghosts in *The Turn of the Screw* in
having no concrete status as a positive force of evil outside
Notterdam but being potent enough as a product of superstition to torture his mind and to invest his world with an almost Gothic atmosphere of nightmare. Because of this basic
absence of conviction, in society as well as in the individual,
the environment becomes dark and death becomes, as in *The
Secret Agent,* an inexplicable horror. Like the suicide of Gilda
Leroy in *Mr. Fleight* the death of Porter, an instance of metropolitan indifference to the disappearance of the individual,
is too small a matter to disturb public apathy; yet as a personal experience affecting the unsteady mind, it may acquire

an exaggerated power to terrify, as Notterdam finds on confronting Porter's body:

> Porter was, dreadfully, in the bathroom, his head reclin-
> ing on the patience-cards with which he had occupied him-
> self whilst waiting for death. His hands were stretched out
> and ice-cold, his thin hair disordered on his white scalp.
> A deep hollow in the nape of the neck above the coat-collar
> denoted his extreme emaciation. The cards alone gave a
> startlingly bright touch of scarlet and black to the sordid
> brown room where even the geyser that had killed him was
> green with verdigris. (p. 167)

Because of the rapid pace of *When the Wicked Man* the
manner in which the themes interlock is not at once evident;
and the prominence of the *doppelgänger* motif tends to over-
shadow the equally significant theme of the absence of communal relationship between Notterdam and Porter, an aspect
of the story that Ford stressed rather awkwardly by the ironical transfer to Notterdam of Porter's identity and the late
shift of scene to England for the purpose of enlarging upon
the idea of homelessness. Since Ford's immediate aim was,
however, to reveal a state of waste-land neurosis, the balance
of the novel leans understandably towards individual disintegration rather than towards the prospect of cultural recovery
and hence of renewed personal ties which becomes a main
issue in the richer mythical setting of the two-part novel of
1933 and 1934, *The Rash Act* and *Henry for Hugh*. In this
work, the most elaborate attempt by Ford to deal in fictional
terms with a symbolic resolution of the passional-religious
dilemma, the art differs not only from the satirical effect of
When the Wicked Man but also from the more openly didactic
handling of matters of contemporary faith in such an early
novel as *Mr. Apollo*.

By incorporating the death-rebirth cycle, *The Rash Act*
and *Henry for Hugh* stand as a refined example of the funerary
art peculiar to the modernism which followed the Great War.

Although the immediate historical atmosphere is that of the depression years in which the novels took shape, the allusions to suicide and communism having topical point, Ford responded to the world crisis by intensifying his efforts to devise a cultural remedy against civilized decline. His setting, therefore, becomes Southern France—his Provençal region—and his characters a small group of people—American, English, Swedish, French—drawn from various parts of Western civilization into that area of the Mediterranean coast commonly the haunt of expatriates and idle rich. The leading roles Ford assigned to an American, Henry Martin, and an Englishman, Hugh Monckton—both lost generation types at the outset exemplifying, as war veterans, the penalties of Nordic descent in their suicidal impulse and traits of Albigensian negation but before the end undergoing a change leading towards that redemptive state which Ford designated by his key word "Provence." Whereas this regenerative process follows to some extent the course of Mediterranean slacking off from New England virtue that Ford prescribed later in *Great Trade Route*, the governing image in the novel of the transformation desired is that of the "Boy of Antibes," whose memory and art Ford later celebrated directly in *Provence:*

But at least I cannot be accused of disliking dancing or of having any contempt for the most lovely as it is the most fugitive of all the Arts. And indeed of all the beautiful and mysterious motives and emotions that go to make up the frame of mind that is Provence the most beautiful, moving and mysterious is that of the Northern Boy of Antibes. The boy danced and gave pleasure, died two thousand years ago and his memorial tablet set into the walls of Antibes which is Antipolis of the Greeks sets forth these salient facts of his life and portrays in the lasting stone the little bag in which he used to make his collections. . . . He indeed along with Herod's daughter who came after and King David who preceded him must be amongst the earliest dancers

upon whom Destiny has conferred the immortality of stone,
papyrus or wax. . . . The most mysterious and the most
beautiful.

And that is the note of the frame of mind that is Provence—[14]

Curiously, with "mysterious," "beautiful," Ford here seems
almost to echo Yeats in the latter's poem on the Coole swans;
and certainly the image of the boy dancer, a figure of sophisticated innocence crystallizing so many of the writer's late
aesthetic and personal ideals, inspired Ford with much the
same awe and delight at the vision of a dominant symbol as
were felt by Yeats in contemplating the swan. Like Yeats, too,
Ford came at last and after having dallied over a variety of
emblems and talismans, from the Tamworth cross in *Ladies
Whose Bright Eyes* to Val Wannop's scrap of Hebrew parch-
ment in *Some Do Not,* to a preoccupation with the dancer,
and if not with the poet's customary bent towards frenzy or
ecstasy, at least with something of the latter's desire to recover lost sources of joy. What Ford chiefly commends is the
living quality of the boy dancer's art, one not only devoid of
violence and egotism but also fulfilled in the free and harmonious gesture of the whole person rather than by means of
an artifact. To some degree, perhaps, Ford thus arrived at
a symbolic equivalent for the equilibrium between art and
action which he had earlier sought restlessly; for the boy
represents a tradition wherein artist and normally functioning individual are one, in which respect his image affords a
standard to offset the dismal corrupting of the arts by commercialism and venality which Ford had touched on in *When
the Wicked Man* but which he notes repeatedly in *The Rash
Act* and *Henry for Hugh.*

But in the light of a body exhibiting fulfilled purpose, the
symbol of the Boy of Antibes also denotes a harmony sufficiently vital to reconcile the conflicts—religious, aesthetic,
even economic—of postwar society. Evidently, too, from al-

lusions in *The Rash Act,* Ford intended to associate the spirit
of the boy with the celebration of self-delight in time which
he had recognized, possibly at the Louvre, in examples of
Cretan art from Cnossos, an art described by one expert as
". . . the most complete acceptance of the grace of life the
world has ever known." [15] Hence the symbol establishes a
connection in the novel between the motif of rebirth and the
Provençal frame of mind; and as a controlling funerary emblem the inscription for the boy long dead becomes a motto
for the renewal of life out of a tomb-like contemporary existence ruled by Nordic habits of thought, as Henry Martin,
while contemplating suicide, reflects on this prevailing mood:

> His mind ran on tombstones. European Teuto-Frankish
> minds still did. Father, in private, thought Holbein's *Dance
> of Death* the finest humor in the world . . . And, when
> Henry Martin came to think of it he was not averse from
> thinking of tombstones himself. There was a mural inscrip-
> tion at Antibes, a few miles from where he then stood. It
> was on the wall of the Roman Theatre—to the memory of
> a boy dancer who had died young.
> "SALTAVIT. PLACUIT. MORTUUS EST."
> "He danced. He gave pleasure. He is dead."
> It would be nice to have that on one's tombstone. But he
> never would. That would no doubt make his real epitaph—
> that he had never given pleasure.[16]

With still a faint recollection of the old antithesis in *The Fifth
Queen*—the medieval Katharine Howard against the Hol-
binesque court of Henry VIII—Ford arrays Provence through
the boy dancer against a Nordic culture that remains subservient to Holbein's Germanic art.

From an image, therefore, of mystery, subdued color, and
grace Ford evoked the mood for his two-volume novel in
which the Boy of Antibes, without being a physical presence,
disseminates the atmosphere for a work purposely removed
from Nordic energy and tension, designedly sensuous rather

than strenuous and seemingly directed by something nearer the magical agencies of an Oriental tale than by the force of will characteristic of Western literature. The pivotal event— the assumption by the American, Martin, of the identity of the Englishman, Monckton—thus occurs as an almost passive transformation marked by strangeness instead of the cruder romanticism of changed identity in books like *A Tale of Two Cities* or *The Prisoner of Zenda*. As a key to the tone that he sought, Ford begins *The Rash Act* admirably by a view of the sailboat, chosen by Martin for his drowning but later to become an instrument of restored life, as it rests at dawn, in a setting reminiscent of Conrad, on the translucent water of the small French port. Still but on the verge of motion, the boat suggests a funerary emblem with classical associations:

> The morning seemed to herald a glorious day. The motionless silver of the sea was ruffled in irregular streaks like watered satin. The light mists were rising from the horizon and the islands. Sunlight from over the stone pines just touched the end of the jetty so that there was a triangle of gold. A boat, anchored beyond, brooded, motionless. On the translucent water it seemed to be suspended in the air. It became vivid—a melon slice of incandescent white, a curved stripe of scarlet. Another, parallel below, was of azure. The boat should have caught the light first. It was further out than the end of the little pier.
> The phenomenon was no doubt occasioned by the irregular outlines of the pines. Or perhaps a beam pierced an interstice in their tops. The prow of the boat stood up, white, shaped like half an open fan. The sail, untidily lowered on the curving felucca-yard was lambent maroon. Then all the light went out of the whole caboodle.
> It was as if he had been vouchsafed a chromolithographic closeup of a prehistoric craft. In miniature the thing had been one of the thousand ships that Helen's face had launched and Homer catalogued. (p. 3)

In surroundings overburdened with history, the boat, poised between death and life, retains the shape of a past with truths known to the boy dancer.

Eventual acquaintance with the spirit of Provence and its concrete symbol in the Boy of Antibes resolves the problem of identity and tradition for Martin, a former Rhodes Scholar and veteran of the British Army, who suffers from an alarming Nordic parentage as the son of a Luxembourg born candy manufacturer, a "wild boar of the Ardennes" lacking consistent character, and a woman of New England conscience from Fall River. After a series of personal disillusionments, marital and professional, Martin obtains his wish to become someone else when, as a wanderer in Southern France during the world crisis, he encounters the Englishman, Monckton, his double in age and appearance but in other respects his opposite: a hero of the first battles of the Great War, the wealthy head of a famous automobile company, and by outward indications a success with women. To Martin, who has known him in the army, Monckton looks as fortunate as a god, an Apollo; (p. 78) yet in subsequent conversations in the Englishman's hotel room Martin learns that Monckton plans suicide to end the intolerable situation resulting from a war wound in the head from a German cavalry sabre which not only causes him ceaseless pain but also renders him incapable of normal pleasures, including those of love with his mistress, the Swedish actress Gloria Malmström, or the French girl, Jeanne Becquerel, once mistress to the governor of Cochin-Annam but now dependent upon Monckton for support. Because of his reputation as a financier and his desire to safeguard his company stockholders, Monckton wishes to conceal his suicide and so proposes that Martin, who has likewise decided upon killing himself following money losses in the Crash and his conviction of futility, should impersonate him after his death, taking for reward all of the Englishman's fortune and possessions. Despite Martin's refusal, the stranding of his sailboat near the place where Monckton later commits suicide leads to an apparent conspiracy of circumstance actually casting him into the role proffered, a transfer of identity facilitated by the seeming coincidence that the real surnames of the two men happen to be Smith.

In this element of the fanciful operative in a contemporary situation the novel has features in common with *When the Wicked Man* just as it also resembles at times work by Charles Williams. Although Ford's intention, as in his simpler *Ladies Whose Bright Eyes*, is to employ the device of transposed identity with its accompanying surprise in order to carry the reader into a field of experience unfamiliar to him and so make him receptive to a rendered conception of the idea of Provence, the presence of archetypal qualities in *The Rash Act* strengthens the general bearing of the action. Of broader import than the more limited relationship between Notterdam and Porter, the international encounter of Martin and Monckton pleads for the reconciling of these agents of Western culture upon a groundwork of Mediterranean tradition; yet the assumption by Martin of Monckton's responsibilities likewise introduces a mythical allusion to the reinstatement of the cycle of kingship, Martin replacing the sick and self-slain hero whose status a pointed reference to the Ariel sea-change line plainly affirms. (p. 95) From the latter standpoint the basic theme of the novel is less internationalistic than redemptive, the Martin-Monckton alliance furnishing a paradigm for the healing of the divided self central to *When the Wicked Man*.

Ford's method of handling such complicated material is both delicate and expert. Throughout the whole of the two-part novel the point of view is entirely that of Martin, his thought process being reported by a Jamesian form of indirect narration occasionally interspersed with passages of direct action and dialogue. This procedure imparts an appropriate tone of soliloquy, less vivid than the nervous monologue of *The Good Soldier* but better adapted to a work consciously evoking an atmosphere of semi-indolence suggestive of Provence and admitting the possibilities of the involuntary and the strange;

and the fact that Martin, like Mark Tietjens in *The Last Post*, remains for a long period immobile physically, invalided by the blow of the sailboat yard in the storm, conduces to a generally elegiac impression. By this technique Ford undertakes the difficult task of relating the change of identity to the field of internal experience and so creating the illusion of a mind finding its habitual mental attitudes transformed by the gradual influx of a different personality as Martin discovers that he is thinking in the manner of the dead Monckton. Although Ford had attempted a similar effect in *Ladies Whose Bright Eyes*, he had there relied, perhaps with an eye to *Heart of Darkness*, upon the more obvious stratagem of turning the mind of his character alternately from present to past, thereby missing the effect of mental activity happening simultaneously on two planes as with Martin, a conception that may have owed something to Conrad's treatment of Razumov in *Under Western Eyes*.

Since at the outset the burden of worry impelling Martin to suicide has originated largely with the war, he must confront his double, the actually wounded Monckton, so that, like the protagonist in Wilfred Owen's *Strange Meeting*, he may recognize the true cause of his own mental distress. The two characters being complementary parts of a single postwar mentality and thus resembling Quester and King in *The Waste Land*, Martin, though physically uninjured, can discern in Monckton's suffering from the cut of the Uhlan sabre at the Marne the reason for his own psychic disability as well as that of civilization in general left enfeebled by the blow dealt by the German invasion of Belgium "near a place called Gemmenich." Once identified with Monckton, therefore, Martin faces the fact that ". . . the fellow in the blue uniform charging down on him on a roan charger was something that he might seem to see at almost any moment of the day. In a sort of substituted memory." (p. 328) But Monckton, in his record of gallantry at the Marne, is likewise the dying hero figure of

Western culture and still the vestigial Christian, so that in representing this declining cultural past he leaves at his death to Martin a collection of European art, financial power, and two women—one from the West, the other from the East. Martin, the American side of the postwar mind, cannot, therefore, rid himself of the problem bequeathed by his war partner.

Significantly, in Ford's parable, what the war has maimed is the brain, the over-taxed Western intellect, and from this results the impotence of the body for love or pleasure. Recovery, therefore, seems to require a fusion at sub-rational level, as Ford implies by the sequence of events in which the accidental storm, causing the sailboat yard to strike the head of Martin and so marking the instant of his psychic interconnection with his double, sends the American in a daze to the dead body of Monckton and to the almost unconscious exchange of passports which closes the compact between the characters. Recalling this crucial incident in *Henry for Hugh*,[17] Martin visualizes his taking of Monckton's passport as a completely involuntary act that exonerates him of guilt as a criminal impostor, even though he acknowledges that the decision, made by a self below the conscious, reveals "the remains within himself of the cave man: the latent possibility within him of the criminal."[18] Here a possible overtone from "The Secret Sharer" is relevant, since the secret pact between Martin and Monckton occurs outside and in disregard of an official and deadening authority. After his baptismal drenching by the storm, the Mediterranean *trombio* which sweeps towards the boat "like a great wall with a whitewashed foot" as if an emanation of Provençal energy, (p. 214) Martin completes what is essentially a life ritual with the falling of a spot of his blood upon Monckton's signature. (p. 225) The involuntary deed, reminiscent of the uniting of Tietjens with the common soldier in the shedding of the latter's blood in *No More Parades*, renews a bond of human fidelity at a source more vital than that of the consciousness impaired by the outbreak of barbarism at Gem-

menich and implies that the Western faith, crippled by the
war, could acquire fresh root in the soil of Provence through
an effort to regain lost communal truths.

The consequence of accepting Monckton's identity is, in
any case, that Martin finds himself the center of a small and
oddly assorted community, if not almost a cult, differing in
nature from the private groups formed by Tietjens or Gringoire.
Neither Monckton nor Martin, both of whom appear to have
dispensed with formal religion, show any traces of the English
mysticism that develops in Tietjens; but before his death
Monckton exhibits signs of an awakening Provençal spirit by
expressing a desire to convert his art treasures into a memorial
to his mistress, Gloria Malmström, who has given pleasure in
the ephemeral art of dancing. In his own way, too, Martin
takes a step towards Provence by becoming attracted to the
French girl, Eudoxie, who has displayed her resistance to
authority by selling cocaine as ". . . a crusade against the
imbecile wickedness of Authority that hated happiness," (p.
353) and who has on the wall of her room the "saltavit et
placuit" motto of the Boy of Antibes. While a subconscious
impulse to ally himself with these people may indirectly thwart
his suicide plan, Martin returns to consciousness after his accident in the boat to find himself in the company of Jeanne
Becquerel and Eudoxie and to enter upon a period of con-
valescence during which, though experiencing Monckton's
pain, he is sufficiently free of his former anxieties to contem-
plate a way of life in which his physical self may reawaken
to neglected sources of pleasure. In the quiet of the Villa Niké
overlooking the Mediterranean, he perceives in Jeanne with
her oriental tastes a graceful exoticism lacking vulgarity and
in both women a propensity for color and unaffected enjoyment that harmonizes in a Hellenic way with the southern
warmth and light:

Jeanne Becquerel stood in the doorway, leaning back
against the door post beside the dark girl. Since the light

from the upper sky was intense she was not in silhouette and her skin was indeed nacreous as the dark girl said. Like mother of pearl. She stretched out one arm to hold the other door post so that it cut the door space in half, like a straight bar, obscuring St. Mondrier. Her head was turned to gaze into the South. The shadows beneath her arms, armpits, busts and knees reflected the blue of the sky; there was a little pink on the base of the neck, the ribs and the lower limbs. But most of the flesh was rice-white. . . . A Hellenic figure done in nacre. The dark girl was like a drop of luminous blood! . . . She would no doubt one day fly away. . . . Like a scarlet sail before disaster.

They had perhaps arranged that contrast so as to be alluring to men. They had perhaps arranged to shade or expose their flesh so as to be the one in red bronze, the other, rice. . . . Why shouldn't they? The allurement of men is the business of these seas and skies. . . . They had to leap and give pleasure. Then to die. (pp. 336–337)

Detached temporarily from his puritan and Nordic past and in a situation like that of a Roman noble of the decadence, Martin comes to appreciate aesthetic effects not from artifacts but from a living beauty comparable to that of the boy dancer. In opposition to modern arts afflicted by cultural sterility, the movements of Eudoxie and Jeanne recall images of classical beauty and follow delicate yet formal rhythms that exhibit the life acceptance of the Cretan figures which Eudoxie at times resembles:

Out on the terrace she juggled with oranges. With one hand she kept six in the air at once. As one fell out of range she caught it with her net and took another from the table beside her. So there were always six in the air at once. Those high up caught the sunlight and were illuminated and golden. Behind her pyjama trousers, from below the terrace the orange trees pushed up their formal and emotional foliage. He could not be certain that Greek women wore pyjama trousers. Perhaps the Cretans did. At Cnossos. Or he seemed to remember an outline on a red platter. In the Louvre.

At any rate the boy of Antibes who danced and gave pleasure had probably juggled six oranges in that way. Perhaps on that very terrace. It was an unchanging landscape. . . . (pp. 337–338)

With his view towards the south, which Jeanne and Eudoxie instinctively face, Martin so far abandons his older self as to grow a beard and wear silk and colors. Relinquishing, too, his former provincialism, he mingles with the foreign crowd in the port below the villa, (p. 369) attaining sympathy with a type of internationalized world not hitherto known to him and outside prevailing systems of authority. On this evidence Ford apparently favored the international spirit in the 1930's but regarded communism dubiously not only as a lapse from the cultural tradition that he valued but also simply as another manifestation of the Nordic blight, since the avowed communists in the novel—Monckton's secretary, Macdonald, and Gloria Malmström—display pugnacious traits and act in boring or disagreeable ways. Whereas Martin speculates on the spread of the movement, his disposition of Monckton's inheritance in keeping with the Englishman's aim to explore the reasons for crises in civilization and to resist them by an adequate theory of finance and monetary exchange [19] implies that the burden of alleviating the ills of the time properly rests with those who, having experienced the war and its baptism of action and suffering, constitute an aristocracy able to restore a cultural heritage which survives through continuity of blood rather than political abstraction.

For this reason the novel, with its subtle tone of Provençal magic, approaches the celebration of a rite calling for the recovery of a lost principle of ideal kingship in human affairs so as to resolve the predicament in the background of novels from *The Fifth Queen* through *The Good Soldier*. Such a change inevitably precedes the restoration of art itself to the cultural status of which it has been deprived in the modern American and Continental worlds; and in this respect *The Rash Act* and *Henry for Hugh* by their attempt to create the impression of a living art conjoined with the image of the boy dancer not only project within the novel an actual conception of a possible art form but also contain Ford's last and most mature statement on a topic which had concerned him from his earliest years. Implicitly, the transfer of Monckton's heritage to Martin bears with it a promise of the re-enactment of tragedy frustrated in books like *Mr. Fleight* and *The Good Soldier*, as may be seen in Martin's conversion from his role of potential suicide at the start of the action to that of a man capable of enduring tribulation, a development marked significantly by his averting of Jeanne Becquerel's suicide shortly after Monckton's death. While preparing to drown from the sailboat, Martin assumes the pose of a death-impelled Nordic hero, so that the watching Eudoxie stands like Isolde waving her lover farewell.[20] Once, however, he has succeeded to Monckton's place, he occupies the center of what approximates to a static classical drama with the two women for chorus. This new role involves, as well, an alteration in his judgment of art objects as represented by the accumulation of museum pieces left in his charge by Monckton. In the strong room at the villa these treasures obsess Martin "like a dumb wound in his mind," [21] since, like the Poynton spoils, they symbolize a luxury that he wishes to be rid of in his growing recognition of the vital and frugal Provençal spirit. Just as Monckton himself had come to wish that the objects be given away, so also his successor renounces luxury in order to adopt the burden of responsibility, what Eudoxie calls "la paume de la gloire."

Martin's final establishment as legitimate heir to Monckton is the principal subject of the second novel in the pair, *Henry for Hugh*, set at the Villa Niké about a year following *The Rash Act*. Even more contemplative in tone than its predecessor by reason of the sustained mood of soliloquy, *Henry for*

Hugh keeps, however, an element of suspense in that Martin is both disturbed by a sense of divided identity in sharing dual selfhood with Monckton and apprehensive that he may be charged with imposture. The book thus opens on a note of tension with the unexpected appearance at the villa of an elderly English aunt of Monckton, a woman capable of penetrating Martin's disguise:

> He could not say that this lady seemed a sinister figure. She resembled a gentle sleuth chasing a butterfly. He had been looking at the exact spot on the house-end where first the brim of her large black hat had appeared. He had turned his head on his cushions to rest his eyes from the white glare of the Mediterranean. The house-end was in the deep shadow from the great Japanese lilac. There that apparition had had the air of something going very quietly. . . . As if he had been watching the opening of a plant.
>
> He seemed to have been watching her for a long time before her eyes met his. He had made a minute examination of every object on the terrace—the urns, the tree in the white sunlight, a pale tea-rose that climbed to the balustrade. Eudoxie had hung her large white palmetto hat on a deck chair in the shadow of the lilac; on the stone table near it was Jeanne Becquerel's black satin pocket that held her manicuring things, beside a large pyramid of oranges in a green earthenware bowl. . . . (p. 10)

Instead, however, of pursuing retribution, Aunt Elizabeth, or the "Lady," as Martin thinks of her, joins the small cast of characters as an intercessor to clarify Martin's position and, rather like a figure in an Eliot play, to help draw the plot to a close on a classical note of resolution and order. Her ready acceptance of him in place of the nephew she has lost and her advice in dealing with the perplexities of his inheritance from Monckton make her indispensable to Martin, who acquires a measure of her own calm and poise; and before dying, prepared by Catholic rites but uttering at the last a Protestant prayer, (p. 299) she removes his sense of guilt by unraveling the complicated genealogical skein which proves not only that he and Monckton were actually related in having a common European great-grandfather but also that Martin has a prior claim over Monckton to stand as head of the Anglo-American family group.

In thus disclosing the truth that promises continued life to a family threatened with extinction by the war, through which she has suffered, she completes for Martin the process of self-recovery begun with his awakening through Jeanne and Eudoxie to the Provençal spirit of life and art and finished with his recognition of the complementary ideal of frugality and responsibility. Her function is, therefore, vital in that her membership in the Martin-Monckton clan together with her sympathy towards Provence represents the rounding of the cultural circuit between the Mediterranean and anglicized worlds. By her attitude of forgiveness and tolerance of both Catholic and Protestant doctrine she points, moreover, to a way of healing such a fatal rift as that in the Tietjens family line, her principal injunction to Martin being simply to observe the standard of individual workmanship asserted by the motto, *Sino Fabro Nihil*—"By Hammer and Hand all Art doth stand"—the original crest of the Faber-Smith lineage from which he descends. Modifying yet blending, as she does by her luminous tone of grey, the exotic Mediterranean colors dominant at her entrance, she becomes the ultimate harmonizing agent in a work purposely invested with an aura of mystery and suggestive of the temper of a Provençal romance. Although the titles of the novels are among Ford's worst, even so elusive a caption as *Henry for Hugh* may impart something of the spirit of a book purposely detached, in its theme of metamorphosis, from sheerly temporal concerns.

Infused as they are, however, with mythical and romantic elements, *The Rash Act* and *Henry for Hugh* still retain features basic to Ford's Impressionism, in particular the restriction to the small group of characters typical of the *Affair*. Be-

sides this note of private history the work also includes, in its
undercurrent of criminality and suspense investing the impostor motif, a modicum of that flavor of popular appeal
which both Ford and Conrad thought essential to the novel.
From the prevailing atmosphere of the introspective and
miraculous Ford appears, nevertheless, to revert in his last
complete novel, *Vive Le Roy* in 1937, to a level of outright
melodrama in a key with Conrad's *The Secret Agent,* so that
this book with a detective figure in the central role may be
classified too hastily as popular entertainment of the thriller
variety if attention ignores the overtone of fable that allies it
with the whole trend in Ford's later output. Ostensibly *Vive
Le Roy* is a contemporary Gothic tale with accompaniments
of the factors of pursuit and political intrigue like those in the
earlier fiction of Greene. During a war between Loyalists and
Communists for rule in Paris, a young American doctor, Walter
Leroy, disappears through a plot to make him serve as double
for the assassinated Loyalist king and is at last rescued by the
efforts of the girl in love with him, Cassie Mathers, an American student of painting, and Penkethman, an elderly international detective. In choosing a plot of this kind, Ford seems
obviously to have responded, in his customary manner, to the
change in literary mode from the depression background
employed in *The Rash Act* to the later 1930's setting of violence
and approaching general war that helped to create a taste
for the politically tinged spy story as written by Greene,
Isherwood, Ambler and others. To a genre of this kind Ford's
Impressionist techniques for involving and surprising the
reader could be adapted with ease; hence in contrast to the
subdued rhythms of *Henry for Hugh, Vive Le Roy,* with
its probable indirect reflection of the Spanish Civil War, not
only calls into play Ford's entire battery of strategical resources
but also moves to an appropriate and spasmodic tempo of
nervous dread, like the staccato of a machine gun, which recalls
in places the war front episodes in the Tietjens tetralogy. Thus

unexpectedly concealed enemies open fire on the Loyalist car
bearing Walter Leroy and his French captor:

> Suddenly his hat was not there . . . M. de la Penthièvre
> had a gun in his hand . . . A blue nickelled gat! Held down
> out of sight of the spectators on the sidewalk. . . . He
> ducked forward suddenly. . . . So did Leroy. . . . The
> horsehair plume of the officer of Cuirassiers sprang sud-
> denly into the air. The officer reeled. . . . The air was full
> of wasps. Droning in long high notes. The crowd was silent
> for a second. . . A "tack-tack-tack," the sound of a mad
> and enlarged typewriter, sounded from a house-front, high
> up and to the right . . . A low house . . . The houses there
> were in part marble-faced banks, in part the tiny houses of
> little cafes. . . .[22]

The absolute conformity to the principle of rendering illustrated in the foregoing passage with its hail of raw sense
data precluding the solace of abstraction characterizes a novel
in which every artifice of shock and suspense bares the nerves
of the reader to the onset of violence and danger from out of
supposedly familiar surroundings, a Conradian technique
with increasing relevance to the disorder of the contemporary
world immersed again in war. Following a main procedure in
The Secret Agent, Ford leads up to but does not present
directly the episode in which *Vive Le Roy* centers, Leroy's
actual experiences while impersonating under duress the dead
Loyalist king, a maneuver by which the reader stands nearly
always in the position of Cassie Mathers and thus participates
in the state of anxiety and dread with which she searches for
the man suddenly lost to her after a short interval of love
making. Ford's most audacious, yet meaningful, feat in this
line is the scene in the Paris morgue where Cassie, under the
guidance of Penkethman who holds the clue to Leroy's disappearance, goes to examine the embalmed body of the king
that the authorities wish to persuade her is her lover's.

Penkethman insists that she bend close enough to the corpse to determine whether the ears are pierced for rings, as Leroy's were:

> She was already almost insensible; but she must do it before insensibility overcame her. An intense beam of light shot from beside her hand, showering over the bier, over the features supine upon it, showering over the arches and bits of the forms that lay beneath them. She had the comforting man's searchlight between the fingers of her right hand; with the other she must touch the bier, to lean forward. That was dreadful; that she never forgot on dark nights. A voice cried:
> "Touch not. . . . By the sacred name. . . ."
> She had had her face within . . . oh, how hideously little distance of . . . She would not have believed she could move. . . . But on the other side she had pushed away a man in white . . . Pushed him away. . . . She was on the other side. . . . She had her face nearly against a blazing . . . wall of musty perfume. Something from her mouth screamed:
> "It is not . . . Mercy of God . . . It is not . . . Not . . . Not . . ."
> All those white things looking upwards listened. And went out. Row on row went out, as candles go out. In the blackness the flagstones hit her temple. (pp. 195–196)

In such an incident the heightened rendering technique goes beyond its mere end in shock and underscores a broader range of meaning, as it does likewise when in *The Secret Agent* Ossipon must confront the corpse of Verloc; in *When the Wicked Man* Notterdam must face the body of Porter; or, perhaps of deeper significance for the later Ford, in *No More Parades* Tietjens must raise with his own hands the dead 09 Morgan. The reader himself has to meet the evidence of death vicariously, just as in Ford's historical novels he undergoes exposure to hidden evil, but with the closest simulation of a real occurrence in order to penetrate to the final truth behind a widespread screen of lies and pretense. As one principal aim, *Vive Le Roy,* especially through the prolonged ordeal of fear in Cassie, demonstrates the outrage done to the private individual in a contemporary world of violence perpetrated by concealed enemies; and when Cassie stands over the corpse in the morgue with its identity purposely confused, she realizes the significance of Penkethman's comment that the particular evil of a supposedly civilized condition is the ease with which the single person may be obliterated without trace or enquiry. To emphasize this point, Ford continues his attack upon the use of scientific weapons by masked agents, as he had begun this in the Tietjens tetralogy, by equipping such political gangsters as the *camelots du roi* with hypodermic syringes loaded with poison or microbes, (p. 226) an ironical thrust at civilized substitutes for the visible menace of dagger or pistol. In *Vive Le Roy* the central fact of individual loss through contemporary insensibility to evil differs little from its statement by Greene in a novel like *The Third Man;* yet Ford had already grasped this issue in dealing with the death of Gilda Leroy in *Mr. Fleight,* just as Conrad had done so earlier in *The Secret Agent.* To the present-day heroine, Cassie Mathers, for whom no straight path leads to the recovery of a vanished lover, the world remains as labyrinthine as the Tudor court for Katharine Howard; and Cassie's search ends in the heart of a maze, the subterranean crypts buried in Paris under layers of history:

> The Caveau Rouge that Walter Leroy had appointed as the meeting-place of Cassie and himself is one of those singular places that only exist in very ancient cities in whose subsoils are to be found, far below the surface, layer on layer of the detritus of dead civilizations. Most of it lies below the church of St. Julian the Poor, which is the oldest church in Paris and the only one of Norman architecture, and some of that part extends to even below the surface of the Seine. In another part of it, where the ground has filled in solid to a

depth of many feet, excavations have laid bare innumerable
relics of thousands of years . . . potsherds and bronze
knives of the Gauls who preceded the Roman occupation;
urns, bones, coins, fibulae of the Romans themselves; thigh-
bones, skulls, crowns, ornaments in gold, the rust of great
swords and spearheads, of the Frankish kings who succeeded
the Romans in the possession of Paris and whose successors
for so long reigned over the whole of the country that is
known as France.

The part beneath the church is a maze of excavated passages that formed the crypt of the religious order that owned
the church. (p. 233)

To the end Ford's art remains labyrinthine and allusive in
defiance of the growing mechanization of the world, and in
this respect *Vive Le Roy* is as rich in funerary symbolism and
mythical overtone as the two novels preceding it. In an obvious rebirth pattern, colored by both Egyptian and classical
associations, Cassie under the protection of the strong and
omniscient Penkethman seeks her lover in the underworld of
contemporary evil; and, having endured the terror of death,
she and Walter emerge at last from the "circular grave" (p.
284) in the maze of history, leaving a passageway excavated
in the war year of 1914, (p. 287) and return to a new life
together in America. The initiation affects Walter as well; for
having in him the trace of royal blood suggested by his surname, he has not found intolerable his compulsory doubling
for the dead Royalist king but, like Martin in *The Rash Act*,
has learned to sympathize with the views of the man he has
impersonated, an intelligent youth with objections as strong as
those of Ford himself to luxury and mass production. Presumably, therefore, Walter, while remaining a doctor, expects
to observe certain of these royalist precepts in the up-state
farm life, "a humanitarian form of communism," that he has
planned for himself and Cassie. (pp. 244–245) Rather than
the ideal of Provençal internationalism favored in *Henry for*

Hugh, Vive Le Roy appears merely to subscribe to the hope that an inevitable communism will follow the line of humanism and traditional ritual rather than that of either communist materialism or fascism, both of which are proceeding to demolish the outer world of culture in Paris without yet reaching to the subterranean life mysteries still accessible to the people who gather for mutual entertainment in the cabaret underground.

Despite these modifications, however, the Provençal myth of restored harmony continues to manifest itself in *Vive Le Roy*, which, like *The Rash Act* and *Henry for Hugh*, is a novel featuring the reconciliation of characters of varying nationality and religious background: Cassie, an American descendant of Cotton Mather and Brigham Young; Walter, partly Canadian and French; and Penkethman, by immediate descent English and Dutch and a member of an international police group. Yet in keeping with his strange name, Penkethman, like Harcourt-Reilly in Eliot's play, is the most problematical and elusive figure in the novel and certainly one of the most complex of Ford's personae. Simply in physical perspective he offers a blend of those attributes that had always attracted Ford, the man of action and the devotee and connoisseur of art and beauty as well as the adherent to lost causes; and his detective role, disfavored by Scotland Yard, is consoling and protective rather than expressive of that fear which the common image of the policeman so often inspires. But Penkethman has, in addition, the traits of a god not only in his almost Herculean strength but also in his superior knowledge which enables him to rescue the lovers and to supply these children of unhappy parentage with an acceptable past when he discloses the true facts of Walter's ancestry and thus removes the young man's dread of insanity as a possible inheritance from a father victimized in commercial rivalry.

In the latter guise Penkethman seems to borrow something of his guardian's function from the Aunt Elizabeth of *Henry for Hugh* while acquiring the authority of a paternal figure representing an antithesis to the Victorian duplicity of Gen-

eral Campion in the Tietjens tetralogy. As the real father of
Walter Leroy, Penkethman has assumed a measure of a
deity's prerogative in producing a child in secret; yet he has
done so out of love for a woman bound to a husband legally
mad and has borne full responsibility in shielding Walter with
the solicitude frequently demonstrated by a parent towards
an illegitimate son. The consequence is a familial relationship
between Penkethman, Walter, and Cassie which by its very
complexity asserts the intricate nature of human affairs at any
level of sophistication above the undifferentiated mean too
frequently and abstractly conceived as an end for a mass society. By his admission of fatherhood Penkethman transmits
to Walter a substantial proof of continuity different from the
temporary association with the person of the dead Royalist
king; and in reality it may be Penkethman, whose password is
the rallying-cry of a martyred king of France, (p. 302) who
bears the true kingly heritage acclaimed in the novel's ambiguous title. If so, his character also draws substance from the
spirit of the Boy of Antibes and the impulse to joy; (p. 200) for
Penkethman not only in his youth danced and gave pleasure
to Walter's mother but also still in his later years can share in
the amusements of the cabaret below the political strife that
rends the metropolis overhead.

That the character embodies traits of Ford himself through
its relation to his personal myth of Provence seems apparent,
though the mask is an elaborate artifice. Something of an outlaw to fixed institutions, an internationalist, and more a patron
to the young than a father in the usual sense, Penkethman's
role approximates to that of Ford in the later years; and the
enigma becomes denser through the close resemblance of the
son, Walter, "a tall, tweed-dressed, good-humored blonde fellow," (p. 14) to the detective, in spite of the latter's massive
bulk. Waiving, however, the autobiographical factor, the
figure of Penkethman constitutes a version of the standard
for individual conduct, the Plutarchian image that Ford had
held in mind through so much of his life, and a more developed

and positive model of the hero than Ford had tried to imagine in his early Apollo or even in Christopher Tietjens with his Victorian involvement. Perhaps some of the assurance and vitality attributed to Penkethman derives from his origin in Ford's private conviction over an extended period of time rather than in borrowed theory; for in a way typical of Ford, Penkethman is not the professional artist or dilettante frequently regarded in the later novels as bound to a sterile society but instead an artist in life, though also a guardian and preserver of the aesthetic impulse credited with a hope of survival in the union of the painter, Cassie, and the doctor-farmer, Leroy. In this light such a character represents an inevitable outcome of Ford's postwar concern with civilized depression and the problem of death which is central to all of the later novels from *When the Wicked Man* on. That Ford's deep and enduring response to the strain of the war, which he had recorded initially in the memorable scene in *No More Parades* where Tietjens witnesses Morgan's death, may be detected in the whole range of his fiction in the 1930's is beyond doubt; and this same anxiety motivates his continuing effort to project dramatically the cultural plight and the means to its cure. In *Vive Le Roy* Penkethman bestows upon the young lovers the specific benefit of a past within which they may achieve identity and thus provides the chief remedy for the ills noted by Ford as besetting modern man, in particular the feeling of homelessness and the burden of mental tension due to growing conflict and disorder. In his later work Ford did not enlarge measurably the catalogue of afflictions that he had begun to recognize in even his earliest novels, but he did advance in resolving them within the scheme of his Nordic contra Provençal myth with its supplementary images like that of the Great Road.

Whereas this accretion of personal myth in the later fiction is a feature peculiar to Ford's postwar phase, it is not of sudden origin, having emerged out of his early preoccupation with matters of faith, nor incompatible with his Impressionism and its use of representative figures and situations. But in taking a mythical direction from a contemporary base, Ford indicated ways in which the novel might occupy new areas of form and sensibility.

Chapter X

The Impressionist Legacy

IN REMARKING that Ford's trouble was an inability to suffer fools gladly, Conrad offered a reasonable explanation not only of Ford's numerous personal imbroglios but also of a main element in his character as a writer. Ford possessed, undeniably, exceptional intelligence, so much, in fact, that Stephen Crane thought him capable of patronizing God. For this reason, he never quite managed to write a stupid book, in this respect being deficient in a quality belonging to a good many of his contemporaries in the field of popular fiction; and even in trivia, like *The Panel,* he could not stop contentedly with sheer nonsense. Nonsense had to be turned against itself so as to provide a *bonne bouche* for the perceptive reader; and by reason of this adroit handling his novels, even the most dated, contain somewhere veins of brilliance. His style was not esoteric after the fashion that came to prevail in the 1920's, since this would have been at variance with his literary creed which today needs expounding if his finer effects of implication and compressed statement are to be grasped at all; but together with an artist's sensitivity, his temperament was natively intellectual, as may be detected in his appreciation of the eighteenth century and in the tendency of his writing, especially the earlier work, towards modes of irony and satire more topical than the cosmic ironies of Hardy or Conrad. Rationalized in literary doctrine as the attitude may have been, he abhorred what seemed to him amorphous or expansive, hence his notorious aversion to Fielding and Thackeray; and in the English novelists that he most praised, James and Conrad, his taste singled out those works distinguished for close and intricate design—*What Maisie Knew, The Turn of the Screw, Heart of Darkness, The Secret Agent, Under*

293

Western Eyes. Clearly he took for granted that the novel must advance from this point, that the modern reader would accept no retreat from this level of complexity. As a consequence he persisted in the endeavor to extend the possibilities of form and to perfect a minute and delicate craftsmanship. Intelligence of this kind, perhaps more than anything else, accounted for the unpopularity of books in which he sought to condition readers to the niceties of the Affair.

In his early work leading to *The Good Soldier* the intelligence gave signs of turning rancorous from lack of proper stimulation or from its exercise in social diatribe; and ironically the war, while it left him for the time being weak in hope of survival, proved more tonic than the Edwardian atmosphere in giving his spirits outlet in genuine sympathies and a real concern with the problem of human recovery. Perhaps, moreover, as with Yeats, the war afforded him the sense of tragedy that he had accused the peacetime world of having lost. In rational terms he opposed late Victorianism on cultural grounds, blaming commercialism and luxury for debased standards in action and the arts; and his increasing bitterness must have been occasioned in great measure by the defeat of his aspirations for the *English Review*. Frustration, as a result, may have vented itself to some degree in his portrayal of characters like Luscombe in *The Simple Life Limited* and Blood in *Mr. Fleight*, men whose strength has no place in a frivolous society.

Although this cultural dissatisfaction had a reasonable basis in his reflections on the course of events as set forth in his books on the state of England and the contemporary scene generally, it may likewise have grown out of his own consciousness of inadequate status in the world of his day and have affected the air of Flaubertian detachment evident particularly in his earlier novels. In Ford the note of expatriation, as of a kind of expatriate at large, seems more insistent than in James and Conrad or Crane, who was never anything but American; and the theme of homelessness is as recurrent in his work as that of the search for a country which led him towards the Provence celebrated in his last books. His early novels have an oddly rarefied tone—a deficiency in the English place sense which came naturally to writers like Wells, Galsworthy, and Lawrence; the main characters are in some way alien, like the partly Greek Grimshaw in *A Call* or the "transatlantic" American Don Kellegg in *An English Girl,* the social view restricted to rather eccentric and frequently idle members of a supposedly privileged class. It is, therefore, perhaps significant that after having identified himself with the Army, Ford wrote most convincingly and tolerantly of English character in *Parade's End* and in the same work created in Tietjens his first real hero in the usual sense. Subsidiary though such matters may be in formal evaluation of the tetralogy, they probably account in considerable measure for the popularity of that novel with the common reader.

In one light, consequently, Ford might be considered a kind of expatriate before the arrival of the lost generation, whose outlook he was well equipped to understand. He was not, in any case, a social novelist as the term is normally understood and as Wells and Forster, Dreiser and Fitzgerald, in varying fashion, could be called. To locate Ford in the literary map of his time, the distinction seems imperative. Whether or not in order to cultivate his special aptitudes and limitations, he endeavored to make himself the exponent of a novel of international relationships, being convinced, seemingly, that modern fiction would tend away from provincialism. Undoubtedly he had discerned this trend in the work of James, notably in such books as *The Golden Bowl,* and in the Conrad who changed direction with *Nostromo;* yet in his independent progress in this line Ford moved out from the mood of regnant Imperialism, still prevailing in a novel of contrasting nationalities like *The Inheritors,* and into the newer atmosphere of lowered Imperial enthusiasm which followed the Boer War and continued into the cosmopolitanism of the Edwardian era. With the latter age, including the rising influence of America, he could deal with more intimate understanding than

Conrad, for example, possessed; and in his novels directly preceding *The Good Soldier* he displays familiarity with the looser manners and uncertain social values of the period. Being anti-Imperialist, he leaned instinctively towards an international position; and from this standpoint his 1907 novel, *An English Girl,* which strives for a broader range than his books set in England, marks the beginning of a course to run through *The Good Soldier* and ultimately on to his postwar novels with their international cast of characters. In this development, his handling of international issues is not merely for the sake of novelty. Already in *An English Girl* he seeks to examine a world peculiar to a post-Imperial generation, and in an approach of this kind he stands almost alone among novelists in English before the international vogue of the 1920's. Although in recent years writers like Lawrence Durrell and P. H. Newby or Frederic Prokosch might be regarded as carrying on more or less in this path, Ford is still distinguished by indifference to the exotic for itself. His concerns do not lie outside the European tradition, except as the United States shares in that inheritance.

This international range came as an accompaniment to Ford's conception of the novelist as historian, a view which brought him close to a main development in fiction at least through the first quarter of the century and especially so in the years preceding the Great War. In adopting this position, Ford responded not only to what seemed to him the important historical changes taking place around the turn of the century and offering a particular obligation to the novelist but also to what he thought essential to raising the novel to serious status and influence in a new and historically conscious age. Although in this opinion he could have looked for precedent to the Goncourts in France, his outlook was undoubtedly formed by the personal attraction to history in itself which made him more adept at ordinary historical fiction than he ever cared to admit and also by his early contact with the tradition of the artist historians of the nineteenth century, a manner of writing which, not without reason, he regarded as more comprehensive in scope and hence more illuminating than the narrow specialization that he saw as becoming the mode in the twentieth. In Ford this historical persuasion appears different not only from the sense of history informing the work of James and Conrad, and amply recognized by Ford, but also from the expression of historical interest in a writer like Bennett, who is in certain respects of Ford's generation.

With Ford the notion of glory or the vestiges of confidence in history which still hold a place in James and Conrad, despite their capacity for scepticism, have begun to wane; and he moves directly into a central current of modernism, as Joyce was doing from another quarter, by his confrontation of the religious dilemma and its bearing upon sexual relationships, for which reason one is always conscious of his relevance to the mainstream of contemporary literature. In this respect his stand as novelist-historian is a fundamental departure from what such a title might have implied in the nineteenth century, as, for example, with Tolstoy or Thackeray, since Ford is eminently, and especially in his earlier work, the historian almost exclusively of the deficiencies of his time, always engrossed in the lapse of tradition which he emphasizes repeatedly by the failure of the paternal figures in his novels. In consequence, he belongs with the younger Joyce and Lawrence as a chief witness to the late Victorian disillusionment, which points his ironies, and, through his role of historian, a more overt witness. From this perspective the course of his literary career reveals itself as sequential and even predictable. After the critical mood of his early books and the decisive shock of the war as a final rebuke to historical confidence, his work moves towards the establishment of personal faith conceived as myth. By and large, his development resembles that of others in the literary generation—including Yeats, Eliot, and Lawrence—mature enough to experience the war as a central crisis in their lives. Ironical, however, as he had been towards inadequacies in the Victorian attitude to passion in

both its sexual and religious bearing, he seems to have retained traits of early century liberalism and aestheticism
strong enough to prevent his turning after the war to either
of the common alternatives of religious orthodoxy or socialism. His personal vision, though it favored an image of the
individual restored through an ethic of disciplined joy, was
still too fastidious to admit the simplicities of dogma; and for
this reason his Provençal myth tends to appear idiosyncratic
in details, even though its ideals of harmony and grace are
attractive. Although the war had left him acquiescent in the
wiping out of the immediate past, he could not in his mythical
program relinquish an older past as source of the cultural
values in which he believed.

It follows, then, that in adopting and perfecting the form
of the Affair, Ford was not simply indulging a fancy for technical artifice but was, instead, evolving a design in conformity
with his own vision, as his long preliminary efforts towards
The Good Soldier go to prove. Much as he owed to James for
inspiration, Ford really took his departure from a relatively
limited segment of the whole Jamesian corpus and interpreted
books like *What Maisie Knew* in accordance with his own
predilections. In his hands the Affair became not a novel of
character or story but a fictional rendering of a representative
datum of history, whether past or present, in which persons
and action were specific in themselves but also to some degree
universalized in meaning. Within this structure Ford attempted
to compress the central preoccupations of civilized life, from
the social to the aesthetic, which prompted his use for the most
part of upper class characters, just as Eliot went to a similar
milieu in order to render contemporary mentality in his early
monologues. Significantly, the Affair, while historical in purpose, is in effect not progressive but static, web-like, and thus
implicitly counter to temporal advance. The movement travels
inward towards a concealed center of intrigue, which ordinarily rests upon grounds of passion and thus opposes the in-
corrigible human heart to the claims of historical optimism, a

pattern that Ford had intimated even in his imperfect first novel, *The Shifting of the Fire*. His reason for acclaiming *The Good Soldier* lay in recognizing that in this book, once and for all, technical excellence had resulted in the consummate Affair, which is not tragedy but an account of sexual and religious disaster. By this measure he could, justifiably, view the Tietjens tetralogy as falling into second place, since the latter work unavoidably approaches the conventional historical mode despite Ford's attempt to shape history to the pattern of an Affair, mainly through the prominence given to the sexual-religious antagonism between Sylvia and Christopher. Magnificent though it is as fictional art, the tetralogy depends for full comprehension on a reader's knowledge of some characteristics of the late Victorian world. By contrast, *The Good Soldier* requires a grasp mainly of the texture of Ford's irony. Hence it may be read at any time, no matter what the reader's disposition towards history.

Whereas both of these works are masterpieces, *The Good Soldier* has so far exerted the greater formal influence, although the tetralogy presents notable features of its own as one of the few types of modern prose epic to warrant comparison with *Ulysses*. With *The Good Soldier* Ford provided a model, which has never been surpassed, for the novel of sexual and religious crisis within a particular cultural setting, a form naturally suited to the concerns of the mature Faulkner, to Greene in *The End of the Affair*, and perhaps also to L. P. Hartley in a work like *The Go-Between*. Whether or not, however, the form can retain in adaptation the original complexity that it drew from the particular historical circumstances might be questioned. Certainly, for example, C. P. Snow's *The Affair*, while a novel of the intricate interplay of human aims and emotions, is primarily social in reference and concerned with institutional intrigue. It has not, by reason of change in period, the sense of cultural apprehension that intensifies Ford's vision in all of his work in addition to *The Good Soldier* and that makes art in itself one of his recurrent themes.

Once again it is his intelligence that here supports him; for whereas his cultural speculations are biased by his personal attitudes and often exceed the particulars normally reserved to the novelist, his intuitive perceptions of the causes and results of the fracturing of Western tradition are keen and arresting. Of special note in this respect is his procedure, with a novelist's instinct, in referring the cultural tensions in force to the mental distress of his characters, a habit indicating his awareness of dealing with an advanced and introspective civilization vulnerable largely through the mind. Although almost from the first he had designated the modern predicament as one of psychic strain resulting from cultural confusion, he gave the matter special emphasis when in *The Rash Act* he symbolized the destruction of the war by the sword wound to Hugh Monckton's brain, thereby rejecting not only the idea of physical impotence attached to Hemingway's Jake Barnes or Lawrence's Clifford Chatterley but also the possibility of scientific solutions to what he thought the deeper problem of cultural barbarism. In pursuing this track, he developed the monologue of psychological duplicity, first employed with Dowell in *The Good Soldier,* and that of religio-secular confusion, remarkably associated with Notterdam in *When the Wicked Man*—certainly two of the notable contributions to fictional style in the present century. But following *The Good Soldier* generally, he became master of a language suited to the evasions and restraints of contemporary life. In one sense it is the muted speech of the English good people that he depicted in *The Good Soldier* and *Parade's End,* the convention in which decorum inhibits emotional outcry; yet it is likewise a demonstration, revealed in a different way by the stream of consciousness technique, of the prevailing modern discrepancy between overt discourse and the broad undersurfaces of unspoken feeling. Rather than seeking as a rule to disclose this private thought directly, as in stream of consciousness, Ford effectively and impressionistically renders its delayed effects, thus providing some of the most forceful episodes in his novels, many of which are richly exemplified in *Parade's End*, though the practice is common to all of his later fiction. In Ford a cultural attitude led to the discovery of technique rather than the process being reversed.

Most, consequently, that Ford had to say regarding the importance of method to the novelist may be construed as an argument that the novel be provided with a tradition to bring it to an equality with the other literary forms. That he favored—though he did not exclusively—the Flaubertian or modern French tendency is a consideration of less moment, since this taste had become familiar after the crusading of George Moore. As a technical critic Ford was able to draw the attention of the practicing novelist to a number of usable devices, all of which have passed into the common fund of the craftsman; but the bulk of these attain immediate interest chiefly insofar as their function relates to the central aims that they further. They are, on the whole, subsidiary to what Ford produced in the way of form, including the mythical constructs of his late years, and in the anecdotal prose style which supplied one of the keys to modern narrative speech. Perhaps his mistake was to assume that the novel would proceed on a main course of greater allusiveness and subtlety, a trend that he saw checked during his lifetime. By instinct he was a refined craftsman, just as he was by nature civilized; and in the end he found himself rather alone in a world where these qualities had less chance of appreciation than with the kind of public he had expected to address in his earlier years. Had he been no more than a fictional historian little of his work might have survived. Instead, being first and foremost an artist, he gave to the novels of his maturity the enduring character of style.

Notes

Chapter II

1. Ford, *Great Trade Route*, p. 204.
2. Ford, *The March of Literature*, p. 793.
3. Joseph Conrad, *Letters to William Blackwood*, p. 129.
4. Goldring, *The Last Pre-Raphaelite*, p. 100.
5. Ford, *Return to Yesterday*, p. 198.
6. Baines, *Joseph Conrad*, pp. 217–20.
7. Jessie Conrad, *Joseph Conrad and His Circle*, pp. 64, 87.
8. *Joseph Conrad*, p. 271.
9. *The Last Pre-Raphaelite*, pp. 153–66.
10. *The Last Pre-Raphaelite*, pp. 176–79.
11. Ford, *It Was the Nightingale*, pp. 63–64.

Chapter III

1. Ford, *Mightier Than the Sword*, pp. 250–51.
2. Ford, *Some Do Not . . .*, p. 18.
3. Ford, *Rossetti*, p. 74.
4. Goldring, *The Last Pre-Raphaelite*, p. 118.
5. Ford, *The March of Literature*, p. 800.
6. Ford, *Ancient Lights*, pp. 154–55.
7. Ford, *It Was the Nightingale*, pp. 76–77.
8. *Ancient Lights*, p. 194.
9. *Ancient Lights*, p. 241.
10. *Ancient Lights*, p. 195.
11. *Ancient Lights*, p. 226.
12. Hunt, *The Flurried Years*, pp. 38–39.
13. *Mightier Than the Sword*, pp. 52–53.
14. *Ancient Lights*, p. 242.
15. Ford, *Joseph Conrad*, p. 121.
16. *Joseph Conrad*, p. 106.
17. *Joseph Conrad*, pp. 56–57.
18. *The March of Literature*, p. 835.
19. *Mightier Than the Sword*, p. 93.
20. Ford, *Thus to Revisit*, p. 87.
21. Ford, *Great Trade Route*, p. 24.
22. *The March of Literature*, pp. 98, 99.

23. *The March of Literature*, p. 473.
24. Ford, *A Little Less Than Gods*, p. viii.
25. *The March of Literature*, p. 793.
26. Ford, *The 'Half Moon,'* p. vi.
27. Ford, *Between St. Denis and St. George*, p. 77.
28. Ford, *Provence*, p. 329.
29. Ford, *No Enemy*, p. 169.
30. Conrad, *Letters to William Blackwood*, p. 44.
31. *Joseph Conrad*, pp. 46–47.
32. Ford, *The Critical Attitude*, pp. 29–30.
33. *The Critical Attitude*, p. 30.
34. Ford, *New York is not America*, p. 35.
35. Ford, *Henry James*, p. 146.
36. *Henry James*, pp. 22–23.
37. Masterman, *The Condition of England*, p. 17.
38. Bennett, *Journals*, pp. 148–49.
39. *Joseph Conrad*, p. 208.
40. *Joseph Conrad*, p. 174.
41. *Great Trade Route*, p. 177.
42. Ford, *The Cinque Ports*, p. 76.
43. *The Critical Attitude*, p. 186.
44. Ford, *The Soul of London*, p. 121.
45. *The Soul of London*, p. 27.
46. *The Soul of London*, p. xii.
47. *The March of Literature*, p. 99.
48. *Mightier Than the Sword*, pp. 94–95.
49. Ford, *The English Novel*, pp. 131–32.
50. *Thus to Revisit*, p. 36.
51. *The March of Literature*, p. 821.
52. *Henry James*, p. 82.
53. *Henry James*, pp. 152–53.
54. Ford, *A Call*, p. 303.
55. *Henry James*, pp. 167–68.
56. *Thus to Revisit*, p. 91.
57. *Between St. Denis and St. George*, pp. 202–03.
58. *Great Trade Route*, p. 212.
59. *Joseph Conrad*, p. 159.
60. *Thus to Revisit*, pp. 52–53.
61. *Thus to Revisit*, p. 40.
62. *Mightier Than the Sword*, p. 278.
63. *Great Trade Route*, p. 395.
64. *Joseph Conrad*, p. 101.
65. Ford, *When Blood is Their Argument*, p. xx.

66. *Mightier Than the Sword,* pp. 76–77.
67. Ford, *A Man Could Stand Up—*, p. 98.

CHAPTER IV

1. Ford, *Thus to Revisit,* p. 139.
2. Ford, *Great Trade Route,* pp. 33–34.
3. Ford, *The English Novel,* pp. 146–47.
4. Ford, *Rossetti,* p. 55.
5. *Thus to Revisit,* p. 44.
6. Conrad, *Letters to William Blackwood,* p. 154.
7. Ford, *Henry James,* p. 161.
8. Ford, *The March of Literature,* p. 116.
9. Ford, *Joseph Conrad,* p. 163.
10. *Thus to Revisit,* p. 46; *The March of Literature,* p. 699.
11. *The March of Literature,* p. 496.
12. *The March of Literature,* p. 603.
13. *The March of Literature,* p. 498.
14. Ford, *A Mirror to France,* pp. 273–74.
15. *Joseph Conrad,* pp. 197–98.
16. *Rossetti,* p. 54.
17. Ford, *No More Parades,* p. 239.
18. *The March of Literature,* p. 808
19. Conrad, *The Secret Agent,* p. 24.
20. Ford, *Mr. Fleight,* p. 165.
21. *The English Novel,* p. 128.
22. *Henry James,* pp. 154–55.
23. *The March of Literature,* p. 374.
24. Ford, *The Critical Attitude,* pp. 91–92.
25. *The March of Literature,* pp. 99–100.
26. Ford, *Ancient Lights,* p. xi.
27. *Joseph Conrad,* pp. 129–30.
28. Flaubert, *Sentimental Education,* pp. 383–84.
29. James, *What Maisie Knew,* p. viii.
30. *What Maisie Knew,* p. 21.
31. James, *The Golden Bowl,* p. 194.
32. *Thus to Revisit,* pp. 150–51.
33. *The Cinque Ports,* p. viii.
34. *The English Novel,* p. 120.
35. *The March of Literature,* p. 602.
36. *The Cinque Ports,* p. 372.
37. Ford, *It Was the Nightingale,* p. 116.
38. *Great Trade Route,* p. 50.

39. Ford, *The Pre-Raphaelite Brotherhood*, pp. 125–26.
40. *Rossetti*, pp. 28–29.
41. *Rossetti*, p. 26.
42. Conrad and Hueffer, *Romance*, pp. 330–31.
43. *Romance*, p. 530.
44. Conrad and Ford, *The Nature of a Crime*, pp. 86–87.
45. James, *The Wings of the Dove*, II, p. 188.
46. *Joseph Conrad*, pp. 180–81.

CHAPTER V

1. Ford, *Joseph Conrad*, p. 176.
2. *Joseph Conrad*, p. 175.
3. Ford, *Rossetti*, pp. 28–29.
4. Goldring, *The Last Pre-Raphaelite*, p. 114.
5. Ford, *Ancient Lights*, pp. 37–38.
6. Ford, *The March of Literature*, pp. 665, 668.
7. *The March of Literature*, pp. 780–81.
8. Lukács, *Der Historische Roman*, pp. 198–201.
9. *Joseph Conrad*, p. 21.
10. Ford, *Return to Yesterday*, p. 284.
11. Ford, *Women and Men*, p. 40.
12. Ford, *The Spirit of the People*, p. 286.
13. Conrad, *Letters to William Blackwood*, p. 129.
14. Conrad and Hueffer, *Romance*, p. 157.
15. *Letters to William Blackwood*, p. 139.
16. *Joseph Conrad*, pp. 46–47.
17. *Romance*, p. 30.
18. *Return to Yesterday*, p. 232.
19. *Joseph Conrad*, p. 14.
20. Ford, *The Fifth Queen*, p. 60.
21. *The Spirit of the People*, p. 284.
22. Ford, *Hans Holbein the Younger*, p. 9.
23. Ford, *The Fifth Queen Crowned*, p. 309.
24. *The Fifth Queen*, p. 20.
25. Ford, *When Blood is Their Argument*, p. 299.
26. *The Fifth Queen*, pp. 178–79.
27. *The Fifth Queen*, pp. 301–02.
28. *Hans Holbein*, p. 11.
29. *Hans Holbein*, pp. 12–13.
30. *Hans Holbein*, p. 80.
31. *Hans Holbein*, pp. 81–82.
32. Ford, *Privy Seal*, pp. 241–42.

33. Ford, *No Enemy*, pp. 177–78.
34. *The Fifth Queen*, pp. 231–32.
35. *The Fifth Queen*, p. 36.
36. *The Fifth Queen Crowned*, pp. 312–13.
37. *The Last Pre-Raphaelite*, p. 137.
38. Ford, *The 'Half Moon,'* p. 197.
39. *The 'Half Moon,'* p. 116.
40. *The 'Half Moon,'* p. 115.
41. *The 'Half Moon,'* pp. 210–11.
42. *Women and Men*, pp. 30; 32–33.
43. *The Spirit of the People*, p. 242.
44. Ford, *The Portrait*, p. 56.
45. *The Portrait*, p. 101.
46. *The Portrait*, p. 101.
47. *The Portrait*, pp. 38–39.
48. *The Portrait*, pp. 205–06.
49. *Rossetti*, pp. 48–49.
50. Ford, *Ladies Whose Bright Eyes*, pp. 10–11.
51. Jessie Conrad, *Joseph Conrad and His Circle*, p. 221.
52. *Joseph Conrad*, pp. 63–64; *Return to Yesterday*, pp. 193–95.
53. Ford, *A Little Less Than Gods*, p. 282.
54. *A Little Less Than Gods*, p. 273.
55. *A Little Less Than Gods*, pp. 255–56.
56. *A Little Less Than Gods*, pp. 282–83.
57. *A Little Less Than Gods*, pp. 148–49.
58. *A Little Less Than Gods,* p. 136.

CHAPTER VI

1. Ford, *The Shifting of the Fire*, pp. 139–40.
2. *The Shifting of the Fire*, p. 257.
3. *The Shifting of the Fire*, pp. 297–98.
4. Conrad and Ford, *The Nature of a Crime*, pp. 32–34.
5. *The Shifting of the Fire*, p. 71.
6. Ford, *Joseph Conrad*, p. 136.
7. *Joseph Conrad*, p. 135.
8. *Joseph Conrad*, p. 133.
9. Conrad and Hueffer, *The Inheritors*, p. 7.
10. *The Inheritors*, p. 84.
11. *The Inheritors*, p. 206.
12. *The Inheritors*, p. 164.
13. *The Inheritors*, p. 38.
14. Ford, *The Benefactor*, p. 10.

15. *The Benefactor,* p. 20.
16. Ford, *An English Girl,* p. 208.
17. *An English Girl,* pp. 116–17.
18. *An English Girl,* p. 146.
19. *An English Girl,* pp. 148–49.
20. Ford, *Mr. Apollo,* p. 118.
21. *Mr. Apollo,* p. 48.
22. Ford, *A Call,* pp. 303–304.
23. *A Call,* p. 160.
24. *A Call,* pp. 46–47.
25. *A Call,* p. 3.
26. *A Call,* p. 274.
27. *A Call,* p. 284.
28. Ford, *The Simple Life Limited,* pp. 74–75.
29. *The Simple Life Limited,* p. 52.
30. *The Simple Life Limited,* p. 5.
31. *The Simple Life Limited,* p. 99.
32. Ford, *The Panel,* pp. 9–10.
33. Ford, *Mr. Fleight,* p. 276.
34. *Mr. Fleight,* p. 133.
35. *Mr. Fleight,* pp. 24–25.
36. *Mr. Fleight,* p. 262.
37. *Mr. Fleight,* p. 176.
38. *Mr. Fleight,* p. 299.
39. *Mr. Fleight,* p. 304.

Chapter VII

1. Ford, *The Good Soldier,* p. xx.
2. Ford, *Return to Yesterday,* p. 399.
3. *The Good Soldier,* p. xix.
4. Hunt, *The Flurried Years,* pp. 135–36.
5. *The Flurried Years,* pp. 134–36.
6. *Return to Yesterday,* p. 265.
7. Ford, *The Cinque Ports,* p. 36.
8. Ford, *The Spirit of the People,* p. 338.
9. *The Spirit of the People,* p. 338.
10. *The Spirit of the People,* pp. 338–39.
11. *Return to Yesterday,* pp. 123–24.
12. *Return to Yesterday,* p. 263–64.
13. *Return to Yesterday,* p. 262.
14. *Return to Yesterday,* pp. 263–64.
15. *Return to Yesterday,* p. 264.

16. *Return to Yesterday,* p. 263.
17. *The Flurried Years,* p. 243.
18. Ford, *Ancient Lights,* pp. xi–xii.
19. Ford, *The English Novel,* p. 117.
20. Ford, *The March of Literature,* p. 804.
21. Ford, *Great Trade Route,* p. 388.

CHAPTER VIII

1. Young, *Ford Madox Ford,* p. 28.
2. Ford, *On Heaven,* p. 19.
3. Ford, *It Was the Nightingale,* p. 193.
4. *It Was the Nightingale,* pp. 98–99.
5. Ford, *The Marsden Case,* p. 197.
6. *The Marsden Case,* p. 261.
7. *The Marsden Case,* pp. 304–05.
8. Ford, *No More Parades,* p. vii.
9. Hunt, *The Flurried Years,* p. 171.
10. Ford, *Return to Yesterday,* pp. 243–44.
11. *It Was the Nightingale,* p. 210.
12. Ford, *The Last Post,* p. 150.
13. Ford, *Some Do Not . . . ,* p. 303.
14. Ford, *Women and Men,* pp. 30; 32–35; *Mightier Than the Sword,* pp. 232–33.
15. *A Man Could Stand Up—,* p. 155.
16. *Some Do Not . . . ,* p. 264.
17. *No More Parades,* p. 20.
18. *It Was the Nightingale,* pp. 206, 214.
19. *No More Parades,* p. 222.
20. *Mightier Than the Sword,* pp. 39–40.
21. *It Was the Nightingale,* p. 162.
22. *Some Do Not . . . ,* p. 3.
23. *Some Do Not . . . ,* p. 328.
24. *Some Do Not . . . ,* p. 90.
25. *Some Do Not . . . ,* p. 143.
26. *Some Do Not . . . ,* p. 159.
27 *Some Do Not . . . ,* p. 159.
28. *No More Parades,* pp. 25–26.
29. *No More Parades,* p. 24.
30. *No More Parades,* p. 227.
31. *Some Do Not . . . ,* p. 24.
32. *No More Parades,* p. 296.
33. *No More Parades,* p. 309.

34. *A Man Could Stand Up—*, p. 335.
35. *A Man Could Stand Up—*, p. 291.
36. *A Man Could Stand Up—*, p. 224.
37. *The Last Post*, p. 50.
38. *The Last Post*, pp. 31, 41.
39. *The Last Post*, p. 283.
40. Ford, *No Enemy*, p. 197.
41. *No Enemy*, pp. 288–89.
42. *No Enemy*, p. 130.
43. *No Enemy*, pp. 59–60.
44. *No Enemy*, p. 23.
45. *No Enemy*, pp. 204–17.
46. *No Enemy*, pp. 184–89.
47. *No Enemy*, pp. 190–93.
48. *No Enemy*, pp. 251–57.
49. *No Enemy*, p. 11.

CHAPTER IX

1. Goldring, *The Last Pre-Raphaelite*, p. 263.
2. *The Last Pre-Raphaelite*, p. 244.
3. Ford, *Provence*, p. 295.
4. *Provence*, p. 308.
5. *Provence*, p. 298.
6. *Provence*, pp. 299–300.
7. Ford, *Great Trade Route*, pp. 29–30.
8. *Great Trade Route*, p. 194.
9. *Great Trade Route*, pp. 117–18.
10. *The Last Pre-Raphaelite*, p. 204.
11. Ford, *When the Wicked Man*, p. 4.
12. Kracauer, *From Caligari to Hitler*, pp. 28–31.
13. James, *Fourteen Stories by Henry James*, p. x.
14. *Provence*, pp. 49–50.
15. Groenewegen-Frankfort, *Arrest and Movement*, p. 216.
16. Ford, *The Rash Act*, pp. 32–33.
17. Ford, *Henry for Hugh*, p. 52.
18. *The Rash Act*, pp. 322–23.
19. *Henry for Hugh*, pp. 218–19.
20. *The Rash Act*, p. 326.
21. *Henry for Hugh*, pp. 70–71.
22. Ford, *Vive Le Roy*, p. 73.

Bibliography

I. Works by Ford Madox Ford

A Little Less Than Gods: A Romance. London: Duckworth, 1928.

A Man Could Stand Up—. New York: Grosset and Dunlap, 1926.

A Mirror to France. New York: Albert and Charles Boni, 1926.

An English Girl: A Romance. London: Methuen and Co., 1907.

Ancient Lights and Certain New Reflections: Being the Memoirs of a Young Man. London: Chapman and Hall, 1911.

The Benefactor: A Tale of a Small Circle. London: Brown, Langham and Co., 1905.

A Call: The Tale of Two Passions. London: Chatto and Windus, 1910.

Between St. Denis and St. George: A Sketch of Three Civilisations. London, New York, Toronto: Hodder and Stoughton, 1915.

The Cinque Ports: A Historical and Descriptive Record. Illustrated by William Hyde. Edinburgh and London: William Blackwood and Sons, 1900.

Collected Poems. London: Martin Secker, 1916.

The Critical Attitude. London: Duckworth and Co., 1911.

England and the English: An Interpretation. New York: McClure, Phillips, and Co., 1907.

The English Novel: From the Earliest Days to the Death of Joseph Conrad. Philadelphia and London: J. B. Lippincott and Co., 1929.

The Fifth Queen Crowned: A Romance. London: Eveleigh Nash, 1910.

Ford Madox Brown: A Record of His Life and Work. London, New York, Bombay: Longmans, Green, and Co., 1896.

The Good Soldier: A Tale of Passion. With an Interpretation by Mark Schorer. New York: Alfred A. Knopf, 1951.

Great Trade Route. New York, Toronto: Oxford University Press, 1937.

The 'Half Moon': A Romance of the Old World and the New. London: Eveleigh Nash, 1909.

Hans Holbein the Younger. London: Duckworth and Co., 1914.

The Heart of the Country: A Survey of a Modern Land. London: Alston Rivers, 1906.

Henry for Hugh: A Novel. Philadelphia, London: J. B. Lippincott, 1934.

Henry James: A Critical Study. New York: Dodd, Mead and Co., 1916.

It Was the Nightingale. Philadelphia and London: J. B. Lippincott, 1933.

Joseph Conrad: A Personal Remembrance. London: Duckworth and Co., 1924.

Ladies Whose Bright Eyes: A Romance. London: Constable and Co., 1931.

The Last Post. New York: The Literary Guild of America, 1928.

The March of Literature: From Confucius' Day to Our Own. New York: The Dial Press, 1938.

The Marsden Case: A Romance. London: Duckworth and Co., 1923.

Mightier Than the Sword: Memories and Criticisms of Henry James, Joseph Conrad, Thomas Hardy, H. G. Wells, Stephen Crane, D. H. Lawrence, John Galsworthy, Ivan Turgenev, W. H. Hudson, Theodore Dreiser, Algernon Charles Swinburne. London: George Allen and Unwin, 1938.

Mr. Apollo: A Just Possible Story. London: Methuen and Co., 1908.

Mister Bosphorus and the Muses: or a Short History of Poetry in Britain Variety Entertainment in Four Acts words by Ford Madox Ford Music by several popular composers With Harlequinade, Transformation Scene, Cinematograph Effects, and Many Other Novelties, as well as Old and Tried Favourites Decorated with Designs Engraved on Wood by Paul Nash. London: Duckworth and Co., 1923.

Mr. Fleight. London: Howard Latimer, 1913.

New York is not America: Being a Mirror to the States. New York: Albert and Charles Boni, 1927.

No Enemy: A Tale of Reconstruction. New York: The Macaulay Company, 1929.

No More Parades. New York: Grosset and Dunlap, 1925.

On Heaven: And Poems Written on Active Service. London, New York: John Lane, 1918.

The Panel. London: Constable and Co., 1912.

Parade's End. New York: Alfred A. Knopf, 1961.

The Portrait. London: Methuen and Co., 1910.

The Pre-Raphaelite Brotherhood: A Critical Monograph. London: Duckworth and Co., 1907.

Privy Seal: His Last Venture. London: Alston Rivers, 1907.

Provence: From Minstrels to the Machine. Philadelphia, London: J. B. Lippincott, 1935.

The Rash Act: A Novel. New York: Ray Long and Richard R. Smith, 1933.

Return to Yesterday. New York: H. Liveright, 1932.
Rossetti: A Critical Essay on His Art. Chicago, New York: Rand, McNally and Co., n.d.
The Shifting of the Fire. London: T. Fisher Unwin, 1892.
The Simple Life Limited by Daniel Chaucer. London, New York: John Lane, 1911.
Some Do Not . . . New York: Grosset and Dunlap, 1927.
Songs From London. London: Elkin Mathews, 1910.
The Soul of London: A Survey of a Modern City. London: Alston Rivers, 1905.
The Spirit of the People. London: Alston Rivers, 1907.
Thus to Revisit: Some Reminiscences. London: Chapman and Hall, 1921.
Vive Le Roy. London: George Allen and Unwin, 1937.
When Blood is Their Argument: An Analysis of Prussian Culture. New York and London: Hodder and Stoughton, 1915.
When the Wicked Man. New York: Horace Liveright, 1931.
Women and Men. Paris: Contact Editions, 1923.
The Young Lovell, A Romance. London: Chatto and Windus, 1913.

II. Secondary References

Aiken, Conrad. *Scepticisms: Notes on Contemporary Poetry.* New York: A. A. Knopf, 1919.
Baines, Jocelyn. *Joseph Conrad: A Critical Biography.* London: Weidenfeld and Nicolson, 1959.
Béhaine, René. *The Survivors.* Translated by Edward Crankshaw. Preface by Ford Madox Ford. London: George Allen and Unwin Ltd., 1938.
Bennett, Arnold. *The Journals of Arnold Bennett.* Selected and edited by Frank Swinnerton. Melbourne, London, Baltimore: Penguin Books, 1954.
Blackmur, R. P. "The King Over the Water: Notes On the Novels of F. M. Hueffer," *The Princeton University Library Chronicle,* IX (April, 1948), 123–27.
Cassell, Richard A. *Ford Madox Ford: A Study of His Novels.* Baltimore: The Johns Hopkins Press, 1961.
Chaucer, Daniel. *The New Humpty Dumpty.* London: John Lane, 1912.
Conrad, Jessie. *Joseph Conrad and His Circle.* New York: E. P. Dutton and Co., 1935.
Conrad, Joseph. *Letters to William Blackwood and David S. Meldrum.* Ed. William Blackburn. Durham, North Carolina: Duke University Press, 1958.

Conrad, Joseph. *Notes on Life and Letters*. London: Gresham Publishing Co., 1925.

Conrad, Joseph. *Conrad's Prefaces to His Works*. London: J. M. Dent and Sons, 1937.

Conrad, Joseph. *The Sisters*. Introduction by Ford Madox Ford. New York: Crosby Gaige, 1928.

Conrad, Joseph and Hueffer, F. M. *The Inheritors: An Extravagant Story*. London: Gresham Publishing Co., 1925.

Conrad, Joseph and Ford, Ford Madox. *The Nature of a Crime*. Garden City, N.Y.: Doubleday, Page and Co., 1924.

Conrad, Joseph and Hueffer, F. M. *Romance: A Novel*. London: Gresham Publishing Co., 1925.

Crankshaw, Edward. "Ford Madox Ford," *The National Review*, CXXXI (August, 1948), 160–67.

de Traz, Georges. *See* Traz, Georges de.

Firebaugh, J. J. "Tietjens and the Tradition," *Pacific Spectator*, VI (Winter, 1952), 23–32.

Flaubert, Gustave, *Salambô*. London: The Pushkin Press, 1947.

―――. *Sentimental Education: The Story of a Young Man*. Introduction by Louis Bogan. New York: New Directions, 1957.

Goldring, Douglas. *The Last Pre-Raphaelite: A Record of the Life and Writings of Ford Madox Ford*. London: Macdonald and Co., 1948. Published in America under the title *Trained for Genius*. New York: E. P. Dutton, 1949.

―――. *Odd Man Out*. London: Chapman and Hall, 1935.

―――. *South Lodge: Reminiscences of Violet Hunt, Ford Madox Ford and the English Review Circle*. London: Constable and Co., 1943.

Gose, Elliott B. "The Strange Irregular Rhythm: An Analysis of *The Good Soldier*," *PMLA*, LXXII (June, 1957), 494–509.

Greene, Graham. *The Lost Childhood: and Other Essays*. New York: The Viking Press, 1952.

Groenewegen-Frankfort, H. A. *Arrest and Movement: An Essay on Space and Time in the representational Art of the ancient Near East*. London: Faber and Faber, 1951.

Hamann, Richard. *Der Impressionismus in Leben und Kunst*. Köln: M. Dumont, 1907.

Hicks, Granville, Richard Aldington, and others. "Homage to Ford Madox Ford; A Symposium." *New Directions*, 1942. Norfolk, Connecticut: New Directions, 1942, pp. 443–94.

Hough, Graham. *The Last Romantics*. London: Gerald Duckworth, 1949.

Hueffer, Francis. *Richard Wagner*. New York: Scribners and Welford, 1881.

――――. The Troubadours: A History of Provençal Life and Literature in the Middle Ages. London: Chatto and Windus, 1878.

Hueffer, Oliver Madox ["Jane Wardle"]. The Artistic Temperament. New York: McClure, Phillips and Co., 1907.

Hunt, Violet. The Flurried Years. London: Hurst and Blackett, 1926.

Hunt, Violet, and Hueffer, Ford Madox. Zeppelin Nights: A London Entertainment. London, New York: John Lane, 1916.

James, Henry. The Art of the Novel: Critical Prefaces. Introduction by Richard P. Blackmur. New York, London: Charles Scribner's Sons, 1947.

――――. Fourteen Stories by Henry James. Selected by David Garnett. London: Rupert Hart-Davis, 1947.

――――. The Golden Bowl. London: Methuen, 1956.

――――. In the Cage. London: Martin Secker, 1928.

――――. The Spoils of Poynton. London: John Lehmann, 1947.

――――. The Turn of the Screw. The Aspern Papers. London: J. M. Dent, 1935.

――――. What Maisie Knew. London: John Lehman, 1947.

――――. The Wings of the Dove. New York: The Modern Library, 1946.

James, William. The Varieties of Religious Experience: A Study in Human Nature. New York: The Modern Library.

Kenner, Hugh. The Poetry of Ezra Pound. London: Faber and Faber, 1951.

Kracauer, Siegfried. From Caligari to Hitler: A Psychological History of the German Film. New York: The Noonday Press, 1959.

Lid, R. W. "Tietjens in Disguise," The Kenyon Review, XXII (Spring, 1960), 265–76.

――――. "On the Time-Scheme of The Good Soldier," English Fiction in Transition, IV, no. 2 (1961), 9–10.

Lubbock, Percy, The Craft of Fiction. New York: Charles Scribner's Sons, 1921.

Ludwig, Richard M. "The Reputation of Ford Madox Ford," PMLA, LXXVI (December, 1961), 544–51.

Lukács, Georg. Der Historische Roman. Berlin: Aufbau-Verlag, 1955.

Macauley, Robie. "The Good Ford," The Kenyon Review, XI (Spring, 1949), 269–88.

MacShane, Frank. "The Pattern of Ford Madox Ford," New Republic, CXXXII (April 4, 1955), 16–17.

Masterman, C. F. G. The Condition of England. London: Methuen and Co., 1909.

Mayne, Ethel Colburn. *Blindman.* London: Chapman and Hall, 1919.

Meixner, John A. "The Saddest Story," *The Kenyon Review,* XXII (Spring, 1960), 234–64.

Norman, Charles. *Ezra Pound.* New York: The Macmillan Co., 1960.

Petronius Arbiter. *The Satyricon of Petronius Arbiter.* Translated by William Burnaby. New York: The Modern Library.

Playne, Caroline E. *The Pre-War Mind in Britain: An Historical Review.* London: George Allen and Unwin, 1928.

Schopenhauer, Arthur. *Essays from the Parerga and Paralipomena.* Translated by T. Bailey Saunders. London: George Allen and Unwin, 1951.

Traz, Georges de ("François Fosca"). *Edmond et Jules de Goncourt.* Paris: Albin Michel, 1941.

Tymms, Ralph. *Doubles in Literary Psychology.* Cambridge: Bowes and Bowes, 1949.

von der Kyrburg, Fritz ("Lieutenant Bilse"). *A Little Garrison: A Realistic Novel of German Army Life of Today.* Translated by Wolf von Schirbrand. New York: Frederick A. Stokes, 1904.

Walter, H. V. "The Political Sense of Ford Madox Ford," *New Republic,* CXXXIV (March 26, 1956), 17–19.

Weininger, Otto. *Sex and Character.* London: William Heinemann, n.d.

Wells, H. G. *Experiment in Autobiography.* New York: Macmillan, 1934.

Williams, William Carlos. "*Parade's End,*" *Sewanee Review,* LIX (January–March, 1951), 154–61.

Young, Kenneth. *Ford Madox Ford.* Published for the British Council and the National Book League. London, New York, Toronto: Longmans, Green and Co., 1956.

Index

Austen, Jane, 58, 194, 202

Beardsley, Aubrey, 116
Bennett, Arnold: as Impressionist, 40–41; mentioned, 15, 16, 82–83, 153
Bowen, Stella, 20, 22
Brown, Ford Madox: and Ford, 11, 27; mentioned, 10, 30, 35–36, 59

Chamberlain, Joseph, 113, 139, 141
Clemens, Samuel, 120, 184
Conrad, Jessie, 123–24
Conrad, Joseph: and Ford, 6–7, 12–14, 31–34, 37–38, 57–58; and *Romance*, 97–101; and *A Little Less Than Gods*, 123–25; Ford and *The Sisters* of, 124; and *The Inheritors*, 139–40; mentioned, 16, 23, 50, 74, 155, and *passim*
Crane, Stephen: and Ford, 39, 49, 83, 221; mentioned, 14, 32, 84, 122, 293

Dickens, Charles, 54
Dostoevski, Feodor, 51, 87, 137, 158, 249, 257
Douglas, Norman, 16
Dreiser, Theodore, 48, 146, 295
Dreyfus trial, 51, 87, 137, 158, 249, 257
Dudley, Dorothy, 251
Dürer, Albrecht, 106, 109
Durrell, Lawrence, 296

Eliot, T. S.: and Ford themes, 256; mentioned, 133, 240, 252, 282, 289, 298

English Review: Ford edits, 15–17, 22–23; mentioned, 39, 153, 159
Euripides, 70

Faulkner, William, 69, 78, 249, 299
Fielding, Henry, 71, 293
Fitzgerald, F. Scott, 260, 262
Flaubert, Gustave: *L'Education sentimentale* of, 38–39, 83, 220; and *Salambô*, 93–96, 98–99; mentioned, 11, 41, 65, 69, 103
Ford, Ford Madox: "Affair" in, 5–6, 52–57, 65–67, 75, 76–77, 298–99; boyhood and youth of, 10–11, 26–27; illness of, 14, 182–84; and America, 15, 23–24, 250–52; war service of, 18–20, 205–07; Sussex farming of, 20–21; and France in 1920's, 21–23, 248–49; and Pre-Raphaelites, 26–29; art and action in, 30–39 *passim;* and luxury, 32; as historian, 34–37; on novelist as historian, 40–42, 295–98; and Impressionism, 42–50; "rendering" in, 43–44, 80–82; and industrialism, 45, 95; "case" in, 50–52; time-shift in, 52, 89–90; prose style in, 56–57, 57–59, 300–01; anecdote in, 59–61, 301; and 18th century, 67, 116, 293; "justification" in, 68–69; *progression d'effet* in, 68; and fate, 69–71; and tragedy, 70–71; surprise in, 71–75; dialogue in, 77–78; psychological effects in, 84–89, 300–01; as historical novelist, 91–95; history in, 95–97; and historical types, 97, 101; and medievalism, 97, 101–02, 129; and Edwardian society, 131–33; and cheap fiction, 163–

317